PRAISE FOR THE GRIEVING GARDEN

"Grieving parents Redfern and Gilbert, along with 20 others, fill a void in the literature of child loss that both discovered after the death of a daughter; having 'devoured every grief-related bit of writing,' they found no relief for their escalating isolation: 'What I needed wasn't information, but company.' Unadorned by 'expert' commentary, Redfern and Gilbert address directly the personal experience of living out 'a parent's worst fear' with the voices of those who have. Organized by issue (24, in six sections) rather than contributor, it's easy to find a wide variety of perspectives on specific challenges ('Surviving the First Few Days,' 'Pursuing Counseling,' 'Encountering the Void' and 'Continuing the Connection'). Parents take turns weighing in on each issue in conversational first-person contributions (most solicited in written interviews), occasionally including journal entries, verse and straightforward guidance (especially helpful is the long view provided by Martin Katz, whose son died in 1981). A 'More About Us' section provides photos and brief profiles. A variety of backgrounds and circumstances, along with a shared dedication to speak out on a notoriously unspeakable loss, make this brave volume cathartic and comforting; grieving parents may well find it invaluable."

—*Publishers Weekly* starred review, March 24, 2008

"It's hard to imagine anything worse than the death of a child. Redfern and Gilbert reflect on their own experiences with such a tragedy and recount the stories of 20 other parents whose children died at a variety of ages and from causes ranging from disease and accidents to suicide and terrorism. The authors organize the interviews in a way that mirrors the stages of the grieving process, including immediate reactions, seeking support, effects on family life and relationships, integrating the loss into one's life, and maintaining connections with a loved one. Simple words, carefully edited, convey eloquent and practical insights into the bereavement experience. Ultimately, this book shows that comfort, healing, and even growth are possible after the death of a child. This powerfully authentic book is highly recommended for large public libraries and counseling collections."

—*Library Journal* starred review, March 24, 2008

The Grieving Garden

LIVING WITH THE DEATH OF A CHILD

SUZANNE REDFERN AND SUSAN K. GILBERT

HAMPTON ROADS
PUBLISHING COMPANY, INC.

The Grieving Garden
Living with the Death of a Child

Cover design by Susan Shapiro
Cover art: *Poplars on the Banks of the Epte, Autumn, 1891*
(oil on canvas) by Claude Monet (1840-1926)
© Private Collection/The Bridgeman Art Library

Hampton Roads Publishing Company, Inc.
Charlottesville, VA 22902
www.hrpub.com

Library of Congress Catalog Card Number: 2007046660

ISBN 978-1-57174-581-1

Printed in the United States of America
WZ
10 9 8 7 6 5 4

All proceeds from the sale of this book will be
donated to KARA, a nonprofit grief support
foundation in Palo Alto, California
(www.kara-grief.org).

DEDICATION

For Aimée and Amanda

TABLE OF CONTENTS

WHY THE GRIEVING GARDEN

After my daughter Aimée died in 1999 of lung cancer at thirty-two, I scoured every self-help and grief section of our local bookstores in a frenzied quest after some sort of lifeline. I soon realized that what I needed wasn't information, but *company,* and that it wasn't to be found on those shelves.

—Suzanne Redfern

When my daughter Amanda was killed in a van rollover in 1993 while returning from a debate competition as a freshman at UCLA, I devoured every grief-related bit of writing I could find. I didn't know exactly what I was searching for: answers to the *whys?* advice? hope? Some of the reading was helpful, but when I turned the last page I was still hungry for something that wasn't there, at least, not enough of it.

—Susan Gilbert

Looking back on those hard days, we can now recognize that our voracious reading came out of our need for relief from the isolation that most bereaved parents suffer. The simple fact that our children had died made us different from all other parents, in our own eyes but especially in theirs. To many we were the personification of a parent's worst fear: the death of his or her own child. When friends or strangers tried to empathize with us, they couldn't help imagining that unthinkable circumstance. Often they would visibly recoil, both from that image and—sometimes subtly and sometimes not—from us.

At times we also felt a societal onus at our having failed at the primary responsibility of all parents: to protect their children from harm. Also, because it is human nature to want to believe that tragedy is something that happens to others, some couldn't conceal their need to step back from us and our fate—uncomfortable reminders that disaster can strike anyone at any time.

But most people who kept their distance did so simply because they didn't know what to do or say. We probably didn't make it any easier for them, overcome as we were with emotions too wild and strange to verbalize. Our behavior was hard to read, as social niceties and everyday matters became for us intolerably trivial against the monstrous and all-encompassing presence of our loss.

The other parents who share in the making of this book say that they, too, felt isolated at one point or another after their child's death. Like us, they found—and still find—the greatest relief from their loneliness in the company of people who have been there. We all concur that hearing or reading the stories of other grieving parents comforts our hearts when nothing else will. Especially in the early days, we longed for that community of common understanding. We needed assurance that others had survived such unthinkable pain, that our bizarre behavior was natural, and that life might one day bring us some peace, and possibly even pleasure.

In our search for such reassurances, the two of us read nearly every book in print on the subject of parental grief. While we found some of them useful, none took the edge off our desire to find ourselves among a diverse group of bereaved mothers and fathers reflecting on their experiences in their own words, without "expert" opinion or undue editorial analysis. That unsatisfied hunger was the seed for *The Grieving Garden*.

But, you may ask, why the *Garden* in the title?

The title grew out of my weekly sessions with Kathryn, my volunteer grief counselor. Every Wednesday for a year, we two passed the afternoon talking about my Mimi and her Nick and reflecting on the many faces of grief—our new companion. When the day was mild we would take our teacups outside to my small brick patio, fringed with camellias and scented with orange blossoms. I came to think of this comforting place as my grieving garden. It became a refuge in which good companionship and shared emotions calmed my raw nerves, eased my loneliness, and relieved my fears.

—Suzanne

After Amanda's death, I was desperate for activities that would capture my attention and divert me for small pieces of time. I found that the creation of a garden—preparing the soil, selecting and adding plants, tending to their growth—was an activity I could manage and it helped to sustain me. As my new garden came into bloom, I liked to imagine that Amanda's spirit dwelled among the plants, nurturing them and helping them grow. I would cut the best flowers to bring to the cemetery. These activities soothed me during the worst of my grief.

—Susan

If you, too, are suffering from the loss of a child, we hope that this book will be a refuge for you. We want you to feel that it's a safe place to enter whenever you need to be among people who have felt what you're feeling. The twenty-two of us represent such a broad range of experience, age, religion, race/ethnicity, occupation, and personality that we think every reader will find within these pages something that rings true or someone who feels like home.

On behalf of all the mothers and fathers you're about to meet, we warmly welcome you to the garden.

HOW TO READ THIS BOOK

Just as there is no one right way to grieve, there is no one right way to approach this book about grieving. You, the reader, will make instinctive choices, depending on your needs at the moment. As those needs change over time, you may pick up the book again and go at it quite differently.

The structure is straightforward. The main body of the book consists of six parts. Each of them explores a related set of issues commonly—and in many cases *uniquely*—faced by bereaved parents, in the form of twenty-four questions participating parents answered. Most wrote their answers, and a few we interviewed. Each respondent was free to choose which questions to answer. Their responses are arranged in alphabetical order.

In "More about Us" you can become better acquainted with the twenty-two parents who appear in the book, including the two authors. Again, names are listed in alphabetical order. You are invited to learn something about each of us and our sons and daughters and to see family photographs. At the bottom of each parent's entry you'll find a list of the page numbers on which that person's answers appear.

You may decide to proceed in one of several ways. You may simply open the book to part 1 and plunge in. But if you are struggling with a particular challenge and need to know how other parents have dealt with it—what we do with our guilt, how the loss affected our marriages, how we mark the anniversaries of our children's deaths— you can find that topic in the table of contents.

Or, if you're looking for someone like yourself—for instance, another grieving father, the parent of a deceased infant, or a person with the same religious tradition—you can identify that person in "More about Us" and use the guide at the bottom of the page to locate the relevant entries.

Finally, you may wish to get a sense of the larger company you'll be keeping before seeing what each has to say. Then we suggest you lose yourself in "More about Us" before returning to the questions and answers.

Regardless of method, we're confident that each of you will discover your own path through this company of wonderful people in a way that is useful and meaningful to you.

To learn more about *The Grieving Garden* or to contact the authors, please go to: www.thegrievinggarden.com

ABOUT US

Most of the participating parents came to us as strangers, referred by friends and acquaintances over a period of five years. Suzanne's volunteer peer grief counselor Kathryn was the first who said *yes,* she would write about Nick and the two years since his death, if the telling would be of use. She thought another recently bereaved parent she knew, Nancy Emro, would be a wonderful contributor if she were interested in talking about her grief following Sean's fatal train accident. She was. Our mutual hairstylist Don English mentioned Anne Logan, who came to Palo Alto from Virginia for haircuts. Don said she was a medical doctor who talked courageously about the death of her daughter Virginia. He wondered whether we'd like him to ask her to take part. We said *indeed.* Martin Katz, Susan's former business colleague, served us tea and cookies in his sunroom and spoke of his struggles after his son Barry's suicide. He also suggested that we contact Lottie Solomon, though it was less than two years after September 11, 2001, when her daughter Naomi had died in the World Trade Center attack. And so it went.

We took in everyone who was willing—amazingly, people were willing, even if the remembering promised to be painful. Then we stepped back to see what we had. We were delighted with the spectrum: sixteen women and six men from five states, ranging in age from their thirties to their eighties. White, Hispanic, Asian, and African American. Jew, agnostic, Buddhist, Roman Catholic, Greek Orthodox, and Protestant. Farmer, corporate executive, scientist, musician, accountant, physician, teacher, social worker, and cattle-woman.

Our grief experiences were as diverse as we ourselves. Ten had lost children to physical or mental illness—some lingering, some viciously brief, some unexplained—and nine to a variety of accidents. Three of the children were victims of violence: murder, street crime, and terrorism. Their ages at the time of death ranged from a fetus *in utero* to a woman of fifty-two.

As we started receiving the written answers to the questions we'd sent out, our participants' independence showed again. First, though we'd asked the participants to tackle only a couple of questions to begin with, most responded to eight or ten, explaining that they'd found the exercise to be therapeutic. Two answered every single question. Then, while some writing was lyrical and carefully crafted, other people responded so matter-of-factly that reading their words was like having a conversation with a friend at Starbucks. At first we worried about it—how could such a variety of styles ever come together into a cohesive whole? Now we see this diversity as the book's greatest strength. We celebrate the authenticity of each distinct voice telling its own truth.

In the end, we came to admire and respect every one of the contributors. We also fell in love with each of them. Though different in nearly every aspect, they—and we—are connected in fundamental ways: first, we have undergone what is widely considered to be the hardest loss in the human experience; second, we have volunteered to reach down into tender and painful memories and to reveal deeply personal details of our lives in hopes of helping another through that loss; and third—whether or not we have outlived our children—we are, and always will be, parents.

IN BRIEF

STATHI AFENDOULIS
His daughter Lainie died of Ewing's Sarcoma at age twelve.

INÉS BETANCOURT ASCENCIO
Her daughter Angelita died *in utero* just before birth.

SUSAN BENVENISTE
Her daughter Shelly was a passenger in a drunk
driving accident at age seventeen.

MARY LOU COFFELT
Her son Matthew was killed by his father's pickup
on a cattle ranch at age three years and seven months.

NANCY EMRO
Her son Sean was struck and killed by a
commuter train at age seventeen.

SHEILA GEORGE
Her son Ronnie was stabbed on the street at age twenty-three.

KEITH D. GILBERT
His daughter Amanda died at age eighteen
as a passenger in a van rollover.

SUSAN K. GILBERT
Her daughter Amanda died at age eighteen
as a passenger in a van rollover.

VAN JEPSON
His son Ian died on a father-son outing in
an off-road vehicle accident at age eight.

MONICA L. JONES
Her daughter Bronwyn died at age nine
of Werdnig-Hoffmann Syndrome.

MARTIN KATZ
His son Barry died at age twenty-one of suicide.

JOHN LECOMPTE
His daughter Aimée (Mimi) died of lung cancer at age thirty-two.

KATHRYN L. LODATO
Her son Nick was a pedestrian, hit and killed by
a car at age twenty-one while at college.

ANNE J. LOGAN
Her daughter Virginia died of a methadone overdose,
secondary to depression, when she was twenty years old.

JOHN PHUA
His son Ryan (a twin) died of Sudden Unexplained
Death in Childhood at age two-and-a-half.

MICHELE PHUA
Her son Ryan (a twin) died of Sudden Unexplained
Death in Childhood at age two-and-a-half.

SUZANNE REDFERN
Her daughter Aimée (Mimi) died of lung cancer at age thirty-two.

PATRICIA W. SHAW
Her daughter Cathy was murdered at age forty-eight
by her husband, who then killed himself.

LOTTIE SOLOMON
Her daughter Naomi died at age fifty-two in the attack on the
World Trade Center on September 11, 2001.

MERRYL WEBER
Her son Adam died in a boating accident in the
Atlantic at age twenty.

KATHLEEN WEED
Her daughter Jenica died at age twenty-one of
meningitis while attending Dartmouth College.

JANE WINSLOW
Her son Peter died at age twenty-six, the
victim of a driver who ran a red light.

ACKNOWLEDGMENTS

*the angels have no wings
they come to you wearing
their own clothes
they have learned to love you
and will keep coming
unless you insist on wings.*
—Lucille Clifton

We are deeply indebted to our mentor and friend Wayne Oler for his tireless advocacy of this book and his determination that it be published, and to Barry and Virginia Weinman for their insight in leading us to Wayne. We are also profoundly grateful to Don English, who believed in the project from its inception, brought the two of us together, and introduced us to several of our parent contributors.

Liz Powell supported our approach to parental bereavement and shared with us the wisdom gleaned from her many years of grief counseling.

Tiffany Randall organized and updated the manuscript with skill and good cheer.

Ruth Endsley, in a lovely gesture of friendship, typed the first draft.

Carolyn Pincus bolstered us with her enthusiasm for the book and, with a light touch, helped us give it more heart.

Robert Redfern-West (when asked) offered his editor's eye and publisher's know-how from a lifetime in the book business.

Doug Hollis volunteered his superb design sense and first suggested Monet for the cover.

Alev Croutier and Jean Hollands gave us sound advice out of their extensive experience in writing and publication.

Jack Jennings and Greg Brandenburgh at Hampton Roads risked taking on a difficult subject matter because they thought it was an important one to air.

The rest of the publishing team at Hampton Roads treated the manuscript as if it had been their own.

Finally, we cannot find words to adequately thank the wonderful mothers and fathers who so generously and beautifully contributed to this book in hopes that their words might comfort or encourage another grieving parent. When the project began, we were not acquainted with most of them; now they feel like family. Since they were largely strangers to each other, we brought everyone together in the spring of 2008 for a joyful afternoon of conversation and book signing. Appropriately, we met in a garden.

PART ONE

HANGING ON

Setting Out

How did you . . . ? What did you . . . ? Part 1 focuses on the agonizing days and weeks immediately following a child's death. Most of us weren't at all sure we could survive it. We look back and wonder how we made crucial decisions, even planned and carried out the funeral, while in such pain. Stathi Afendoulis calls this phenomenon an "autopilot kind of thing."

Then, as we slowly emerged from our state of shock, feeling raw and vulnerable, we found ourselves in situations for which we were entirely unprepared. One of the first dreadful moments all of us encountered was being asked by a stranger how many children we had. Initially tongue-tied and stricken, we eventually developed strategies to field this dreaded question, but we still struggle with it.

Another unthinkable but inevitable challenge, which a few faced early on, was how to mark the anniversaries of our child's birth and death. You will learn that even after many years parents still experience waves of sadness as those days approach. As Michele Phua wrote in her journal on the second anniversary of Ryan's death, "It is just another day to the rest of the world and is such a life-changing day for our family." Some describe the ways their family has found to commemorate these milestones with rituals and even celebrations.

Finally, we explore the bittersweet experience of being in the company of friends of our children, and find that most parents seek out that company despite its poignant reminders.

Those people who answered questions in part 1 say that going back to the beginning was very hard, yet healing. They were grateful to have had a reason to remember the first days and, in a sense, to honor them.

As you venture into the recollections of people's early grieving and on into the book, please keep in mind that some are remembering from a distant perspective—twenty years or more after the death—and others after only a year or two. Because grief is an organic experience, we all grow through it. If we were asked the same questions today, many of our answers would be different. The reflections you will be reading, vivid as they may be, are only a snapshot in time.

Surviving the First Few Days

In the period following a shocking loss, people survive the only way they know how. To those around us, our behavior may appear either utterly bizarre or eerily normal. One friend reports being unable to cry after her son was killed except in church, where she sat wordless, Sunday after Sunday, awash in tears. Another, having lost an infant, stood at the playground every morning telling all the other mothers—friends or perfect strangers—about her baby boy. *During the first days and weeks after your loss, how did you survive?*

STATHI AFENDOULIS

I don't remember being conscious of anything that helped me cope with Lainie's death, especially in the days immediately following her passing. We always talked about keeping life "normal" and that's what I did. It was really an autopilot kind of thing. I could barely think about getting out of bed in those early days, let alone pick a coping method. Although at her memorial dinner following the funeral, I toasted her and spoke of the courage she displayed during her battle with cancer. I talked about so many things, even describing to the mourners the actual death and what happened. What I *really* wanted was to share with everyone there the experience we went through, not only on the day she died but the whole ordeal. I wanted everyone to know my pain, to share it with me and make it their own, so I wouldn't feel so alone.

Loneliness is what I felt the most in those early days. An isolation so profound it seemed to envelop my whole being. At the dinner, I spoke of starting a foundation, Lainie's Foundation, to help the parents of children who have cancer and blood disorders. It was something I had been doing at the hospital before Lainie's death and I wanted to continue. I don't know why, but it seemed the only logical thing to do. The only thing that made sense to me was to go back to that world. Most parents want to leave it all behind, but it was the one thing that still connected me to Lainie in a concrete way. For most of her illness, I was her primary caretaker, and in that time we spent together I experienced the most intimate and personal relationship I will ever have. The privilege of caring for this child was the pinnacle of my life. I could do no more good than to care for her. When she was gone, I had to keep on caring. I just couldn't turn it off.

My wife Emily was very angry, as I was at that time, and this further created a sense of isolation and emptiness. Work was a terrible place to be, especially since we are self-employed and our employees are our friends. It was so tough to face them every day. The early days are so enshrouded by grief that every waking moment is about the loss. Friends and relatives always warned us to be careful, to go slowly, but it's silly advice, because you're already at a dead stop. Like being in a waking coma. It's amazing I got anything accomplished during those first three months. Lainie died in June, on the last day of school, and we had the summer to escape. We fled the confines of home and work and headed out to other places, where people didn't know us or we were more alone. It was easier to deal with the constant ache of loss by being alone.

Being alone is a good thing, at least for me. I had time to wrestle with all the emotions boiling inside of me. My anger was so strong, my bitterness so deep, my loss so painful.

I could barely stand it. I used to sit or stand somewhere and be overcome by this feeling of helplessness so powerful it rendered me mute and frozen. Incapable of doing anything, I wanted to scream and punch and kick and destroy everything around me. I wanted to blame something and then destroy it for taking my girl away from me, but there was nothing. Nothing I could grab onto and crush to dust. In fact, that's what I felt like, dust. Ashes. Totally burned away yet still living. I remember when Lainie was diagnosed and I had this physical reaction to the news. I felt like my body had been gutted, like when you clean a fish. Somebody just took my guts out. My torso felt empty! There was nothing inside me. I would stand with my fists clenched, thrusting them upward to heaven, waiting for God to help me and cursing him with every fiber of my being. My mouth would be wide open, but my rage choked any sound I could make. It was like the painting *The Silent Scream.* I had a physical body with no soul. I was just an abyss.

I shared these feelings with very few people. Most, when they heard me speak of it, immediately jumped to conclusions about my wellbeing and worried after me. It's not what I needed. I really needed them to stand there and scream and cry with me, to be as sad as I was, but it's impossible. Even my wife grieves so differently from me. Understanding another person's grief is a huge mystery. Now, when I meet people like myself, I make no attempt to understand or even help them. In fact, I am mostly silent, and when I do share, it is to share grief and nothing more. I cannot bring back for them what they have lost. When I realized that for myself, it was the end of one kind of grieving and the beginning of another.

INÉS ASCENCIO
[From an interview]

I was at the end of a pregnancy and went to the doctor; I was a young, pregnant woman.

The doctor put this monitor on and I could see her face and I knew. She asked if my husband were there. I said, "No," and she said, "Why don't you call him?" The baby died on Monday and I did not give birth until Wednesday. The autopsy people and the doctor said that the blood stopped flowing and it got clotted, but that was not necessarily the cause.

The doctor gave me options. She said, "You can just stay in the hospital if you want." She would schedule me to come into the hospital and induce labor or do a C-section if I did not want to go through labor. I decided to have the induction, and it was hard, really painful labor. It was weird. They tied me up to a monitor; there was no concern about the baby. And I was going into this despair and suddenly I felt her spirit like it was out there. It was almost like I saw her. I felt she was still around. I felt her support.

The hospital I had her in was very sensitive. They let me bathe her and dress her, take pictures. So at least I have those memories. My mother says they never even brought her the first daughter to whom she gave birth. She didn't know the baby had died—they told my father first and then my father had to tell my mom, and the doctors and nurses never did say anything. Some people might think, *Oh, it's morbid, I don't want to see the baby,* or they might not have the courage to ask.

On the day of the funeral service, we brought her coffin to the house; we made an altar and people brought flowers. In the Latino culture there's that wake where you stay with the baby. We had her there all weekend.

I have a whole album of her pictures, and that's all I have. In her short life, she really touched a lot of people. My sister-in-law already had three children and was expecting her fourth. It taught her to be grateful for what she had.

Her name was going to be Camila or Camila Angelita. And my husband wanted to change it. The fact is her name is Angelita, little angel. She gave us so much, not just her dad and me but others who know us.

I remember how hard it was when I first went out after her death. I was seeing strollers and wondering where they had all been before.

EL ÚLTIMO LATIDO

Cuando la doctora nos dijo
tengo malas noticias . . .
Su corazón
dejo de latir
Lloré
Me sentí destrozada y sola

Te fuiste . . .
Sentí las manos de tu padre sobre mi
vientre
tratando de alcanzarte

La doctora me abrazó
los latidos de su corazón
fuertes y firmes
me calmaron

En ese momento
supe
que mientras tu corazón latía
dentro de mí
Encostraste la paz en mis latidos . . .
Entonces . . . me sentí mejor.

JUST A HEARTBEAT

When the doctor told us
I have bad news . . .
There is no longer
a heartbeat
I cried
I felt devastated and alone

You left
I remember your father
rubbing my stomach and crying

When the doctor came back
she hugged me
I remember hearing her
heart beating
strong and steady
it soothed me

And then
I thought
My heartbeat must have soothed you
while yours still beat
within me . . .
And I felt better

—Inés B. Ascencio

MARY LOU COFFELT

When Mattie died, I was joyfully eight months pregnant with our second son. Life was at its peak for us. We had been happily married for fourteen years and, after a lifetime of working for other people in the ranching industry, we had finally been able to successfully maintain our own cattle enterprise, a great accomplishment in this sometimes tenuous business. We had just purchased our first home, a fixer-upper with six acres, and we were ecstatic land barons! Our lives had reached the "top" and we were grateful.

Then, *The Day.* Our world completely stopped . . . dead in its tracks. Never, ever to return to the "normal" we thought we once knew.

(The good news is people do return to life if they can make the treacherous journey and tough choices. It has been nine years now. I am a survivor.)

The beginning of our ordeal was surreal. Much of it is a blur for me, although I remember some things as clearly as if they are happening to me this very minute. I feel fortunate that instinctively, from the very beginning, my husband and I made choices and took actions that allowed us to work through and live our grief. Bob was able to hold our dead son for a long time, alone and at the sacred place that he passed. I was able to go there too, and as horrible as it was at the time, hold him and be present to that experience. Had I not been allowed to go to the scene of the accident, I think I would have had a much more difficult time accepting the reality of his death.

The pictures flash painfully through my head, brought up by the slightest provocation, but I have learned to replace them with kinder, gentler ones. This was a conscious decision. The horror of our pictures of our precious little Mattie, his "misshapen head" (as Bob called it), and the accident that ended his life. We knew that there was no hope for any semblance of peace if those pictures continually flashed in our heads. So in the beginning when they flashed, we cried and talked and died a little more inside each time. Then one day we talked of how we had to "turn the channel on our TV," "flip the page," and make the decision to change the horror thoughts. It didn't always work at first and then, when it was appropriate, we would gently remind the other to *try* to turn the page. I say *appropriate* because this exercise was not about denial, but survival. I did not want to be consumed by the horror. We needed to have some sort of "control" of our life back (although I realized at the moment of Mattie's death that we don't really have control of our lives, but we can control what we do with the life we are given). I believe this page-turning "exercise" was the beginning of an effective strategy that helped us walk through our first days of grief. It was the first step that allowed me to walk the treacherous journey, but keep myself from being swallowed up in it and drowned.

Our first days were numb, of course, but somehow—probably because both of us are doers by nature—we took action. In ways that I look back on and marvel at. We encouraged our "whims." Our first step was to choose a casket. We had a masterful, rugged, almost-four-going-on-fourteen-year-old cowboy to buy a "box" for, a final resting place, symbolic of his uniqueness, and what we saw were a frilly white odd-shaped box and a cold vinyl-looking one. We stood in the mortuary, stunned. It had *never* occurred to us that we would ever be standing in that place. John, our funeral director, looked at us and softly said, "There are no rules. You can make your own casket if you want." Well, we were off. We would make our own. Of course, the reality was we had very little energy or ability to function at that time. Our minds designed a beautiful box for our little Mattie and we shared the idea with friends. Our dear friend Ed offered to help us. He was an incredible woodworker who lived on a neighboring ranch. Ed and his cousin Marty and Bob and I would create this masterpiece. Bob and I gathered the wood and met at Ed's wood shop. We designed the box, but they did most of the cutting and fitting. We pounded a few nails and sanded a bit, but mostly we cried and talked and stood there silent. The love poured out. Our Mattie was there, I could feel him smiling at us. It was magical. We placed our cattle brand on the outside in two spots. We each cut a piece of our lariats and tied them on the end for handles. For the inside we each gave up our favorite saddle blanket, and my husband's worn flannel over-shirt became Mattie's pillow. Ed's wife Pattie, who had been in the process of sewing Mattie a special cowboy quilt for his room, crafted a smaller version of the quilt she had hoped to give him and laid it on him.

It was beautiful. It was fitting. And it helped us send our child out in style. These things were and still are important to us. We did not stop at that. In the days before our service, we visited our child regularly and often, something the typical funeral director would not encourage. It was an infringement on his life, I am sure. We dressed Mattie ourselves, one last time. Our family visited and brought important mementos and placed them with Mattie, in his beautiful casket.

We put some energy into the service, although my sister and our priest did all the work. I am very aware that in those early days it was very important to us to ritualize the experience as fully as we could. However, we were not physically capable of executing much. We needed and had friends and loved ones with legs. We had the need, they made it happen. And when and where we were able, they somehow had the grace to leave us alone, to do it ourselves.

Those first days were a blur and a blessing:

To have a "perfect" goodbye.

To have the love and support of an entire community.

To have no regrets.

All of this gave us the strength to begin our wake-up call and to realize what had just happened to us.

SHEILA GEORGE
[From an interview]

Ronnie was twenty-three and got murdered. He died only a block from my house. And I was away on vacation—that was '88. He died the day before Thanksgiving, so Thanksgiving to me was a tumultuous journey. I didn't celebrate Thanksgiving for about ten years. I left and I started helping feed the homeless. I just wanted to be anyplace but home, because that was his favorite holiday—not all my other kids—that was *his* favorite holiday. I don't care where he was, he'd come back and eat.

When Ronnie was murdered, I was not here. First of all, I was on vacation with my parents and they got the news. And when I got home with my cousin, they just told me my son was hurt and may not make it. So they had to sedate me, they gave me nerve pills and stuff like that. I didn't know why . . . well, though I think when I first got that information, in hindsight as I look back, I knew he was dead. It was just the way things went down, but at the time my mind couldn't grasp it, it wouldn't let me believe that, so I had to hold on to the hope that he was still in the hospital, but I think I knew he wasn't. And then my brother in Oklahoma got us all packed up and everybody drove with me. The closer we got here—we drove because they wouldn't let me fly, that was another trigger that I tried to block out—I said, "I want you to let me go to my son."

So as it turns out, when we got about thirty miles from here my mom told me in the car. I lost it. I don't remember *anything*. I guess all the pills I was taking weren't putting me to sleep, but when I got that news I couldn't breathe. I will never forget. I could not *breathe*. They had to pull off to the side of the road so I could breathe, and I don't remember getting back in the car, but for that thirty minutes I was out, and I woke up again in my driveway. I woke up and started screaming again. They brought me in the house and from then on everything was just a blur—I don't remember anything. I didn't plan the funeral, I didn't do anything. I just didn't do anything. My mom, my dad, and my cousin planned the funeral, though I had to pay for it all. They did everything, I did nothing. I was just off.

Everybody knows I like to shop, so my girlfriends came over and tried to take me shopping. I went—they say I went, anyway—I can't tell you anymore what I was feeling. I know I cried a lot.

I'm a community activist, and so everybody was there. I couldn't tell you who was there. Even my neighbor, who I knew but didn't know, she was in and out of my house all the time. I didn't know anything. I was just there.

Susan Gilbert

Amanda died on March 1, 1993, just a few weeks short of her nineteenth birthday. The night before she died, she called home from Las Vegas, where she was competing for UCLA in a debate competition. She was excited and happy on the telephone and declared Las Vegas "sleazy but fun." It was the last time I spoke with her, and I remember I was anxious to get back to my dinner, which was sitting on the table as we spoke. How ordinary it was.

A policeman came to the door early on a Tuesday morning and informed us there had been an accident and that Amanda was killed on the road between Las Vegas and Los Angeles. I tried so hard to convince him that he was wrong. "How do you know it was Amanda? Maybe she was the driver." (The driver survived.) This period of total denial passed in a few minutes, and then I understood. I remember looking at my husband, who appeared as shocked as I felt, and feeling my knees almost give out. I still remember my first thought: *I must make my mind up right now to survive.* It was then, and sometimes still is, unimaginable to live without her. Our lives had always been intertwined and I pictured my future with her: helping her to raise her children, talking on the phone wherever she was, going to movies. I felt totally secure in the knowledge that she would always be there. And then she was not.

Shock set in within an hour or so, and I began to go through the motions of dealing with death. One of my sisters lives nearby and she and my brother-in-law were exceedingly helpful to us. They were the first to come to our home, probably within an hour of the notification. My sister already had the telephone numbers for the funeral home, church, and cemetery. I called so many people in those first hours, repeating the story over and over, but not having it sink in. Later, I would read the newspaper headlines and obituaries and it still would not seem real.

Fortunately, I made a new and now treasured friend in those first hours. Susan had lost her daughter, a classmate of Amanda's, the previous year. Simply seeing her carry on, watching her extend herself to me and others, and heeding her suggestions helped so much. Knowing that someone else could survive helped me to do so. She suggested books for me to read, which helped divert me and which spoke to what I was experiencing. I later met others who had lost children, and I find we have an immediate and deep kinship and understanding.

In the first few days, I somehow carried on. I did not cry, and was not deeply aware of Amanda's death. I could not sleep, ate little, and lost about ten pounds in two weeks. It was very important to me to plan her memorial service, with the help of my family and others. We chose music she liked and several of her friends kindly offered to speak at the service.

I was unable to cry for almost four months. Finally, my husband Keith and I were in Washington, D.C., on his business trip and I was on my own during the day with few distractions. I began to cry to an extent that my clothing was soaked with tears; I cried steadily for several months.

After the funeral, I made myself get up every day; I busied myself with thank you notes for all the kindnesses shown to us and responded to all condolence letters and cards. An impatient CEO wanted me back at work and I tried to comply. I was ragged and felt so unproductive. My company was in the process of raising money and I was responsible for this aspect of the business in a way that required me to speak to large and small groups with enthusiasm. I managed to do so for a while, and then my mother died unexpectedly three months after Amanda. I knew then that I simply could not go on working. I also knew that it could be dangerous to my wellbeing not to have productive activity. I chose to apply to and later attend graduate school in a subject that had always intrigued me: counseling psychology. School helped to occupy my mind and I could go strictly at my own pace. I never intended to have another career but something that I hoped would safely fill the hours.

Those early months held a lot of fear for me. I did not know if I could go on living or ever find a way of coming to terms with Amanda's death. I felt that if I let the impact really hit me that I would be consumed and I felt in danger of harming myself. It took several years before this fear totally left me, and there were times that I needed psychiatric counseling to deal with grief and to help me adjust to a new life. During the first few years I learned that there was simply no comfort for how I was feeling. Not friends, not ministers, not prayer, not medication, not meditation. Nothing helped. I learned that the waves of pain needed to be borne and could not be stopped or dismissed. One elderly lady of my acquaintance said that when her child died, she needed to pretend she was on a subway, standing and holding onto the strap. She just held on.

Almost exactly a year before her death, at age seventeen, Amanda wrote a poem entitled "Man Will Prevail." When I found it just after her death, it seemed to speak directly to me, to tell me to keep hanging on.

MAN WILL PREVAIL

Close your eyes and endure the terror
Realize it all will pass
Hold on to your hidden dreams
And see the future in the glass
Close your eyes to the darkness
The patience is within your soul
Its presence you can mark
For on the inside you are whole
—Amanda Gilbert, 1992

VAN JEPSON

The only thing that worked for me was to stay in the present moment. Thoughts or memories of the past or anticipations of the future were so painful that I could not go there. I was drawn into the comfort of the present moment, knowing that with each breath and with each step I was drawn more closely to an awareness that I had lost touch with, to a set of senses that could sense where my son was. Being in the present moment brought my mind to a quiet place, it brought my physical body into the breath that I was breathing, and it brought my emotions into the fact that I was alive and well and that those I loved were still close to me.

There was an outpouring of support from friends, family, and the community. The only way we could interact with the community was to set up an inner circle of four to six friends to buffer us from the calls, letters, flowers, and food offered. Ninety percent of the calls were an outpouring of sympathy for loss, 10 percent of the calls were people wanting to know when the memorial service was. We asked people not to send flowers. If people felt like giving, we set up an education fund in honor of our son. We also had a person opening our mail and surfacing any particularly appropriate cards for us to read. We also had a person who was the coordinator of food. This person created the schedule that stretched out for weeks. This inner circle of friends kept us from being emotionally, mentally, and physically overwhelmed by the events of the first several weeks.

MONICA JONES

Our daughter Bronwyn was not only paralyzed, but also required much nursing care for years. We enjoyed caring for her and she was never in great pain, although she did have difficulty in breathing and choked frequently. When she died on a Good Friday, my husband and I were not only exhausted from providing intensive medical care during the last weeks of her life but also relieved that her suffering was over. We were then faced with making phone calls to family and friends, who had not known how sick Bronwyn had become. Although we had discussed calling out-of-town family, we didn't call them sooner because we did not know what they could do to help. We also had to plan and take part in one memorial service for the children who were her friends and one for adults on Easter Sunday. It was difficult for me to interact with others, because I didn't think I should burst into tears and also because I found people just didn't know what to say.

My husband Desmond went back to work on Monday, while my son Gareth and I spent a week camping on the Colorado River with friends. When we got back, Desmond and Gareth were gone during the day and I was alone at home.

I remembered that Bronwyn once told me that when she died we should have a party and be happy. I knew that I would honor her life and her memory more by being cheerful rather than morose. And I realized that I was feeling more sorry for myself than I was for her. In essence, I could, as Shelley wrote, "look before and after and pine for what is not" or I could pick myself up, dust myself off, live in the present, and be grateful for what I had. That being said, the challenge was to exemplify my beliefs in practice, for how I felt and acted was inevitably colored by how I viewed the world in general and Bronwyn's life in particular.

Initially, I'd wake up in a panic at night because I didn't hear her noisy electric bed rolling her and I didn't hear her breathing or choking on the intercom. During the day I did the normal jobs associated with running a household as well as sorting out medical insurance details and Bronwyn's things. Most of her clothes I gave to friends with daughters her size. I also invited many of her friends over and let them choose a piece of her "jewelry." We kept most of the toys, as Gareth still played with them. While I definitely did not want to turn her room into a shrine, I did keep a shoebox full of some of her "treasures," little things that reminded me of her.

My husband and I also had to decide if we wanted more children. As Bronwyn had a hereditary birth defect, we had decided at the time of her diagnosis not to have another biological child and had adopted Gareth as an infant in 1971 when Bronwyn was three years old. By 1977 there were very few infants available for adoption, especially to what were considered older parents (Desmond was forty and I was thirty-six). We did take two foster children, whose single mother had been unable to cope. During the next six months we found the children were very needy and would have required much love, care, and attention for years to come. We knew we could provide the care, but we had to decide whether it would be the appropriate thing for us to do after almost ten years of twenty-four-hour-a-day nursing care, during which time Bronwyn's immediate needs usually had to take precedence over Gareth's. We finally reluctantly decided to be a family of three. With time we discovered that having—and being—an only child is not categorically better or worse, just different.

MARTIN KATZ

Alas for those who cannot sing
But die with all their music in them
—Gates of Repentance, p. 484

My son was a young adult, twenty-one years old, who committed suicide. So much of what I will have to say will have a more specific orientation to this cause of death. The death of any child is horrendous. Forgive my own biased perception that suicide is an order of magnitude worse because of the guilt and rejection that accompany it.

When we left home for the San Francisco airport that day, there was an extra long farewell hug for me and particularly for his mother. He knew what he was going to do. Why didn't we sense it? Why didn't he say something, ask for help? We stayed at a friend's home. I went running the next morning along the Long Island Sound. It was ominously dark, dreary, rainy, and windy.

We were in a theater lobby that evening when an announcement came for us to immediately call our friend's home. We rushed out to a pay phone in the street and then came the cataclysmic news. My younger daughter had found his body. My wife collapsed in the street. I drove back and then made arrangements for our immediate return home.

His farewell note was short and simple. Basically, he did not want any memorial and requested that his remains be cremated.

So many people came to the service. I was still in shock and so was able to speak and tell about how much he meant to me and about many of the wonderful things he had done for me in opening my eyes to things I had ignored. Our parents could not understand why we were not going to a cemetery, and must have been dismayed at the thought of cremation, which is not countenanced by the older Jewish tradition.

ANNE LOGAN

Early one Saturday the telephone call came, the one every parent fears. It was a perfect October morning in Virginia. The air was crisp, the sky cloudless, the fall flowers still in bloom in the garden, and the trees beginning their spectacular autumn display. Our large extended family was assembled for the wedding of my brother's son. The previous evening we had attended the rehearsal dinner, with rounds of toasts and joyous celebration. The wedding was that afternoon. Arising early to fix coffee and start breakfast, I was in the kitchen when the phone rang.

"Hello. May I speak to Anne or Mark Logan?" *Too early for the telemarketers*, I thought. "This is Anne." "This is Bobby Vagt, the president of Davidson College." I felt an instant chill, that profound foreboding that we experience at moments of fear. The college president does not call at 7:00 a.m. for happy reasons. "I have the most terrible news . . . Virginia has died." I'm not sure of my words then, but he went on to tell me that she had been found by a friend who could not get her to wake up. Friends started CPR; the rescue squad arrived. She was taken to the emergency room, where further efforts to revive her failed. "Can I call you back?" I finally whispered.

A long, keening moan came from my mouth as I hung up the phone. "No, no, no . . . ," I kept saying. Our granddaughter was watching TV and heard my sounds. She became alarmed and got her father, our son, who came to see what was wrong. We collapsed in each other's arms, disbelief and horror in our hearts, tears streaming down our faces. "It's not possible!" he said. I then went to tell Mark, who had slept later than usual. Disbelief, panic, fear all registered on his face. "What shall we do?" he cried.

Though I was not inexperienced in facing death—both personally with the death of my father when I was in college and professionally in my medical practice—there is no event as life shattering as the death of one's child. I don't know where I got the strength to continue in those first days and weeks. But in our family and faith tradition, there is much to do when death occurs. And I occupied myself with setting to those tasks.

There were people to notify. There was more to investigate about Virginia's death and funeral arrangements to discuss. There would need to be food, a lot of food, much of which would be brought by friends and neighbors. In the South, one is always to provide a meal to people who visit, especially at times of family crisis. And there would be crowds of people. Some folks would need a place to stay. Can we get some more cots? What friends have extra rooms they could share? And on and on and on. The focus became not what had happened, but what do I do now. I let myself go into "automatic" mode, seeing to all these issues, focusing on tasks, not feelings. It kept me from thinking too much. That would come later.

There is comfort in the traditions and routines that we observe, and this is particularly true at the time of death. Part of this comfort is knowing what to expect, what needs to happen, what decisions must be made. I spent a night alone thinking about and selecting scripture and music for Virginia's funeral. And we as a family spent hours talking over how we would honor her at this service. Though we thought about what she might have liked, real efforts were made to speak to our needs and those of her friends.

In addition to attending to the necessary and practical events at this time, I was surrounded by a host of family and friends. Husband, son, daughter, brothers, sisters, nieces, nephews, cousins, and friends beyond my imagining. Not all grieving parents relish the attention, however. Many needed to be alone, and this was so for my husband. Though I missed his presence when the visitors came, I understood his need to grieve in solitude.

During this time I think I was perceived as a "pillar of strength." Able to function and, in fact, coordinating it all fairly smoothly, I occupied myself with "keeping on keeping on," not allowing myself to feel. I ate nothing, slept only when exhausted. And then it was over. She was buried. Relatives had returned home. Friends had resumed their normal activities. The refrigerator was empty. What now? The house was quiet, the rooms empty, her room as she had left it when leaving for college, her things a painful reminder that she would need them no more, would not be coming home for Thanksgiving, a holiday that she loved, or Christmas, when she delighted in the silly gifts that stuffed her stocking and always insisted on the biggest, most perfect tree. This was the time that I felt the reality of her death and what it would mean to us for the rest of our lives. The aching emptiness that will not go away. The tears that come unbidden and unexpected. The hoping that it was all a mistake; waiting for to her to walk through the door with that infectious smile on her face. The enormous physical effort required to get out of bed in the morning. The concern about other family, her father, brother, sister, niece. The waking in the night to a mind racing with *whys, what ifs,* and *if onlys.*

I remember thinking, *It's got to get better.* And so I faced one day at a time, not trying to plan too far ahead, as I usually did. My horizons were shortened, and I tried to focus on getting through tonight, this afternoon, this week. Many of my activities were automatic, but there were times when I simply ceased to function, when I was so overwhelmed with sadness that it was an effort to breathe. I took long walks and deep breaths, and wrote thank you letters. It didn't get better, but it got different. The tears became fewer. I started resuming work and activities, going through the motions of normality. But aching inside. Still.

JOHN PHUA

In the days and weeks following the loss of Ryan, I fell into deep sadness and grief. I felt the need to explore the pain and deep inner feelings, as hard as it was. I believed that by reaching the lowest point, perhaps I could find answers. I knew I could not patch and begin to rebuild my new life without rebuilding my soul from the ground up. The foundation on which I had lived all these years had shattered, and I did not have an explanation for what had happened. Life couldn't continue as it was. I did not know where this would take me or how I would come out at the other end. *[The following is an edited excerpt from John's journal, one month after Ryan's death.]*

July 22, 2003: I haven't been resting well since Ryan left us. I was doing my normal routines and I was hoping that action would help me climb from my pit. I was just going through the motions. I needed to make a choice. I may not control what goes on, but I do have the option to make a choice. There are no rules in this process.

I recalled that when I was diagnosed with cancer five years ago, I made a choice of what to do about the situation. I guess you can say I had some of the same thoughts of *Why did this happen?* but not as deep and painful as this. Now I felt like I was in quicksand; I surrendered and I let it pull me down without a struggle . . . why should I fight? With cancer, I chose to try to survive, to try to live, not to give up. I embraced life. I wanted to have hope and survive. I asked myself if I was doing that now . . . NO. I needed to make that choice.

I can understand why people who lose a loved one sometimes make the choice to not move. The pain just to lift a finger or get up is too great. It is sometimes easier just to sit. Like anything we do that is hard, we have to try and try and try again, even though the odds seem like they are against us, eventually we will be able to do it.

One has to make that choice.

MICHELE PHUA

During the early days, I let my heart take me to the different stages of grief. I was in shock and numb, in a fog since Ryan died so suddenly and without explanation. However, because I still had Matthew, a toddler, Ryan's surviving twin brother, I had to continue to do the normal activities with him. I just remember each morning when I awoke, I would need to "adjust" myself. Is this tragedy real, or is it a dream? Is Ryan coming back? How can anyone be so cruel to have presented us with the most precious gifts and then take one of those gifts back? I kept replaying the night of Ryan's death and evaluating if I had done everything I was supposed to do. I felt guilty that the canopy that we had provided Ryan had been destroyed and someone cruel had snatched him away from me. I wanted my feelings to be authentic. I owed that to Ryan. The morning following Ryan's death, I typed an e-mail to my Mothers of Twins Club and asked for resources. I needed information and resources on grief. Help poured in.

[The following are edited journal entries Michele made shortly after Ryan's death.]

July 16, 2003: Today I played in the park with Matthew and John as a family of three. Life, supposed to be normal, is so out of routine for me now. I saw Ryan's reflection—smiling at me, running around nearby with his unique walk (Ryan liked to turn his head to the side as he walked forward). I then realized that my life is forever altered. That sense of emptiness, of not having Ryan physically here, is so hard to swallow, so hard to imagine, now that my heart has been ripped apart. The once so joyful, bubbly mom of two little boys, the one who initiated hellos to other happy moms, the one who watched her boys' interaction with other children so excitedly, is now feeling empty. Looking at these moms having their "normal" lives and their not knowing how my life is so not "normal" anymore, I tried to avoid exchanging eye contact with them. I realized how happy they are, spending time with their little ones, and how painful I am feeling without Ryan. It is also difficult to answer friends who ask, "How are you doing, Michele?" How do I describe my emptiness, disbelief, anger, my longing for my son to them? The answer would require a long explanation.

August 22, 2003 [One month later]: Having a ritual calms me. I have been coming to the cemetery daily with John, and I now know that we each need our private time with Ryan. I came to the cemetery today on my own and looked at the ground and told myself that I gave birth to this little body; I held this little body every day with love and care, and now earth is separating us. The body is now deteriorated underneath the ground. Though Ryan's body is a shell, I grieve that I can never hold that body anymore.

Suzanne Redfern

For the first few weeks, I ducked. Literally. I hunched down between the spokes of the steering wheel, slipped around corners, squatted behind grocery store checkout counters, scurried across the street mid-block, all to avoid meeting someone who had appeared unexpectedly, someone I hadn't run into since Mimi got sick. I lived in fear of seeing that person's stricken face, of watching her nervously approach to offer awkward condolences. I dreaded coming across someone who didn't know she'd died and hearing him ask, "How's Mimi?"

It seems strange now that, after all the unthinkable trials we'd faced in the months following her diagnosis, I was thrown into panic over something as banal as coming across an old acquaintance. Yet as dreadful as much of that period had been, somehow the insularity of the experience had offered us a safety zone. As we gathered around her and took on new roles as caregivers and watchdogs, a sort of cocoon had formed around us all: Mimi herself, her husband, her father, her brothers, a few close friends, her medical and spiritual advisors, and me. The power of that sheltering cocoon was palpable when we were at her bedside, and when we ventured out it continued to protect us from seeing too clearly the full implications of the situation. We lost ourselves in meeting the practical challenges implicit in maintaining a viable environment for a terribly ill young woman. Thanks to her grace and gratitude and to our mutual love, we were to some degree distanced from the tragedy of what was happening then and would happen in the future.

When she died and we all went back to our own houses and lives, we didn't talk much—I'm unclear as to why. Maybe we kept to ourselves because after such intense togetherness we needed some time alone. I know *I* did, I was desperate for solitude, but I also needed the sense of security generated by our powerful little unit. So, tucked into my Palo Alto cottage, I consciously placed myself back into that metaphorical cocoon. It kept me close to Mimi, whose energy had created it, and to the warmth that had radiated among us all. Remembering the strength we'd drawn from each other was a natural sedative. Each morning I'd pull those memories around me like a slicker and then move into my day. Right then I needed that insulation, even if I knew it was only temporary shelter and that soon enough the energy would dissipate and I'd have to start confronting head on not only the loss of my daughter but also the loss of purpose created by the abrupt end of our long, all-consuming preoccupation. Soon enough I'd have to stop ducking.

The ducking instinct gradually waned, replaced by a compulsion to dance. *Not* literally. Not gracefully, either, but a frenetic spin I began and was afraid to stop. I said "yes" to everything that came along, fearing that if I slowed down, I might crash through the brittle surface between me and the bottomless sorrow that lay below.

For two years the dance looked like this: I bought a racing bike (yet unridden) and skin-tight biking outfit (yet unworn); went with friends to Maui, to Paris, and to New York City; bought a used convertible; lived in a garage addition for three months during a kitchen remodel; and undertook the restoration of our mountain cabin. I attended two water conferences, joined a new gym and a new church, began hiking, and visited a friend on Balboa Island, where I took up quilting. I sold a lot in Santa Cruz and reinvested in a tiny Capitola diner, which I decorated and leased out. I joined a writing salon in San Francisco and started this book project.

As I look back now at that manic whirl it makes me laugh, but it also makes me sad because it gave my friends the signal that I was just fine and preferred to be left alone, when the fact was that I sorely needed shoring up. On the practical side, it was the most productive period of my life—and the most expensive. Psychologically, I don't know whether the dancing kept me sane or if it simply delayed the important work of beginning to process Mimi's death. I don't know about that ducking thing, either—it was just what I did. I've come to trust that the ways we manage to hang on during our greatest trials are instinctive and ultimately right for each of us as individuals.

Patty Shaw

Frankly, I do not know how I survived that horrid phone call. We were on travel and consequently there were no close friends nearby . . . just my husband and myself. I was in the throes of a violent inner ear infection, so was already reeling and unsteady on my feet. My husband and I had only been married a short time and he had only met my daughter twice. There was nobody there who had known her and that was very painful. Very. I do remember the sorrow being so great when I was given the news over the phone that I collapsed onto the floor feeling like I had been kicked in the stomach . . . hard! And I never truly knew the meaning of "keening" and realized that that was what I was doing . . . and did for days. I was told of the funeral plans, but since I could not fly due to the ear infection, driving was our only alternative. We drove home from Mississippi to Toledo, repacked our suitcases with warm clothes, and headed out for Colorado, where the funeral was to take place. It was a travesty and I wept constantly, not only because my daughter had been brutally murdered by her husband, but also because her many remarks over the years had been that Alaska (her home) was where she was meant to be and that when she died, she wanted to be cremated and her ashes scattered over her favorite places. Why, she even took me to those places so I could see them for myself and could envision her happily there for eternity.

We returned to Toledo (we had only lived there a very short time and knew practically nobody so neighbors were no comfort). My husband and I had previously decided that we wanted to move to a warmer clime, so he suggested (urged most vehemently) we go south, find a place, decide upon a location and a house which would be built after the selection was made. I felt totally not up to that, but I think that he was determined to get my mind off my loss. Nice try, but not truly realistic. The upshot was that we did go south and we did decide upon Sun City in South Carolina, and I did select a house plan from twelve different ones (you realize that I could not yet concentrate on anything . . . not even articles in the newspaper or a magazine). We returned to Toledo to sell that house, did, and then moved here. Unfortunately, the house I chose was not the one I wanted so another blow had to be absorbed.

Perhaps all these things did divert my thoughts and I am not giving them their due. All I know is that those six months after her murder were the worst in my life . . . almost a complete thick, black fog . . . every once in a while a break in the murk and then back into a black fog of despair.

I felt a desperate need to have family close at such a time. That would have been of enormous comfort to me. Someone who had known her so that my grief could be understood. Receiving the news of her murder could never be an easy thing to bear, but perhaps if I had, say, my mother or perhaps father there, that would have helped. Then again, perhaps I would have had my personal grief diverted consoling them at the brutal loss of the first and beloved granddaughter. And that, perhaps, would not have been so bad. We could have shared our loss.

One thing that added to my having a hard time accepting this awful news was that, rightfully, Cathy's oldest son was the one that had to shoulder the majority of the decisions that had to be made. What he did was call me the next day after her death and asked me if I would mind if he had his mother's ashes mixed with his father's, and then they would be buried together and therefore be together forever. At the Air Force Academy! Well, I could not believe my ears! I had been on walks with Cathy and her oldest son Sean, when she had pointed out the places where she wished some of her ashes would be scattered one day. She loved Alaska and she never wanted to leave it. During her lifetime or in her afterlife. Well, I recalled for him his mother's wishes and when she had shown him special places of hers. He remembered, but said that his father would want his mother by his side for eternity. I was almost sick to my stomach right there on the phone. I urged him not to do that, but he was adamant. Then I offered the suggestion that perhaps he could put his mother in one urn and his father in another and then have the urns buried next to one another that way. If he ever changed his mind, he could retrieve her ashes and redistribute them to her requested burial spot. His only answer was that this is the way his father would have wanted it. I pointed out to him that this was not necessarily what his mother would want. My statements fell on deaf ears, and I was so in pain from the shock of Cathy's death, my aching heart, my painful ear infection, and making the trek from Toledo to Colorado Springs in February to attend an outside grave service in the midst of a sleet storm.

Then the reception was held in an office building's conference room and was attended by many of my son-in-law's friends who eulogized Jed for what a wonderful guy he was, what a great friend, etc. Awful, just awful. And in all the speeches that were made and the toasts that were offered, only one of the officers mentioned what a terrific wife Cathy had been. I thought that day would never end.

Another thing that was awkward and uncomfortable was that nobody seemed to know what to do with Jed's mother or with me, so they lumped us together and sat us together and had us appear next to one another in the receiving line, etc. I am certain that she was as uncomfortable as I was. I had to smile and have pictures taken next to the mother of the man who murdered my daughter, and she had to stand next to the mother of the woman who could not stand her son and whose desire for a divorce caused her son to act as he did. It caused him to kill not only her, but himself as well.

If this were a soap opera, I would think that this would be typical. But it happened in real life to my beloved firstborn and only daughter.

LOTTIE SOLOMON
[From an interview*]

Although I am consoled by the thought of all Naomi did in her life, there is terrible loneliness for me. She never missed a day calling me, whether it was Morocco, Egypt . . . I got calls from all over the world. That was the first thing she did almost every day. The women who take care of my husband* knew on September 11, 2001, that *that* day she did not call.

It did not dawn on me that she was in that building. Because I'd talked to her on the Monday before that Tuesday, and sometimes she'd say, you know, I'm going here, but she never mentioned it, it was just part of doing her job. She was going to a technical meeting, computer side, just one of the elite side . . . they lost seventy or eighty people from that society. I got a letter from them, condolence letter, I guess you'd call it . . . seventy or eighty people had come to that meeting, they were the best brains in New York in computer science—that's some event.

Oh, I remember exactly how I heard about Naomi on September 11. My sons both walked in dressed in solemn clothes, it was about 9:30 because they heard from her office, and they walked in to tell me. I had just turned on the TV—one of the women who came to work said, "You don't have the TV on." I said, "What happened?" She said, "Let's get it on." She had just turned the TV on when the plane was going in . . . that sight I shall see 'til my dying day, and it will never leave me. The sight is right in the front, all the time, because I know she was on the 106th floor, just where the plane went in, and the thought of it, I mean, it's so excruciating. I

---

*At the time of the interview, Lottie's late husband Herb was still living at home in the late stages of Parkinson's disease.

know you know the feeling, the helpless feeling, that's all, that's what I feel now.

I've been ill since "it," whatever it means to call it "it." Actually, what happened was I had a hip replacement in that month of June before September 11, and I just about began to recover from it. Then, after September 11, I developed a compression fracture in my lower back, so I'm ailing . . . I've had a second hip surgery, that's why the walker is here. It seems that I have a number of rheumatic ailments about which little is known. Losing Naomi has affected my health tremendously. I lost the ability to recover as effectively.

Merryl Weber

The mind/heart have no sense of linear time. At the moment I heard the words, "Adam is dead," my sense of time expanded as if I were moving through a gaseous world, one where nothing seemed important or real but the sharp pain of my son's loss. At the same time, an inexplicable presence that felt like it connected me to everyone and everything past, present, and future flooded my being. Reality took on a completely different meaning. All previous cares, worries, interests, and attachments to what I did, or had thought were important before Adam's death, became meaningless.

Whatever reflected in some way that presence—a caring thought, a loving gesture, the kindness of the people who came to help us—these filled my heart alongside of that searing and constant pain. An urgent desire to keep the remainder of my little family together while we lived through what I knew were going to be hard times was my constant companion in those first moments and months.

I also vowed not to isolate myself, to let people help me in whatever ways they could, to accept whatever was offered with an open heart. Just after the call that told me Adam was dead, I clearly heard an inner voice that reassured me I was not alone. All the mothers in the world, in all the worlds, who have had children die, all the women whose children have been killed in wars, by illnesses, in accidents throughout all the aeons, swept into my mind. I took this as a reminder to allow the caring and love of others to be with me and not push them away out of anger, fear, or judgment, to allow people to help in whatever ways they were capable of helping. I knew beyond a doubt that I was going to need all the help I could get.

For most of my adult life I had kept a journal. When I think over my life, there are two distinct periods of my life: before Adam's death and after. Starting a new book reflected the new period that had started with that phone call. Once we returned home from picking up Adam's body in North Carolina, two days after his death and the night before his funeral, I wrote these words at the start of a new book:

> *Please don't try and say the unspeakable*
> *There is no comfort*
> *Hold us in your hearts and arms*
> *Go home and love your children,*
> *Your mates, your neighbors . . .*
> *Time runs away.*
> *Only memories are left*
> *Too beautiful to hurt enough.*

Those first weeks and months I chose to let myself feel my grief as it washed up and over me, crying and keening whenever possible, letting my heart break open, crying out for help, for mercy. I had to remind myself to keep breathing in order to get through whatever feelings and thoughts presented themselves. The pain was constant, so constant that I remember thinking that this must be some strange version of what it is like to be drunk with divine consciousness, never forgetting for a moment our connection to whatever one calls that web of being that sustains life. Adam's face, his being, was so palpable I felt I could almost see him, but not quite, and so I would weep for my child who had crossed into a world where I couldn't see, hear, touch, or smell him with my physical senses. Though I wanted to die to be with him, I refused to give in to entertaining the thought of it. I told myself, *This is a suicidal thought. It will pass.* I wanted to get to the other side of this horrendous experience more alive than I was before, not more shut down and afraid. I decided the only thing that made any sense at all was to dedicate my life somehow to be of service to others. The accumulation of material things, of status of any kind, was clearly a dead end. Life became too precious to waste in any way. My heart had broken in a way I could never have imagined.

How did other people see me those first few weeks and months? I couldn't really say. One friend told me I stayed present with the grief in a way that she almost couldn't fathom, that it would have been more "normal" to shut everyone out. Another friend said she found it wonderful that I retained a sense of humor. I do remember my husband telling me I wasn't being "nice" when I refused to keep doing the things that made others happy, things I couldn't stomach anymore. The social niceties fell away. I did only what I had to do for my family and for myself to survive; beyond that I only did what felt right to me in the moment. Everything else was below my radar.

Answering
THE QUESTION

One of the incidents many of us dread most is being hit with THE QUESTION when a stranger asks about our children. It feels like a body blow to our most tender and vulnerable places. THE QUESTION is excruciating when it assaults us in situations like a dinner party, the dentist's chair, or an airplane seat. *What do you say when you're asked, "How many children do you have?"* What considerations come up for you—anger over being put in that spot, guilt of betrayal when you lie, fear of weeping in public? Do you have one stock answer, or several, and when do you use each?

STATHI AFENDOULIS

I founded a foundation in Lainie's memory. It's called Lainie's Angels. Our mission is to provide peer support for parents whose kids have cancer or a blood disorder. We do this through the use of parent advocates, parents whose kids have had these diseases. By bringing these parents together, we provide a network of support and the parent advocate, part of a team of health care providers in the hospital, represents these moms and dads to the health care team. One of the biggest worries practitioners have about parent advocates who have lost their children is, "What will you say when the parents ask how your child is doing?" My answer is always the same. I tell them the truth. I don't always explain or drag out my personal experiences, but I put it out there, no holds barred.

But one of the reasons I might not tell someone that my oldest daughter died is because they patronize me with their sympathy. I hate sympathy. I really do. Lainie hated being felt sorry for, she could tell immediately if someone was doing it to her and she hated it. I feel the same way when I talk to people about my kids. Will I tell them? Won't I tell them? It all depends on the vibe I'm getting and, more important, if I do tell them, will they get it? Will they understand they don't need to feel sorry and they don't have to tell me how sorry they are? Of course, they have to but it's better if they don't. In fact, the only thing they are thinking, if they are parents, is thank God it didn't happen to them.

The reality of THE QUESTION is that it is not really a question at all. For the most part, we all ask THE QUESTION automatically, with no thought to the consequence of the answer we might get. "Hey, how long you been married?" "Got any children?" Rote questions, asked a million mind-numbing times, until we all just say, "Ten years, three kids." "Oh, my God, I got you beat, twenty years, four kids, one just graduated college." So, the real zinger in my mind is THE ANSWER! "I had three daughters, my oldest died of cancer when she was twelve." Silence. The eyes go down. The conversation ends. Reality stops everything dead in its tracks. All of a sudden, the enormity of a banal icebreaker question comes crashing down around both of us, and you either digress into the sad story you've told before or pretend how grateful you are to have surviving children. Either way, it stinks! You feel guilty for being honest or for not telling the whole truth. Who do you strike with the doubled-edged sword that is your answer?

MARY LOU COFFELT

Even now, nine years later, this question stings . . . what do I say?

In my mind I have three boys, but if I say so, the next question is usually, "How old?" Is Mattie almost thirteen years old, or is he still three years and seven months? Do I say my oldest son has died? Oh, then the silence and the looks. People who do not know this loss generally have a very hard time speaking of death. I don't. It is a part, a very big part, of who I am. It is a part of our family.

In the beginning we did not have to face this problem very often. Our community is so tight and small enough that it was a known fact and required no explaining. No one asked. Everyone just loved and supported us, and Mattie. But as my children grew and our world expanded and we were faced with new people, this question, the dreaded question, became more common. My husband seemed to tell everyone matter-of-factly. Sometimes that solved the problem for me because I didn't have to say anything and sometimes it made me uncomfortable. I was a bit more selective about who I shared what with. I realized that the people that I thought I might continue a relationship with were "deserving" to hear about my precious Mattie. When those that I did not care to know beyond this initial encounter, even if I might see them in the future, asked THE QUESTION, I would say weakly, "Two." This answer always made me feel dishonest and uneasy, but it surely was easier than hearing a response from someone I was not at ease with in any case. However, in this situation, if one of my boys was present, they would quickly chime in about their older brother Mattie in Heaven! The beauty of this was how alive their brother was to them, and at that point I did not care who heard our story. To kindly, comfortable people who may have unknowingly asked, I often answered, "Three boys," and when they pursued with the next obvious question "How old?" I seemed to respond with Mattie's current age, for instance, "He would be almost thirteen years old, but he is in Heaven now." There is usually no response to this, only silence, but I have learned to live with it. I wish people could just respond with how they feel, but we are all doing the best we can. The important thing to me is that I am true to my child.

NANCY EMRO

At first, I felt that strangers didn't need to know and I didn't care to go into detail over how many children I had. I didn't feel like creating awkward moments with the stranger in the airplane seat next to me who I'd never see again. That strategy worked all right until a few months after Sean's death when I was taking an all-day class, a continuing education class for my CPA license, with a small group of people who I'd probably never see again. Lunch was included in the class fee. Usually for the people in these accounting-related continuing education classes, a question such as how many kids you had or where you lived was an icebreaker, nothing more, with the conversation returning after a few minutes to the discussion of business. So when THE QUESTION arose at my table of eight, I said I had no children so that I didn't have to "explain." A strange thing happened during that lunch break. Quite unusually, conversation stayed focused on the topic of raising kids, but because I said I had no children my comments were not taken seriously by the group. I was not considered a parent, an expert on child raising. I felt very left out, stripped of my role of motherhood. In addition, I felt I had dishonored my son, pretending that he never existed, which struck the heart of me.

After this meeting, I strongly felt I had to come up with a better solution. First, I felt it was important to me to honor my son by remembering him, even to strangers, and if they were uncomfortable with my disclosure, so be it. Second, I had to come up with a way to tell people about Sean that was comfortable to me.

Now I tell them I have a thirty-four-year-old stepdaughter who has two beautiful girls, and I had a son who would have been nineteen if he had not been killed in an accident two years ago when he was seventeen. Most of the time the discussion ends there, but if pressed, I will tell them about the accident (Sean was hit by a train), and I am comfortable doing that.

KEITH GILBERT

Over the years, my answer to THE QUESTION has evolved, and I now am comfortable with how I respond:

"We have one daughter, Amanda, but she was killed in an automobile accident in 1993 when she was a freshman at UCLA." I like to affirm to the other person that while Amanda's physical life may have ended, her spirit is still alive. Her almost nineteen years were enough to make a difference in the world, especially to me and to my wife.

Even though I know my answer, I still dread hearing THE QUESTION. Most of the time I can feel it coming. It's often especially hard, as for many people discussions of their children (and grandchildren) are "happy talk," relating how much they enjoy watching their children grow and be happy. I know my answer is going to change the atmosphere from happy to horror, as all suddenly contemplate the worst fear of every parent—loss of a child.

After "the answer" from me, there's "the reaction." All of us have experienced the reaction of totally ignoring what's been said. Maybe the other party even immediately changes the subject. Maybe a quick acknowledgment and then back to "happy talk."

What I long for is for the conversation to become about Amanda: what her life was like; what she meant to me; even what she was doing when she died. Maybe that's unusual for someone who has lost a child, but that's what I long for. And I can guess that only those who have experienced a loss can understand the desire to keep the spirit alive.

I've learned that the expression of feelings about the death of a child is often distorted by the horror of the event. Good friends, including some who knew our daughter well, were often seemingly speechless when trying to talk about what happened. They clearly wanted to change the subject.

Throughout our ordeal, we learned that the most satisfying connections we could make were with others who had lost a child. These people were incredibly generous and have become good friends. Even today, more than ten years after our losses, we look at each other and realize that we understand what it's really like.

VAN JEPSON

For me, I start with the root of THE QUESTION, which I always interpreted as how many children do I have *on Earth?* In the beginning weeks and months I answered it "two," and continued the conversation. Sometimes the questioning would go into what sports they liked. If given the opportunity to gently release the information about their likes and dislikes and sports they liked, I would say that one of them is on Earth and one of them is in Heaven and they both play the sports of the season daily. In terms of the emotions that come up and how the mind sorts which ones to share, this has been the greatest challenge for me. For I know that on the earthly plane my son's body no longer exists. I also know that his spirit is alive and well in Heaven. As the months passed—and now it is two years since my son passed on—I find myself still wanting to describe it as two and my choice to split my response depends on the sensitivity level of the person to whom I am speaking. If they are a person that is connected to their heart, I will answer, "Two, one on Earth and one in Heaven."

MICHELE PHUA
[The following are edited journal entries]

July 8, 2004: Today we went to Beresford Park where Ryan's tree is. Matthew made friends with a three-and-a-half-year-old girl, and I was carrying on a conversation with the mother. She asked me if Matthew was an only child and I said yes (this time I didn't feel guilty). I will always acknowledge Ryan in my heart, but this mother just did not need to know. The mother was thirty-nine and wanted a second child. She told me she already had the names planned out for a boy or a girl. I listened and realized that I was able to handle the whole conversation. I admired her innocence, which I personally have lost.

October 15, 2005: Two years have gone by. Now I select my answers depending on my audience. If I am talking to someone whom I don't expect to meet again, I often nod my head when asked if Matthew is the only child and change the subject. However, often when a new mom that I've met in Matthew's preschool asks if Matthew has any other siblings, I tell her that Matthew is a surviving twin and his brother Ryan died at two years of Sudden Unexplained Death in Childhood. Of course, there is the fear that the conversation may make the mother so uncomfortable that she will avoid talking to me in the future. But this is Matthew's life and they need to be informed. If only people knew how much courage it takes for a bereaved parent to reveal that.

PATTY SHAW

It has taken a while to not tear up when the question arises about how many children I have. I now respond with, "I had three, now I have two. My daughter died, but my two sons are fine." Usually that is all that I need to say and they offer their condolences. Some ask for details. That's tough. I have been, and remain, very bitter toward my late son-in-law who did the killing of my Cathy, and have, with great effort, trained myself to say "died" instead of "murdered." The word *murder* causes such a reaction that those who posed the question become uncomfortable and, if not, want to know details. Both scenarios are difficult for me.

I am frustrated with finding another word acceptable enough to explain her death. I recently told someone about the wedding of my oldest grandchild (Cathy's firstborn son) who is getting married in June. I heard myself say that Sean was my dead daughter's oldest. Horror of horrors! Well, that is the truth and as shocking as it is to hear, that is that. I have been told that *deceased* might be kinder. I try.

I have always loved to laugh and for that I am grateful. And such an outrageous thing occurred right after her death that upon reflection I burst out laughing, and I laugh still to this day.

As I mentioned, we drove back to Toledo after the funeral in Colorado Springs. I spent quite a few days weeping, moaning, under hot showers, not always dressed, etc. You know the drill. Finally, poor Don, trying his best to cheer me up at least a little bit, suggested that I shower, do my hair, and get dressed up and we could go to the country club for dinner. Not my idea of a fun thing to do at that particular time, but I did so appreciate his thinking of me so I did as he suggested. We drove to the club and were seated in the dining room. We had no more gotten our menus when a couple appeared at the door. Don had played golf with him, but neither of us had met his wife. They came over to our table and asked if they could join us and of course we said yes. The men started talking and she turned to me and said, "Well, how are you doing?" Thinking that she had heard of our tragedy, I replied, "Thank you for asking. I am getting better, I think." She replied, "What's the matter with you?" I answered, "Well, tonight is the third-week anniversary of the day that my daughter was murdered." Within about a three-second time span she looked me straight in the eyes and said, "Do you know that Kroger is having the most fabulous sale of saltine crackers?" She then turned to the men and entered into their conversation and never looked at nor spoke to me again. Once home, upon reflection, I broke into peals of laughter. It was so very thoughtless, so crass, so unkind. How could one mother say such a thing to another mother? So now whenever someone says something thoughtless that hurts, I intentionally recall that woman's remark so I can keep my composure on the outside and be chuckling on the inside.

MERRYL WEBER

As I moved back into the world of people who didn't know me, I dreaded meeting new people, having them ask me about my children. Of course, as I've gotten older that happens less frequently, but at the time of my son's death, I was only forty-six years old and still had a teenage daughter. At first I would just answer the question and not elaborate. Most people wouldn't ask further, but if anyone kept asking questions, I would tell them, two children, one living and one who died. If that led to my telling them about Adam's death, then I would tell them how, when, where. Normally, I wouldn't hold back the tears that often would well up, but then each time it was a different experience.

I don't know when I occasionally began saying "one daughter" when asked. It all depended on if I felt like dealing with someone else's pity, indifference, shock, or my own feelings of grief in that particular moment. Sometimes I would have a stab of guilt, as if I were somehow betraying Adam, but most of the time I just felt I was protecting myself from slipping down an emotional slope in an inappropriate situation. To this day, I have different answers to the question of how many children I have, and my answers still depend on the circumstances, though most of the time I say "two children" and leave it at that, or "I have one child living and a son who died." After ten years, I am not uncomfortable at all telling anyone that my son died. I feel people need to hear this truth: for some of us, our children die before we do.

JANE WINSLOW
[From an interview]

At first, being asked whether I have children was very distressing to me . . . I felt tense that someone would either not know Peter had died or would ask if I have children. Since I appear different (I wear a brace due to having had polio as a child) people remember me. Acquaintances still come up to me in the street or in the coffee shop and ask how Peter is. At the wedding of a friend's son, a psychiatrist whom Peter saw for a while asked about him. She said something very nice about him and I just crumbled. Once, after Peter had been dead for three or four years, someone asked me, "How is your son?" It took me by such surprise and I was dumbfounded by how it affected me, but as painful as the questions may be, I am so happy and grateful that people remember him. They remember him as a baby, as a young man, and you want them to remember.

Something happened that helped change my reactions in this regard. I was working in the San Francisco Library when Peter died, and I found myself drawn to books that were written for bereaved parents; I found several books quite helpful. Over time, I realized that while I do not have a child now, so much of my life was affected by having a child, by raising a child and doing all the things one does with children. I am as much a mother as any woman whose children are alive, and this will always be so. I can now say in response to questions, "Yes, I have a son who died when he was twenty-six."

Marking Anniversaries

During the first year, all of us must face the inconceivable task of deciding how to mark the anniversaries of our children's birth and death. Those two dates bring up in us deeper, more complex emotions than perhaps any others. We may feel compelled to establish rituals that we can follow every year hence, then find over time that they don't fit anymore. *What traditions have you created to mark these wrenching anniversaries? In what ways are they appropriate for you and for your child? Are they something your family shares in? Wholeheartedly?*

STATHI AFENDOULIS

The whole idea of anniversaries, when it comes to your child's death, seems ludicrous. Even more so their birth after they have died. I am a Greek Orthodox Christian and our church offers beautiful rituals to mark the passing of loved ones with prayer, hymn, and church services. We have graveside readings and numerous traditions that bring families together to share in their bereavement.

We honor the dead with a forty-day memorial, then one-, three-, and five-year memorials where we gather to pray and then spend the day together, eating and remembering.

Ritual works for me on many levels, because creating my own seems contrived in many ways. What could I possibly do to mark the days? My therapist told me to try and find some kind of action I could perform in order to make these anniversaries productive passages for my feelings, rather than bitter reminders. I couldn't do it. No, I have not been able to muster an original way to deal with the days of Lainie's birth and death.

Three years have passed and all the big days and holidays bring with them a dread. Not so much of fear or great pain, but of having to face the joy of others and not being able to experience it yourself. Like a kid with his nose pressed to the candy store window, so full of treats, but unable to partake, only to look and wish.

INÉS ASCENCIO
[From an interview]

Because the anniversary of Angelita's death is Ash Wednesday it makes the anniversaries more prominent in my mind than they otherwise would be. It was extraordinarily hard to give birth. I had to go through all this pain and then nothing, and I am reminded each year.

I start feeling the anniversary weeks and months before the actual day. For the sake of my children and me, I like to go the beach and write messages in the sand. Making that connection. We always get candles—I don't do a cake, but I always do candles. We make an altar too, and sometimes for the Day of the Dead (November 2) as well. So there's that other tradition.

Now that the kids have gotten older, I try to incorporate their ideas in anniversaries. I also often write poetry.

MARY LOU COFFELT

It is and always has been more difficult for my husband Bob to walk through each anniversary and birthday than for me. Why that is may be more a matter of personality than anything else but, as a consequence, I tend to defer to his needs more than my own on these particular days. Our rituals have changed slightly over time but surprisingly have been fairly constant over the last nine years. Mattie died on June 4, 1997, and five months later, with a four-month-old newborn in tow, we were faced with this normally special day, Mattie's birthday, on November 7. Our first son would have turned four years old. As life would provide, David, a very dear friend who had had a special relationship with Mattie, also shared that birthday. David and Renee spent the day with us that year. We had pizza (Mattie's favorite dinner) and apple cake (a cake I had made for his birthday every year). We talked and talked and cried and the day slipped by. It was dark by the time we got around to heading out to the cemetery, "Mattie's Place," as we had come to call it. As it was November, it was a cold and dark night, but we didn't really care. I bundled up our baby Joe (who by this time was already familiar with "Mattie's Place" and with constant visits to a spot that seemed to bring us all to our knees with tears and grief). We brought our cake and candles, sat huddled together against the wind and the pain, and sang "Happy Birthday" to our deceased child. David blew out the candles and we passed out pieces of cake, including a piece for our Mattie, setting it carefully on his stone. We choked down cake and milk and sat talking, or crying, or just holding each other in the stillness and silence. It felt healing. It was a ritual that we carried on for a few more years, always sharing the day with those two people.

Time passed, as it does, despite our inattention to it, and people change and move on (not that we felt like *we* were), and as our friends' lives changed, one year it did not happen that they were with us for our birthday ritual. We noticed it, but the ritual sustained us, and as our little Joe was growing and willing and able to share this special birthday, we smoothly made the transition to our own "celebration." Today, as our Mattie now has two brothers, the four of us continue the ritual each year. The brothers love it, honor it, expect it. We always eat pizza, we always trek to "Mattie's Place," we always sing "Happy Birthday" and eat cake, and we always leave a piece with Mattie. It is Mattie's birthday and although he is gone from our sight, he is alive in our hearts and we cherish this celebration ritual each year. It helps us feel the good of the day—to remember the birth of such a special person, to feel his presence, to feel the closeness of our family.

The anniversary of Mattie's death is not as "happy" a day as his birthday, as it brings back so many of those horror memories that we have worked to erase or at least to tame. It is a day on which each of us is very aware of the fragility of life and how in an instant our lives, our persons, were changed forever from a charmed to a scarred existence. Because the horror is probably even greater for my husband, I instinctively began early on to look toward his needs, not to the exclusion of my own, but it is easy to allow him "the most needy spot" on this particular anniversary. It has been his call as to how we spend it. This day of days altered both of our lives, but Bob will live with his own demons (undeservedly) from then on, and I respect and empathize with that. Mattie's death day has always been our time to retreat from the world, to hide, to gather in our immediate family and hang out—however, wherever, and with whatever we want or need. Early on, we tended to do something symbolic. Some years we visited the spot where he died, others we sat holding each other and relived the day. We always visit his grave. We always stay close to one another and spend a sad, reflective, quiet time together. We tend to relive the darkness, but each year we bring to it a little more strength. It really has become less wretched. Thank God.

SHEILA GEORGE
[From an interview]

I find that even today this happens. As it gets closer to the time of his death, I feel like life is . . . I start feeling depressed, I don't have any energy. Once I identify it, I can get over it, but up until then, I'm like depressed, when people say something I fall apart, I don't know why, and yet all of a sudden, like a trigger, "Click, man, Ronnie's death anniversary is coming up!" And I can't get on with my life until I figure out that's what's going on in my mind.

SUSAN GILBERT

Amanda was born on March 20, the first day of spring, and I always think of her as my spring baby: full of hope and optimism, bright and cheerful. The harbingers of spring begin to arrive in February in California: the tulips and daffodils begin to bloom, birds signal the coming spring, and the weather begins to change. I find this season so very poignant—full of hope yet tinged with sad regret.

In preparation for spring, each fall I plant literally hundreds of daffodil and other narcissus bulbs and tulips. They come into bloom in February, so they are ready for me to pick in March and bring to the cemetery for the anniversaries. Amanda loved the spring bulbs and I like to think that she is pleased.

Amanda also died in March, on the 1st, so we have two anniversaries close together. Sometimes we go away for the death anniversary and some years we are home. I am occasionally troubled with flashbacks, but this happens less often now. There are usually a few very bad days near the anniversary on which I become both depressed and anxious, and I need to keep my schedule very light so that I do not have added stress. Finding the balance between having something planned for diversion and doing too much is important for me. We always go to the cemetery, and then a good movie often helps.

The sharpness of the pain has lessened between the awful first anniversary filled with hurting to the tenth. It was a slow lessening, but the anniversaries are definitely more bearable. One of my friends commemorates the anniversary of her daughter's death by watching videos of the life of her child. Maybe one day I will be able to look at videos of Amanda, but to date I have not been able to do so because they remind me more strongly than I can bear of what we have lost.

We are so grateful for the ways in which in other family members honor her memory around the anniversaries. Some make contributions to charities such as Doctors Without Borders or to the ACLU; others send flowers to the cemetery; some call us or send notes. I am touched that many people remember her so well.

VAN JEPSON

Well, the first year was easy for us, because my son Ian had pre-planned his ninth birthday. The family knew, his friends knew, we all knew exactly what he wanted to do. We all knew exactly which children to invite, and the only last-minute addition was the purchase and release of helium balloons with messages to Ian written on them. The first-year anniversary of his passing was again clear and easy for me, because of the heart connection that I maintained with him through my daily meditations. He made it clear to me that he wanted a large boulder with a plaque with a specific inscription on it. He wanted me to invite the school to come together for a "moment of remembrance." He wanted me to write the first chapter of a children's book, publish it, and hand it out to his friends in his class. He wanted me to provide a large balloon to each class so they could write notes to him on it and then we would release those into the heavens. And although it was clear to me to do these things, it was very difficult emotionally, and specifically to move myself aside enough to allow his will to move through me. But what I was clear on was that it needed to be done for others to remember him and to recognize the beauty that he had extended into this earthly world. This same first anniversary was difficult for my wife and my living son. They chose not to participate in any of the preparations, and outwardly stated that they did not want to come to the moment of remembrance at the school. Though as the moment of remembrance started, my wife arrived.

Because my spouse and I had very different grieving processes, we had separated, so by the second birthday after Ian's passing, we remembered as an abbreviated family. It was Ian's tenth birthday. My living son and I spent it watching videos of Ian's past birthdays, and of the special moments where my sons were together. We also bought a birthday cake and had Ian's two best friends over for dessert. We did not sing "Happy Birthday," as we had at the first birthday after his passing. It was a day of celebrating the remembrance of a beautiful life, more than a day of celebrating an existing life. We had an odd dialogue that never got off the ground, one that centered on the memories of Ian being with us on Earth. Ian's earthly life is only part of the story, because for me his ongoing spirit's life is the miracle and one that all of us should be talking about. Yet, in our society in the United States, it is a topic that is less supported, and this is sad because it contains the greatest hope for all people who have lost loved ones.

MONICA JONES

To commemorate the first anniversary of Bronwyn's death I made scrapbooks with photos and little writings of Bronwyn to give to family and friends. A few years later, I published a Dr. Spock–type book, *Home Care for the Chronically Ill or Disabled Child*, that I wished someone had written for our family, in the hopes that it would help others.

MARTIN KATZ

Today is November 7, 2003. It is "Yahrzeit," the day of the year commemorating the death of a loved one. Each year, my wife and I go to our home on the beach at Pajaro Dunes on the Santa Cruz Bay. No special ceremony, just a retreat. Each of us has our own pictures of guilt and rejection to remember. Each of us has our own individual sorrow, pain, and anger to overcome. What we do is individualized and separate and I wish it were otherwise. Don't necessarily expect a movie version of duality.

I am sitting here on the deck looking out to sea. It is raining and windy and dark like it was the morning of November 7, 1980. I am using my Mac laptop for writing down some of my thoughts for the proposed book for parents who have lost children. (Barry, I just realized that you never really saw the computer revolution, a PC, a laptop computer, the Internet, and e-mail. You would have enjoyed these developments.) I see Barry sitting there that summer on the edge of the deck, legs dangling onto the sand and staring out to sea with a strange, faraway look, not sharing with anyone. Why didn't I see that something was wrong?

Later this afternoon, I took a solitary walk on the beach in the pouring rain to where the river and the ocean meet in a mutual act of renewing and replenishing. I saw and listened to the waves crashing on the beach and the bird calls. It was sunset time and I said "Kaddish," the traditional Jewish prayer of mourning, which does not mention any specific soul but, with its rhythmical incantation, extols the glories of the Universe and prays for peace for all mankind. (Who will say "Kaddish" for me?) I was looking out to sea where you were looking and where, in compliance with your farewell note, we scattered your ashes.

JOHN PHUA
*[An edited journal entry from John's diary
on the first anniversary of Ryan's death]*

As I sit a moment alone, one year from the last night I held Ryan, I think of the joy and the laughter he brought to Matthew, Mommy, and me. We miss what could have been, what should have been. I held him close that night before he went to bed. He held me tight. I will always carry the hole in me. Nothing can fill it.

I cannot explain "why." I just need to keep walking forward, but one day when it is my time, I will "know why." I can now live my life without fear of the future or of my own death.

MICHELE PHUA
[The following are edited journal entries Michele wrote a year after Ryan's death]

July 6, 2004: We went to Carmel, California, for a few days. Carmel was very appropriate. The air cleansed our minds and the foggy weather matched our melancholy moods. As hard as it was, we took Matthew to see the fireworks. I remember vividly that last year Matthew had a high fever and the two of us stayed home while John took Ryan to the fireworks, his third. Who knew that it would be John's last opportunity to do that with Ryan and that one year later I wouldn't have that chance anymore? This year July 4th has a different mood for us.

Later that day: I just went to Ryan's resting place. I have not been there in a long time. I saw a pinwheel left by my friend for Ryan. The pinwheel has a smiley face, reminding me of Ryan. I sat there in this serene and peaceful place, holding Bertie the bus, one of Ryan's favorites. John showed me the teeth mark that Ryan had imprinted on Bertie. I held Bertie and realized that that is the closest physical presence I have with Ryan now, his teeth mark. I sat there and I cried and cried. I miss him. That yearning for holding him does not fade a year later. In fact, it hurts more now knowing that it cannot be a reality.

July 7, 2004: I am sitting here tonight, just crying . . . the night is haunting but Matthew gave me the strength, and he is asleep now. Tonight Matthew sang "Twinkle, Twinkle" to Gor Gor (Ryan). He almost forgot the lyrics since he has not sung that for a while. He talked to Gor Gor, which he also hasn't done in a while. "Gor Gor, Daddy loves you, Mommy loves you, I love you, everyone loves you." And he blew a kiss to the ceiling. Tonight Ryan's death seems so real. I am thinking about 12:40 a.m., or in anticipation of it. My therapist said I would be doing that for the rest of my life, reliving that night at each anniversary. This moment is so hard and I can do nothing to make it easier.

July 9, 2004: Well, we have survived Ryan's first-year anniversary. Now I am able to tell you that Ryan's anniversary was the toughest day among all the major events during the past year. John's parents, Matthew, and I brought Ryan's favorite food and snack to the cemetery. I was heartbroken and angry to see the grandparents presenting their love by placing food on the ground. It just should not be that way. They are supposed to play and spoil Ryan. Sometimes I think John and I can endure the pain, but it is heartbreaking to see the grandparents suffer. I just wanted to be alone, but I was with John's parents and Matthew.

[Edited journal entries in anticipation of and following the second anniversary of Ryan's death]

July 7, 2005: Today is a very difficult day. I went to work. Tried to focus and kept traveling back to 7/7/03 . . . remembering I was at work and returned home to see the boys at 5 p.m. It was a very warm summer day and Ryan and Matthew were in the back yard playing with our nanny. John came home shortly after and held Ryan while watching "Uncle Lance" in the Tour de France. Before I got Ryan to sleep, I felt his temple and thought he was warm. He had a temperature so I gave him some Tylenol. I checked on him every hour until 12:40, when our lives changed forever. How do we make sense of that? Today I felt the enormous mother-to-child love. I felt my intense love for my little boy and I yearned for that and I couldn't have it. I worked and cried, hoping nobody would catch me. It is such a private moment. This year, I didn't do any e-mail blast asking for support, reminding people tomorrow would be Ryan's second anniversary. It is just another day to the rest of the world and is such a life-changing day for our family. I survived the day with a lump in my throat, recalling the sequence of events that had happened on "that" day.

September 14, 2005: Spending two anniversaries without Ryan made us realize what is effective for us: it is important for us to get out of our regular routine so we can feel. We find being in nature, such as the ocean in Carmel or the mountains at Tahoe, allows us to reconnect to Ryan, and we find peace. On that day, I forward all calls to voice mail and spend the day in private with the family.

SUZANNE REDFERN

Mimi's birthday is September 17. The last one we spent with her was her thirty-second. It was less than three months before she died. Her cancer had advanced to a stage that confined her to her room, either in bed or in her recliner chair. She was on oxygen twenty-four hours a day. But she wasn't in pain and her spirit was alive and well—thriving, in fact, nourished by the love and care we'd all showered upon her. She and I had enjoyed planning her party. We would hang streamers from the ceiling fan, we'd decided, then set them spinning. We'd have soup and bread and a carob cake, and invite her husband Brett's parents, and there would be presents. No one loved giving or getting presents more than Mimi.

I'd carried out the details as planned and had a surprise in the wings: a rhyming skit I would deliver in fairy godmother costume, complete with a magic wand and a hidden bicycle bell that her brother Peter would ring as I touched the wand to each gift. The group was gathered and chatting when the phone rang. Brett took it in his adjacent office. We could tell by his tone that it was a medical call, no doubt the report from a recent scan that would reveal the efficacy of the latest chemotherapy cocktail, which was considered our last resort. When Brett came back we fell silent and watched in horror as he sank to his knees beside Mimi's chair and told her that her cancer was devouring both lungs and that it would be only a matter of weeks.

As Mimi took it in, I stood in terror that this news would finally break her. I could face her physical death, but not her spiritual one. If ever there was a pivotal moment, this was it. We watched her digest the information, then make a decision. She looked at me and asked, in a normal tone, "So, what now?" Brett mumbled something about clinical trials, but she shook him off. I said, "She means right now. She means what about her party!" She shot me a grateful look and we picked up where we'd left off. The party spun on late into the night, wrapped in a cloud of love so thick it shut out all thoughts of tomorrow. We knew at the time we'd never again experience love so palpably. None of us will ever forget it.

At Mimi's request, we scattered her ashes near our mountain cabin. We waited to do it until the snow melted, when the South Fork of the Merced River was roaring by the cabin in a joyous shout of rebirth. Brett, John, Peter, David, and I were joined by Mimi's two most trusted advisors—Jon Hake, a medical doctor, and Jackie Cortright, a Methodist minister. Before making our way to the circle of stones near the river where we'd hold our simple ceremony, each of us chose a container of some sort from around the house, something that Mimi had enjoyed over the years: a measuring cup, a wineglass, a coffee mug, or a dice cup. We carried them to the river, heard a prayer, and said our final goodbyes. Then Jackie portioned out into each receptacle a scoop of Mimi's ashes from the box where they'd spent the winter. When she had finished, we struck out on our own, each with our portion of ashes, and we set them free, scattering them wherever it seemed right: around the flagpole, on the Indian grinding rock, or into the pounding river itself. We incorporated her forever into this place she loved more than any other.

Because she loved it so, and because of that physical connection, we feel her powerfully present at the cabin. So on September 17, 2000, her thirty-third birthday, we started the tradition of meeting there again. There were visitors during the day, but by evening that first year, Peter, David, and I found ourselves alone. As is our way, we settled in around the games table. Someone mentioned Liar's Dice, and off we went in search of three sets of dice and three cups. Settling back into our places, we shook and shook our cups, then upended and slammed them down hard. From David's poured out, along with the dice, a shower of gray sediment. "What the . . . ?" said Dave. "Mimi," said I.

Remembering the spirit of the birthday a year earlier and our Mimi, none of us bolted, wept, or made a move to wipe the ashes from the table. We just played on.

PATTY SHAW

I don't know if *traditions* is the word I would use for my actions on the day of the slaying, February 2. What I usually do is say extra prayers, and the first one is always a fervent one that Cathy, for some reason, had her eyes shut and did not see the gun coming up to shoot her face away. Of course, that is my nightly prayer as well. Usually both my sons remember and call, and/or send a card. My grandsons, her sons, used to call but no longer do. I am certain that I am quieter that day more than any other of the year.

Now, her birthday, April 17, is another matter entirely. I cele-brate her birth and send prayers heavenward for having her with me for all of her forty-eight years. She was such an "up" person with a wicked sense of humor and a positive outlook on life. Her husband, being an air force pilot, had five overseas assignments for ten to twelve years, and I missed a lot of those grandsons' growing up. There were assignments in the States between the overseas ones, and I certainly made up for lost time during those months.

When I think of Cathy, I remember how sensitive she was, and how during any gathering of people she would always be with the one(s) who needed some encouragement or who were lonely or who were feeling out of place. Children followed her like she was a pied piper. Her career as a first-grade teacher was perfect for her and how very dedicated she was! She was very creative. All in all, she made me very proud and I loved her dearly. Not only was she my only daugh-ter, she was my firstborn. I try to make her birthday a celebration of her life.

MERRYL WEBER

I thought about creating rituals around the days of Adam's birth and death, but I was incapable of doing it. Since I was involved in a Jewish practice, I was able to plug into ancient and deeply nourish-ing rituals around grief and grieving that helped me get through each day as well as the many days of celebration and the anniversaries of Adam's dying. My husband also found these rituals to be helpful for many years, and so I was not alone most of the time. While we found solace in the rituals, our daughter Sonya did not. At Adam's death she found the rituals to be intrusive, too many people in our home night after night, prayers that didn't speak to her, people talking about Adam and their memories of him that she couldn't relate to.

To this day, Steve and I go to Adam's grave together on the anniversary of his death and his birthday. Our daughter has never gone with me to his grave at any time other than the funeral. Until this year I always called his girlfriend as well as Sonya on those days. We would speak about what was going on for each one of us around Adam's birthday or death day. But as time goes on, only Steve and I are always completely aware of the day as it approaches. I feel lucky that we still share these moments in whatever ways we agree upon each time.

KATHLEEN WEED

I have noticed that if a child's birthday and the date of her death fall within an approximate three-month period the parent experiences a "season of grief." For some the season is short and brutal. There is a week each year in February when my friend Kaylea Bakker must touch her son Anton's death, Anton's birthday, and her own birthday.

My season—June 10, the day of Jenica's death, until her birthday on September 14—swallows up most of the summer. The two anniversaries are still every bit as difficult even though it's been six years. I always try to do something to honor Jenica. One time I flew my mom out for a dinner with Jenica's closest friends. Another time I wanted to be all alone. My husband stayed at our country cottage, and I spent the day going through boxes of Jenica's schoolwork and artwork from as far back as preschool. Since my plan changes from year to year, I can't say I have created any traditions. Except for one.

I wear the same black linen sundress that I slid over my shoulders the day we buried Jenica. The dress was well worn, even then, but nothing could have taken its place in my heart. I had seen it for the first time during a school-clothes shopping expedition with

Jenica the summer before her sophomore year in high school. We both loved this shopping ritual, which found us in San Francisco's Union Square at around this same time every year. We always ate lunch at a chic little deli on Maiden Lane, where we picked out our menu together and shared whatever we ordered. Invariably we wore ourselves out going through as many department stores and boutiques as we possibly could. Then over a latte for me, and mocha for her, Jenica would make the delightful, excruciating decision as to which new school outfit she just couldn't live without. She knew my budget, and never asked for more than I could afford.

This day, while we were at J. Crew and Jenica was piling possible selections into a dressing room, I spied a soft, loose-fitting sundress, with deep, hidden pockets. I tried it on, and loved it. It was the sort of dress I could live in on hot, summer days. I didn't buy it though, partly because it was Jenica's shopping day and partly because I just couldn't justify spending the money to indulge myself.

Months later, on Mother's Day, Jenica handed me a present. I could hardly believe my eyes when I opened the package and saw the dress. Jenica was grinning from ear to ear. When I finished hugging her, I asked, "How could you possibly have afforded it?" I knew the dress had cost over a hundred dollars—a lot of money to a fifteen-year-old.

"I knew you loved the dress," Jenica explained, "so I asked the saleswoman if she could put it on layaway." Over the following nine months, Jenica had saved money from her allowance in order to buy the dress for me.

Invisible, the air supports life. I won't forget the shiver of black linen grazing my calves as I stared into Jenica's hollowed-out grave. I wondered, in that harsh moment, if her love that had not only blessed me—it had sustained me—was gone forever. Or could I believe that even as we moved to place Jenica's coffin beneath earth, her love, like the vacant sky, could still rise and fall in my breast. I wear the dress three days of the year—her death anniversary, her birthday, and Mother's Day.

Meeting Your Child's Friends

When we lose children, we lose along with them the lives they led, the friends who were in their orbit, the energy of that age. Being exposed to young people of the same generation as our children may prove to be a bittersweet experience for us. *How do you react when finding yourself in the company of your child's contemporaries?*

Stathi Afendoulis

One of my greatest joys and most difficult tasks is confronting the reality of Lainie's friends and the progression of their lives, without Lainie. In the weeks immediately following her death, some of Lainie's friends came to me and wanted to know how I was doing. They would e-mail me on her address and inquire about her sisters and the family. And then they would begin to tell me how Lainie affected their lives. Not through big acts, but in the small aspects of their friendship with her. They would recount her sense of humor and especially the verbal wit she possessed. When they were feeling insecure, she reassured them they could overcome their obstacles. Even her teachers would share their feelings and observations on what she did for others in school.

I began to realize the person I knew as a daughter was also a friend, confidante, advisor to so many kids. I wanted to know that person! The person Lainie was after she left the house for school each day. I decided to contact the friends who had approached me and ask if they would be willing to meet at school, to share their experiences of Lainie with me.

At about the same time I was formulating this plan, Lainie's English teacher called and told me many of her friends wanted to write about their feelings. I shared my idea with her, and this coincidence led to the formation of a writing group. We set our first meeting at the junior high Lainie attended and waited to see how many kids would show up.

I remember wondering what it would be like to sit in a room full of her friends and ask them to share the life they had with Lainie. I did not know what to expect, since these were twelve-year-old children, getting ready to enter the seventh grade. What would they tell me of the child I had? What would I learn about her that would bring me closer to her now that she was gone?

The first meeting of the writing club took place in Lainie's English classroom, the one in which she had shared so many good times. It turned out the English class was the best forum for her personality to shine and most of the stories recounted by her friends came out of this environment. Twenty-two kids attended that first meeting, and though not all of them continued to participate after the first meeting, it was for me the beginning of seeing and learning about Lainie in a whole new light.

In many ways, the stories recounted by her friends brought to life a whole new person. How bittersweet it was to me that the person her friends knew was someone I did not completely get a chance to meet. As the kids told of their personal interactions and observations of Lainie, I began to envision the teenager and adult she would have been. All the stories spoke of her ability to inspire confidence, her willingness to help others, her humor that brought laughter and insight into their lives. She made her friends laugh at themselves and be comfortable about it. She helped them put things in perspective. All this while battling a disease that would ultimately take her life, and yet, through it all, she was able to give. I believe this is what her friends truly knew and respected, her ability and willingness to give the best of herself and leave the suffering out of it. She never wanted to be pitied or given special treatment. This is the most predominant fact that came from all the conversations in the writing club. Lainie would tolerate no such behavior. She was the same as everyone else and wanted to be treated as such. What her friends knew, and what I'm sure she would have come to realize in time, was just how special and remarkable a person she was.

Three years have passed since the writing club met and I still keep in contact with many of her friends. When I am with them, I see the girl, growing into maturity and womanhood. I imagine what she would look like, the clothes she would wear. I hear her voice and laughter mixing with the other voices, taking its rightful place in life. I see myself, my family, whole again, and in my mind, we are all fine. There is no loss, no void, no sadness, only us. Happy again.

NANCY EMRO

When Sean died, he was a senior in high school. I didn't know any of his friends until after his death, when they rallied around me. Sean never brought his friends home to our condominium, instead meeting them in front of our building if they were going someplace or going over to their houses to hang out instead. I often feel guilty that I didn't have a chance to meet his friends while he was alive, never insisted that Sean bring them to the house. I don't know why Sean never invited them over to his own house, except that he always said our house was "boring" and found their homes much more interesting. (Sean was an only child living with his single-parent mother.)

The day after Sean's death, I brought my family down to the high school to meet with some of the students who were Sean's friends and to visit the place where Sean spent so much of his time, backstage in the high school theater. My memories of that meeting are almost surreal; I think I must have been in shock. Tim, Sean's theater teacher, introduced me to all the kids who had come to support each other in their grief, but I remember little of meeting them.

A few days after his death, I needed to go down to the high school for some reason and saw all those high school kids making their way to school. I remember automatically looking for my son, scanning the crowds of kids, looking for my son, momentarily forgetting he was gone. And then the reality hit me—Sean is not here anymore. I remember the terrible ache I felt in my chest. I remember I had to pass by the open doors of the auditorium. Upon hearing the whine of the power saw, I could not go in, even though Tim and the kids were there and would have embraced me. I was just reminded too much of Sean, of his presence in this place he loved so much, and that he wasn't the one wielding the power saw.

Over time, at Tim's invitation, I spent more and more time at the theater, getting to know the kids. I came down for tech crew calls and watched the kids put the set together. They were working on the set for *The Crucible.* Sean had created the set design for the show but never had the opportunity to see his first (and last) creation built and used in production. I loved being at the theater, watching the kids. All the rest of the school year (Sean had died in early October) I spent a lot of time at the theater, talking to Tim, talking to the kids, watching the sets come to life. I saw every show they did that year.

Come June, the end of the school year was looming and I was absolutely bereft. I didn't want to give up what had become a big part of my support system. Luckily for me, Tim decided to teach summer school that year and I was able to continue my connection with the high school theater over the summer. Come fall, there were new kids in Tim's class. But I still knew a lot of the old ones, because kids can take theater for all four years of high school if they want to, and most of them who develop a love of theater take it for as long as they can or as often as their parents let them. I still came down to the school the second year, but less often, stopping by only for the crew call the week before the show. I still attended every show the second year, praising and hugging the kids in the production after each show, for me the best part of coming to see the show.

It's now June again. I am no longer feeling bereft at the coming of the end of the school year. Most of the kids I know will be graduating, although a handful will be coming back next year. I don't even know (yet) if Tim will be teaching summer school and it doesn't bother me especially not to know. Either way, I know I will survive emotionally. And I will go back next fall, probably skipping the crew calls but continuing to come to the shows and hugging the kids I know afterward.

It wasn't (isn't) always easy for me to spend time at the theater. Most of the time, I just see teenagers. But sometimes the boys remind me painfully of my son.

I wrote the following to Tim after the crew call for the last show I attended:

Seeing the boys at Homestead today really made me think of Sean. I think of him every day, but usually not for long periods of time as I am trying to move forward with my life. But seeing the boys today, Chris and Devin and Kenny and Dan—they all reminded me of Sean in some way, in ways that fifteen- to seventeen-year-old boys are alike. Tall and gawky and thin and strong with an eye for mischief, a desire to do things mechanical, doing things just to amuse themselves.

Dan physically reminds me of Sean—his build, the short hair, the goatee, the cargo pants and tee shirt. Chris with his shorts and skinny hairy legs and brand-new steel-toed boots (just like Sean's). Devin's self-consciousness and awkwardness remind me a lot of Sean when he was fourteen or fifteen. Kenny's strength, Chris's mechanical ability and sense of humor. Amusing themselves by rolling Dan down the concrete walkway in that great big tube.

It doesn't matter who they are, if I know them or not, seeing them will always remind me of Sean in one way or another, these adolescent boys on their way to becoming men.

I'm not sure I will be coming down to watch the crew calls anymore. It's too heart wrenching, it keeps pulling me back into the past. I see Sean in all of these young men. At the same time, watching the crew calls has given me a tremendous understanding of my son and why he loved technical theater, why it was so important to him. I cherish all those times I spent in the auditorium and I am eternally grateful to you for letting me do this.

There were painful times: going home after the show without my child, when all the other parents go home with theirs; seeing a young man in front of me at a theater show, who from the back looked exactly like my son, a young man with his girlfriend, something my son would never have; seeing Sean's close friends huddled together, sharing some joke, and Sean not among them; Thespian awards night, and Sean not there to get the award that would have been his that year, the Best Tech award.

Still, I have such great memories of the kids and the shows that warm me when I think about them. I think the warm memories I have of the high school kids outweigh the painful memories that were and continue to be sometimes evoked. And I know spending time in the theater with the high school kids served a need I had, to understand what my son loved most about theater, to know my son better after his death, to maintain some connection with what he loved most, to maintain a connection with Sean.

Susan Gilbert

Through the years we have lost touch with most of Amanda's friends. I confess I did not make a huge effort in their direction because I thought it might be difficult for them. I am very grateful for those who remember us with Christmas cards or acknowledge us when our paths cross; these events happen less frequently as the years pass.

Although I do not often see contemporaries, I have lovely memories of them. For example, I am still touched at the many acts of kindness her friends showed us when Amanda died. They packed up all her belongings and delivered them to us when they came to her funeral. They wanted to spare us the pain of closing out her life in that way.

Other friends gave extraordinary eulogies at her funeral. A young woman with whom she had been friends for several years said something I will never forget for its insight and poignancy: "I always knew that when I looked back at the tears there would be laughter; I never knew that when I looked back at the laughter there would be tears."

We still see one friend of Amanda's occasionally. A close friend, Jill, was also in the accident that took our daughter's life. They were so close that she named her first child, a daughter, Amanda Kelley after our Amanda. In fact, on the last day of Amanda's life she and Jill were having lunch along with some other friends. Jill turned to Amanda and told her that she would one day name her daughter Amanda; our Amanda replied, "No, you must give her my full name: Amanda Kelley." Two hours later Amanda was dead. Whenever I think of this incident I feel a strong sense of wonder at the ways in which the Universe works and I receive enormous comfort.

When we see Jill and other contemporaries of Amanda we cannot help but think about what Amanda's life would be like now. What career would she have chosen? Whom would she have married, how many children would she have had, and where would she be living? We need to steel ourselves for weddings, seeing new babies, and all the joys of life that Amanda will never have. She had prepared herself so well and so maturely for a good life, and we cry with all bereaved parents, "It is just not fair."

So many of our friends now have grandchildren and I see the joy they take in their relationships with them. I always looked forward to Amanda's children and in my innocence assumed this stage of life would definitely come. I have tried to forge relationships with surrogate grandchildren, but have found that it is a difficult thing to do. I have volunteered at a grammar school, offered to baby-sit for friends and relatives, and so forth. But the reality is that these children already have parents and grandparents and I can only be a distant second at best.

VAN JEPSON

This one is especially easy for me to answer because I coached Ian's friends in soccer, basketball, and baseball. The connection I had with these boys was through Ian, and the sports that I coached or the sleepovers that we had. So I'd definitely miss the contact with these thriving bundles of love at the wonderful age of ten. Though these "coaching" experiences were the most intense for me. This group of eight boys gaggle together every morning before school starts in a central area of the campus. On occasion, when my heart calls me to, I go and find them and get my head down to their level, so I can look directly into their eyes and I say hello and ask them what they're doing and what they like. Because of a rapport that we built over the years of coaching, they all answer quickly and sometimes at once. The interaction takes maybe a minute or two, but it is so nourishing and rapid-fire for me that it completely satisfies me.

Even though I've stayed in contact with the parents of Ian's friends, the main contact is with this group of eight boys. I must relay a situation that just occurred last week as I went to watch my older son play basketball in the school gym. His game ended early and as the next boys took the floor, it turned out to be this group of eight of Ian's friends. It was an overwhelming joy to walk into the gym and see all Ian's friends playing basketball. They all stopped and quickly said hello and then went back to playing. It was a moment of overwhelming joy, and there were moments I thought I could sense Ian's energy among them.

MICHELE PHUA

Because of the twin dynamic, every day Matthew reminds me of Ryan. During the first couple of years, I would feel Matthew's face, feet, and hands while he was asleep and imagine he was Ryan as I explored the "what ifs?" How would he have grown? At almost five years old, Matthew has grown so much and I cannot imagine him to be the two-and-a-half-year-old Ryan anymore.

I still spend my Tuesday afternoons with my twin playgroup. This group consists of thirteen sets of twins, all around Ryan and Matthew's age. We formed the group when the children were infants. These are my friends who really understand the dynamic of twins and can relate at some level to the loss of one. They are the mothers I can open my emotions to. However, seeing twins in public—especially those who are two-and-a-half and those who are Asian boys—is a difficult experience to swallow. I look at the parents of the twins and remind myself that that was my past. I never can compliment the parents on how cute their twins are. I stand in the elevator quietly and pretend that I am ignoring them. After all, they have the privilege that was taken away from me.

LOTTIE SOLOMON
[From an interview]

Naomi's friend Vivian gave one of the talks at her memorial. They were at Bank of America together and now Vivian is a vice president of Prudential. I had a memorial service at Beth Am, and about seven hundred people came. Word spread, and people just came; I had prepared a dinner reception. I said, "This is the last opportunity I will have to honor Naomi." *So.* And she loved things done just right; I made sure it was done just right. It was magnificent, and everybody came. I don't know . . . people came out of love, out of sadness, out of curiosity, out of shock!

We had people talking, aunts gave some words, and her uncle talked, because Herb can't talk, of course, and her brothers talked, and three or four friends. One of them, Vivian, was her closest friend, they lived one block apart, and Vivian had gone through a rancorous divorce, and Naomi had supported her through this whole thing—they were friends for twenty-five years, there wasn't a day . . . but Vivian wrote a letter to her, "Dear Naomi . . ." that was the speech she gave. The place was crying, the whole audience was crying, because of course it was well done, but so did all the speakers. They are all kind of special girls.

MERRYL WEBER

In the first few years after Adam's death I neither sought out nor avoided the company of our son's contemporaries other than my relationship with Melanie, his girlfriend. I missed the energy that he had always brought around us, the many friends he played music with, the crowd of young people in our home hanging out and talking, jumping in and out of our backyard pool, breaking bread with us. Our door had always been open to kids and they were over a lot. A few of the rest of his friends drifted in and out of our lives occasionally and often uncomfortably. Only two friends kept up continuous contact with us over the years: Melanie, whose company we had always enjoyed, and one of his dearest friends, Lars, who always made a point to see us when he was in town from school. I found it deeply touching that this young man would take time to come over and "hang out" with us, and for me it was a reminder of how wonderful a friend our son had been to him, what a good judge of character Adam had been to have picked such a thoughtful friend at just twelve years old. To this day Steve and I are still close with Melanie though I know it must be hard on her to be with us now that she is married with children of her own. Lars and our daughter Sonya ended up falling in love and marrying just a few years ago, so now we are often surrounded by Adam's friends, since Lars and he were friends with many of the same people.

I enjoy the company of Adam's friends more of the time than not but there are moments when being with them is emotionally exhausting. That old "why" grief tape will start replaying in my head: why did Adam have to die? Then I must go off alone, weep to regain my sense of balance, my composure, by allowing the feelings to surface and recede still once again. The paradox is that, except for my own family, it is only among his peers I can speak of him without reservation, remembering him in an anecdote about something he did or said. Better yet, I am privy to hear their stories of who he was to them, what they did together, how he might have touched their lives. Though this very same situation often unleashes a shorter version of horrible pain from the beginning, the unbearable loss of his presence in my life, I am still happy to be with them all. I've learned how to live with the way my emotions play out each time.

JANE WINSLOW
[From an interview]

I have such a difficult time with this. I still live in the same neighborhood where Peter was born and raised. I have lived here for over thirty years. His friends invite me to their weddings and I often run into people he knew in the street. Some have children, and while I am happy for my friends with grandchildren, it hurts and saddens me to realize that I will never have any.

Peter was very much a part of our local community and I see so many people of all ages who remember him. This is what he said in a high school paper: "As the people in a family live together they will surely see a lot of the same people in the neighborhood. My mom and I both recognize store owners, café people, the butcher, a few bus drivers, and the old neighborhood fellows who habitually meet every night on the street corner to discuss the topic of the day. Common friends are part of the 'family experience.'" So it is not only contemporaries that bring back memories, but so many people in our neighborhood.

Taking Stock

In part 1, you've met all but three of the parents whose stories make up this book. You may have noticed that our experiences, and the way we talk about them, are unique to each of us, as are our survival instincts under great duress. During those first weeks and months, we depend on those primitive instincts to get us through. Our behavior may appear irrational to others, and even to ourselves. Suzanne Redfern ducked and danced. Merryl Weber, according to her husband, wasn't very "nice." Sheila George went shopping. If there's one conclusion you might draw, it's that there is not one *right* way of grieving. In fact, the only *wrong* way is not to allow yourself to grieve at all.

Reading through these remembrances of the early days, you may also have become aware of a common thread running through the various stories: a conscious decision that fundamentally informed the way many of us took on life in the new reality. The decisions themselves may have differed in their focus—Susan Gilbert made up her mind to survive, Van Jepson to stay in the present moment, Michele Phua to be authentic in her feelings, John Phua to let himself fall to the bottom of his sorrow, Monica Jones to exemplify her faith in practice, Mary Lou Coffelt to turn off the horror thoughts and replace them with gentler ones, Merryl Weber to come out more alive than before—but the effect was the same. At their lowest point, all of these people resolved not to be defeated by their fate. That jaw-setting commitment seems to have carried them through the wrenching onset of grieving and into their faltering return to life.

As you move on to part 2, you may find more mention of these intentional decisions as we parents talk about our search for support systems during a difficult reentry into the everyday.

PART TWO

SEEKING SUPPORT

Setting Out

Sometime during the first year, after we had absorbed the initial shock and made our first ventures into a world without our children, our grief work changed. We moved from just getting through each day, barely taking care of the daily business of life, to beginning the more internal work of incorporating our loss into our being. To help us in that process we looked to a number of sources for support.

Religious beliefs, once taken for granted, came into question. Some of us felt betrayed by church or by God; others found their faith changed, or even strengthened. Several parents say they consciously held on to a belief in the survival of the spirit because it promised an eventual reunion with their children.

Many of us sought the help of professional counseling, with mixed results. Also mixed were the well-meaning attempts of our friends and colleagues to express sympathy. Although their efforts were appreciated, too often insensitive remarks, platitudes, or false assurances left us feeling empty and isolated. Some of us felt burdened by expectations that we should just "get over it." On the rare occasion, however, an unexpected gesture gave us just the right nudge or the lift that we needed.

Out of our longing to believe that our children's spirits still existed somewhere, several of us turned to psychic mediums. Two tapped into their own psychic abilities to develop an ongoing communication with the spirits of their children.

These traditional and nontraditional resources sometimes relieved our sorrow, at least temporarily. When they didn't, and we felt we couldn't carry on, some of us considered taking our own lives. We're grateful that all of us found reasons to go on living.

Rethinking Faith

In their deepest despair human beings often turn to a power greater than themselves for explanations, for hope, for comfort. Some have strong religious traditions that support them (or don't) during these times. Others who haven't an established faith sometimes find one under duress. It is probably during times of their deepest anguish that most people discover or abandon God. *How has your experience affected your own religious or spiritual beliefs? What did you believe before your loss; what do you believe today?*

STATHI AFENDOULIS

Three months before Lainie died, my wife left the hospital with her and headed to church. It was the Wednesday of Holy Week in the Greek Orthodox Church, and on this day, we receive the sacrament of Holy Unction. We go to church and are anointed by the priest after a ceremony blessing the oil. The oil heals the sick and blesses the body and soul. Lainie protested that she was tired and, now confined to a wheelchair, did not want to go to church. My wife, desperate to find some solace and comfort, and mired in traditions we grew up with when we were young, would hear none of it. They were off to church, to petition God once again for a miracle

When they got there, it was raining. Transferring Lainie to the wheelchair was hard for Emily and rain made the whole process worse. The doors to the church are heavy and as they tried to enter, they encountered difficulty with the weight and the small steps over which the wheelchair had to pass. Emily looked around the church for help. There was a group of men, all who knew us, standing across the narthex. While Emily struggled with the doors and the wheelchair, no one made a move to help. After a few frustrating minutes, she finally called out to them, shaking them from their blindness, and they helped get Lainie inside.

The fury in Emily grew as she entered the church and not a head turned to recognize the child. The line was long, so she proceeded directly to the front, not wanting to keep Lainie, who was now mortified by the whole situation, there any longer than necessary. At this point, Emily felt the torment of all parents with very sick children. You will do anything to save them, body and soul, so you try to do what's right and get slammed for it. She turned to her church, the one institution she believed would never fail her, and was greeted with silent stares. It was the day her faith died.

When she recounted the story to me later, I sat in mute testimony to the fact that our church as an institution had failed us. Our faith, although still intact, was struggling to survive. We questioned everything, mad at God, the only thing we could blame. All we knew of our spiritual beliefs came into question. Many times we wanted to turn away from it all, certain that God had abandoned us. The only thing that keeps us in touch with our faith is Lainie. If we don't believe she is out there, waiting for us, then where is our hope? Where is the soul we look to be reunited with again? It is easy to reject the manmade version of faith, with its rituals and anointing; it is another thing to reject the mystery of the life of the soul.

We believe Lainie lives. We must. In our only conversation about death, shortly after her cancer returned, she told me it might be better to die and be in Heaven than to have to endure the pain of treatment and disease. I told her I believed she was right, and when the time came, she would make that decision. On Wednesday, June 14, 2000, she decided and moved on, leaving us to continue believing as she believed, and to wait for our reunion.

INÉS ASCENCIO
[From an interview]

I think faith helps. Whatever your beliefs are, if you can put it into a context it helps.

In my work in El Salvador, people would tell me they were in contact with the deceased; a lot of people had lost people in the war. So, that's the general reporting you heard from other people—the spirit would contact them. We talked about this subject this week at our staff meeting because one of our staff member's sister-in-law passed. She waited for certain people to come before she died. I think people know they are leaving before they pass away. Someone I know was hit by a car while crossing the street, perfectly legally in the crosswalk on Market Street. with the light and everything. But before he passed, he visited with many of us. It was very strange because it wasn't a friend that I saw regularly. He had redone his will . . . just certain acts of preparation. Then when we saw his journal there were some quotes in there from a few weeks before about death. It was just really strange.

Mary Lou Coffelt

When Mattie died, we were not actively involved in our church. I had been raised in a very close and comfortable Catholic family and the church had been a very stable part of my growing up, but as an adult I had not been drawn to the church community partly out of logistics (we did not always live very close to town) and partly because I felt no strong need to be a part of a congregation. I found my God in the hills in which I lived and worked. As a result, our churchgoing was sporadic and without commitment. When Mattie died, the pastor of our little Catholic church in Tres Piños, without questions or hesitations, came to us as though we had been his most devoted of followers. He was a dynamo, a high-energy, caring, matter-of-fact kind of person. He respected our needs and offered an open door. He knew what to say and when to say it, and he was very comfortable with death; this was refreshing and very helpful to us, as we were trying desperately to get used to the concept of a dead child. This man brought a piece of God's peace to us without a lot of preaching or gobbledegook! We had Mattie's funeral at our little church and God's presence was everywhere. He was in every person crowded in that small church. I could see it in their eyes. I could feel it all around me.

I have always felt loved by God, and the God I grew up with was always a loving and kind God, not a fearful, judgmental God, but I have never felt as uplifted by my God as I was on that day. I had never really needed God in such a way. I had never been reduced to such a charred human being and, at this lowest time in my life, I was able to witness God's love in so many ways that it amazes me still. God used his people to spread his love . . . the kindness was everywhere we went. Family, friends, strangers. God sent some of the strangest messages through some of the oddest folks! For this I am eternally grateful and ever aware of the work of our God. He didn't take my pain away. I still suffered what seems to me, at times, endlessly. And God did not bring my Mattie back, although that would have been my hope. God helped me walk through my grief. He gave me strength to take each step. He graced me with people who could hold me up when I could not make it on my own. As time went on he gave me little tiny glimpses of peace. Today he keeps me traveling my unknown road. Now that time has helped me feel a little more sane, he helps me learn to walk a little (ever so slightly) closer to him.

In the months after Mattie died we did not return to our little church. It only symbolized our day of Mattie's funeral and nothing more. Little by little we decided we wanted to return, and on the day we attended our first Mass we were overwhelmed with emotions and tears. But we made it through, and gradually we began to return to church. Sunday Mass became important to me. And has continued to be. I now value the community of support. I need a place to go to share in the grace of God. It was and is people who held us together, the people of God. These folks are not only at church, they are everywhere, but gathering together with some of these people to honor God continues to give me strength and I appreciate that.

SHEILA GEORGE
[From an interview]

It wasn't altered at all. I'm a Seventh Day Adventist, and they rallied around me 100 percent. If anything it made it stronger, my belief in God. But my daughter was the one who had to go and identify my son. And she's never been right since. She blamed God, and she did the flip, while I hung in there with him. She hated everything about God at that time. But I didn't have to go identify Ronnie, so I can't say why she feels the way she does.

SUSAN GILBERT

My spiritual beliefs have changed and grown. I experienced several deaths and other big challenges early, and had a childish and naive belief that God would not take anything more from me. Surely, I thought, I had suffered a lifetime's worth of grief by the time I was forty. I never contemplated that Amanda could die since I saw her as a reward for the grave difficulties I had experienced.

As a result, I felt very much betrayed by God when Amanda died. Yet, as angry as I was, I knew almost immediately that I could not face the future without some philosophy and a belief in a supreme being. So, I decided I had better find a different view. As I searched, I felt that I received reassurance. There were several times when I believe I was sent the reassuring message, "I am here."

Sometimes reassuring stories and messages do not seem as vibrant in the retelling as they do when they are happening. Nonetheless, I will relate several of the most meaningful:

Very soon after Amanda's death, a friend told me a fable of dragonfly nymphs that suddenly disappear and leave their friends in the pond. One day the nymphs make a pact that the next nymph to leave would come back and tell the others where he had gone. Sure enough, one soon left, and he came back and beat his wings against the pond trying to no avail to capture the attention of his friends. He finally realized that he could not reach them and flew away. Right after I first heard this fable, I was surrounded by dragonflies; they were everywhere. One day, one that seemed as large as a helicopter flew into the house, swarmed around, and then flew out again. Dragonflies will always have special meaning for me.

In the first year after Amanda's death I was driving down the highway on a day that was partly rainy and partly sunny. There was a huge rainbow in the sky that moved toward me, ultimately enveloping me in the car. I felt comforted.

We went to church the Sunday after Amanda's death, a church which we had never attended before. The exact same music we had chosen for her memorial service was played, even though the hymns were somewhat unusual. It was a pure coincidence. Three months later my mother died and we attended her funeral 250 miles away. The following Sunday we went to the same church and the music played for my mother was played in the church. Again, a coincidence and one that seemed to tell us that we were being watched over.

We all experience synchronicities in life, which we sometimes dismiss as happenstance. I have come to believe that there are few real coincidences. If I am paying attention, I see people who are brought into my life at just the right time, or answers that just seem to come from nowhere to help me solve problems.

In the final analysis, I do think that I have no choice but to submit to the will of God as I understand him. It is in this submission that I have found what I consider a more mature system of beliefs.

Sometimes I feel offended when other people are so very sure they know all that God is or could be. Some mean well and say things like, "She's in a better place." I sincerely hope so, but that does not help here and now. I do not think any of us truly knows the reasons why things happen or can explain the ultimate realities of life or God. Many faiths and beliefs try to do so, but that sort of belief does not work for me. I find that there is a big difference between obedience to the will of God and more superstitious beliefs that like to think that nothing bad can happen to us if we follow a specific formula.

VAN JEPSON

Although I had been raised Christian with a strong family unit of four children and two parents who are still alive and married after fifty-five years together, I had few ongoing religious practices. I did believe in God and the Holy Spirit and Jesus Christ. I had faith that they existed because of the stories in the Bible written about them. I did not have any strong direct experiences that moved me beyond belief or faith and into knowing. I went to church twice a year, on

Christmas and on Easter. I had ongoing discussions with my wife, who was a nonbeliever, about the proper religious or spiritual way to bring our children up. These included questions about baptism, Sunday school, and prayer.

Even though my religious beliefs have not been altered by Ian's passing, my direct spiritual experiences have transformed me and every facet of my life. I have been forever altered by the experiences that I had during the tragic events of his death, and the minutes, hours, days, weeks, and months thereafter, continuing to this very moment. Through my daily meditation, prayer, and writing routine I have come to a place of knowing, where I have a strong heart connection with Ian. This is astonishing to me, and I will say that the process of grief has cracked open my heart and let the love between us keep it open. This is true even when he and I are separated by the distances of life and death, or Heaven and Earth.

I have reread the Bible and have gone to church regularly since Ian's passing and have found that what has been written in the Bible is a clear and perfect validation of the direct experience that I have every day that Ian is alive and well in Heaven and, more astonishing, can communicate with me while I'm on Earth.

MONICA JONES

Was I ready at the age of twenty-eight to be told that our ten-month-old daughter Bronwyn had a progressive neurological disorder that would cause total paralysis and death before she was two? Yes and no. As it turned out, Bronwyn lived to be nine, so we had plenty of time to learn what we needed to know.

I certainly knew nothing about things medical, but I was prepared to care for Bronwyn in three respects. First of all, as the child of German political refugees I was encouraged by my parents to ask questions, to try to understand what was happening (or had happened) and why, and not to be satisfied with easy answers. Therefore, although I knew very little about science, I learned in those pre-Internet days how to ferret out factual information and evaluate it. I also learned to work with doctors and to persist until I understood what I thought I needed to know.

Secondly, due to genetics or good luck, I just happened to be not only a rather optimistic and persevering person, but also someone who genuinely enjoyed being with my daughter and caring for her at home. I initially was able to work around the rather flexible schedule of a graduate student and later was fortunate to be able to be a full-time mother and nurse, as my husband had a full-time job with medical benefits.

Finally, and perhaps more important, I did have philosophical and spiritual beliefs, which not only supported me but strengthened over time. As a teenager I had seriously considered not only the meaning of life, but also why some children suffer and die young.

When considering what happened when one died, I figured out there were only three basic alternatives:

1. You go to Heaven or Hell. This was the alternative presented to me by the Methodist Church, but I found solace neither in the idea that transgressions would cause some to suffer for all eternity nor that others might live short and/or difficult lives but be rewarded with eternal life in Heaven.

2. Life ends at death. If everything in nature is cyclical—the days, the seasons, and so on—why should humans live and then just cease to exist?

3. Karma and reincarnation or the biblical concept of sowing and reaping extend over more than one lifetime. My husband and I were introduced to these ideas in college before Bronwyn was born and to us they made sense. To me karma meant that there is always a relationship between cause and effect.

When Bronwyn was diagnosed as having Werdnig-Hoffmann's Syndrome, I did not question why bad things happen to good people, nor did I wonder why she was the victim of nasty, cruel fate.

Rather, her condition led me to consider the validity of my belief in a law-governed Universe, in which everything happens for a reason, although that is not to say one always knows why. Indeed, if one looks at an individual's life, it is often difficult to understand why things have happened as they have, particularly why children suffer or die young. However, if one thinks in terms of more than one lifetime, then each new life provides new opportunities to learn and grow. One could argue that individuals suffer misfortune because of misdeeds in the past, but one could equally well propose that what might appear as misfortune might actually be an opportunity to learn.

In Bronwyn's case, she must have occasionally found it frustrating to be so paralyzed that she couldn't even scratch her nose, let alone feed herself or move. However, perhaps what she learned was patience and an ability to accept help from others. I often thought that we, as parents, learned much from caring for her, perhaps more than she learned from us.

We did what we saw as our duty. In a sense life was easy because we got up every morning and knew exactly what to do. We learned how to keep things in perspective. As Bronwyn was so handicapped and ill, we had a very small margin of error. Consequently, little mistakes were often life-threatening. We had to learn that we, as parents and caregivers, could only do our best. As our pediatrician sagely told us each time Bronwyn would become very ill, "She'll get better, get worse, or stay the same." So while we had no control over the results of our actions and efforts, we did have control over our attitude.

Before Bronwyn was born I had read much about Mahatma Gandhi and found a wonderful translation of Gandhi's favorite text, *The Bhagavad-Gita*. Krishna points out that those who are wise in spiritual things grieve neither for the dead nor the living, for death is certain to all things that are born and rebirth is certain to all mortals. Krishna goes on to say:

A man is said to be confirmed in spiritual knowledge when he forsaketh every desire which entereth into his heart, and of himself is happy and content in the Self through the Self. His mind is undisturbed in adver-

sity; he is happy and contented in prosperity, and he is a stranger to anxiety, fear, and anger.

I think that the difficulties we face in life test our faith. Although one might profess to hold beliefs, the real challenge is whether one can exemplify such beliefs in action. While we must find our own way, I ultimately memorized much of Krishna's soliloquy, and when frustrated or unable to sleep, I would keep coming back to these ideas, which I found to be most helpful.

When Bronwyn was alive, in the early 1970s, there were no parent support groups in our area, although I did have two other mothers with whom I spoke by phone. However, I was fortunate to be a member of a group that regularly considered philosophical and spiritual ideas, and these discussions helped deepen my understanding of karma and reincarnation.

One big advantage of a progressive illness is that one is not physically and emotionally faced with everything at once. Rather, our family slowly adapted to new conditions, living and learning from day to day. Long illnesses also have the advantage of allowing parents time to become reconciled to the idea of a child's dying. Nevertheless, when death occurs, the living, particularly if they have been twenty-four-hour-a-day caregivers, have to reconstitute their lives. While this takes time—not days, or weeks, or months, but probably at least a year or two—I continued to hold fast to the ideas that had sustained me.

In retrospect, while I did not choose Bronwyn to be the way she was, I'm very grateful she was a part of my life. I became very close to her in part because I physically had to do everything for her. Yet, because she was bright and articulate and had a wonderful sense of humor, we also became the best of friends. I think our family learned to see difficulties not as enormous burdens, but as opportunities to learn, and we are the better for it.

When asked recently if I had wanted Bronwyn to be normal, I was a bit flummoxed. While logically I would have to say yes, I must admit I never pictured her as "normal" and was never filled with longing for her to be someone else.

MARTIN KATZ

Our rabbi was a personal friend and contemporary with the same aged children. He was a welcome visitor and listener. I did not have many. I have a relatively strong Jewish background and am proud of the religion and its customs, traditions, values, and accomplishments. I also went to a Catholic university and studied ethics and religion, which I was able to blend with my Jewish concepts. I do not believe in a physical hereafter or personal reunion. My rationale for being is that you live on in the good deeds you have performed. I love to read and be awed by articles on cosmology. My overriding and simple conclusion is a question. *Why?*

KATHRYN LODATO

I live but a mile or two from Leland Stanford Junior University, commonly just called Stanford. The university was founded by the Stanfords in honor of their only child, who died when he was fifteen years old. They are all buried on the grounds, and there's a statue by the mausoleum that stops my heart for a moment each time I see it. The Angel of Grief, it's called. A larger-than-life white stone angel, on her knees, her head bowed and resting on an altar, her strong, beautiful face all but hidden, her huge, graceful wings folded and drooping. There is nothing cute or charming about this angel. She is awesome, fierce, with a grief huge enough to hold the broken hearts of all the bereft mothers. I keep a picture of her on my altar, where I sit when I meditate and pray. The altar is set up on a small redwood table that my son Nick made for me as a place to set my margarita when I was relaxing in a lounge chair after a summer Saturday working in the yard. Nick had just six more years of life than Leland Junior had.

I was raised in a very secular family. For my first forty years, religion, spirituality, and God were not a conscious part of my life. I never considered myself to be an atheist, but was too caught up in the day-to-day of my life to give God or matters of ultimate concern more than a passing thought. Looking back, I recognize a vague longing and moments of dim insight, but nothing I followed up on.

When Nick died, my life and my heart were blasted apart. One of the things I knew early on, knew with a certainty that goes beyond logic, was that I could not survive this alone, that I needed a force much larger than any I knew to help me survive. And so I began a long, halting journey toward faith. For the first two years after Nick died, I could only read two sorts of books: books about death, and especially about the death of children, and books about spirituality. Everything else just seemed utterly petty. I felt called to a meditation practice and tried to figure out what it means to pray.

A book that impacted me deeply, *Living Buddha, Living Christ* by Thich Nhat Hanh, said that we should all, rather than seeking after new traditions, sink our roots down into our own tradition and make it live within us. I thought deeply about that and realized that, to the extent I had a tradition, it was Christian. At least I knew the major holidays and some of the vocabulary. I started to go to church. I would cry through the entire service and go home so exhausted I had to lie down. It took several tries, but I found a church that combined a rich and beautiful liturgy with an explicit stance that we are *all* spiritual beings seeking to know God, and that all religions at their heart are true, and that they are all also flawed. I have found real community there, and deep solace. It has become a source of strength and an important part of my life.

I don't have a lot of detailed beliefs about life and death and how God works in the world. I ascribe to the wisdom of what the poet John Keats called "negative capability," which is the ability to rest in, to *be* in, "uncertainties, mysteries, doubts, without any irritable reaching after fact and reason." I believe that what I don't know vastly outweighs what I do know. But I have slowly, painfully, come to be a person of faith. A person who believes, who *knows* in some sense that can't be explained or quantified, that there is much more to reality than what we can perceive with our senses or measure with our scientific instruments. And that that "more"—call it God or Spirit—is *good,* is deeply and ineffably good and sacred and holy, despite our sorrow and suffering. I believe that we are grasped and held and permeated with God. And I believe that death is not the end, although I don't profess to know what exactly is beyond the portal of death.

It has been hard for me to accept that it took the death of my son for me to be open to the gifts of Spirit. But to deny these gifts would compound the tragedy, would, in some odd but very real sense, let Nick down, betray his life and his death. The Angel, fierce and passionate, has become a sort of totem for me, a symbol to help me hold, even if I don't understand, the awesome mysteries of life and death.

A couple of years ago I wrote a poem about this Angel:

THIS IS THE ANGEL

This is the angel who stands at your door
and slices you open
and tears out your heart
and strips out your nerves to flay them upon
your exposed and broken bones

This is the angel without a smile
with a blinding sword
and deep eyes that burn
and make you tremble
and shatter your world

This is the angel who watches you gasp
and stands by while you weep
and sees when you crumble and lie on the floor

This is the angel who bows her bright head
and reaches her hand out
and strokes your damp hair

This is the angel who sings you a song
just before waking
and when you think you will fall

—to tumble forever—
into the abyss that gapes at your feet

This is the angel who touches your hand
    and lifts up your chin so you look in her eyes
    and shows you the path
        that leads straight through their depths

This is the angel who stays by your side
    and holds her sword steady
    and holds her gaze fierce
    and waits when you falter
    and nods when you rise

This is the angel who holds your heart and your breath
    your tears and your bones
    your dreams and your sorrows
    and all of your being
        in the tender, callused palms of her hands

This is the angel

MICHELE PHUA
[From an interview]

As for church: we went to a service once. What happened was we met lots of people who didn't give us comfort. That just isn't going to give us a single answer. The priest said that so-and-so had had a death and then they had another baby.

PATTY SHAW

My religious beliefs have not changed. I believe in God and believe in Heaven. My Cathy was my parents' first grandchild and she was dearly, dearly loved. It comforts me to know that she is with them and not alone. I also believe that there are plenty of children up there who died for some reason or another and that she is seeing to them and their needs.

MERRYL WEBER

More than any other experience I have had in my life Adam's death deepened my understanding of the interconnectedness of all life and changed the way I thought about the role of spirit in all our lives. His death brought me to my knees, quite literally, and I found that by necessity I had to surrender to something indefinable and unfathomable. The sea was stormy and yet full of light and a love that was both subtle and powerful. Even the anger I felt did not mitigate the experience of being connected to everyone and everything around me, even people I couldn't stand being around too much!

The morning Adam died was beautiful. I had been on an early morning walk in the mountains with a friend, and was sitting at a stoplight just enjoying the day. As I waited for the light to change, I distinctly heard an inner voice say, "Our lives are not in our hands, our lives are not in our hands." Experience has taught me to pay attention when something like that repeats twice or more. I thought, *I wonder if I am going to die today,* though I wasn't particularly bothered by that thought. Not too long after I got home, I received the call telling me Adam was dead. His death had taken place within an hour of that inner voice at the stoplight.

More than once family, friends, and acquaintances alike asked me if I was angry at God over Adam's death. My answer is the same now as it was then. I was angry at his death, at his being gone forever from my life, from our lives, for the emptiness that was left and the sorrow we must carry with us, but to this day I have never been angry at "God." I had always felt that my children were borrowed, that they were/are a gift given to me, a gift that brought the flow of love into my life. They were not "mine," though, of course, I thought of Adam as "my son." I just never framed my ideas about birth and death from the point of view of God having taken him from me as some sort of punishment, any more than I had felt God had "given" him to me in the beginning as some sort of reward.

I have spent so much time in my life just watching the way all life arises from nothing really and then melts back into nothing again. Even as a small child playing in the dirt, squishing ants as they came out of their ant hills, watching the insects caught in a spider web, having a beloved dog hit by a car and die, I wondered at the capriciousness of life and death, the "here one moment, gone the next" quality of it. For me it just became "the way it is." This understanding stood me well when Adam died.

JANE WINSLOW
[From an interview]

I sometimes feel that both Peter and his father knew that they would not have long lives. It makes me feel better knowing that they would not have thought they had lost a great deal of experience. They both felt that they lived rich lives and if they were short, then that would be okay. I find relief in this thought.

Shortly after Peter died, there was a dove that would come and sit on the railing of my balcony. He would just sit and look at me and I felt that Peter was close.

Pursuing Counseling

As a result of the isolation most bereaved parents feel, many of us seek group support or counseling. *Did/do you attend a grief support group or professional grief/psychological counseling? How does it help you? Fail you? How will you know when it's time to stop?*

STATHI AFENDOULIS

During my third visit to the therapist, I had a life-altering experience. I was in the room and talking about something, when she stopped me cold and said, "I want you to stop saying 'we.'" Apparently, when I was talking in the sessions, I would always refer to myself and my experiences in the first-person plural. "I want you to start saying 'I' when you talk about yourself." Well, it took the rest of the hour for me to make this adjustment. I found myself having to think about it, physically think about it, by leaning forward or pausing, and then correcting myself when I let a *we* slip out.

When I left her office, it was all I could think about. You see, all my life I have been raised to believe I was part of a greater whole. I belonged to a family, a community, a church. All these things served me and I served them. They were as much a part of the person that I was as my own individual traits. I was defined by the things that I served. That is, until cancer came to my life.

They say there is strength in numbers and I believed that position to be true. All the pillars of my life, the "we" part of my life, held me up and kept me going. All through Lainie's struggle I used them to find strength. Then she died. And all the "we" parts of me died with her. You see, I had never looked truly to myself to find the strength I needed in life. I had always used the "we" parts and saved myself from the reality of my own feelings. My therapist, with a seemingly simple request, made me view my life, for the first time, from my own very personal and private perspective. The strength that I thought came from "we" really came from "me." But I had to embrace it, find it, and put it back into my life.

I sought therapy because I felt myself slipping away. I had to find the real me, or at least begin the search. I thought that therapy would be about Lainie and me and all the other "we's" in my life, but it ended up being about me only, and that is good! Lainie was gone, whether I liked it or not, and I had to be able to make that reality a part of my life. I stopped therapy after nine months and the search continues, but I wouldn't trade those months for anything. I feel I was reborn, ironically, in that time. I learned that by serving myself first, I could still serve others and cope with my own grief. In fact, learning to say *I* instead of *we* helped me to grieve more openly and honestly than I had ever done before.

MARY LOU COFFELT

We were fortunate—available in our community at the time was a six-week information grief group led by a local counselor who had lived her own grief. She provided a safe place to share a lot of our grief, but mostly receive a ton of information guiding us through some of the "stages" of grieving. It was helpful to us to understand more about the process, learning that some of the bizarre feelings, thoughts, and behaviors are "normal," a natural consequence of grief. Beyond that we had no other formal assistance.

SHEILA GEORGE
[From an interview]

At that time there was an organization called Mothers Against Drugs, so I joined that organization and from that point I became president and that's what changed my life. In the process, I met a lot of people from real life, staffers, social workers, and so on who came around, and we started what we called "Friends Healing Friends," same as you're doing, only you're writing a book and I wanted to get the mothers like us together. Because nobody knew how I felt, nobody can identify with the pain. So I started a group just for mothers and family members to heal, just to talk about the pain.

But I found that in the black community nobody wanted to talk about it, that it wasn't reality to them, so it only lasted about a year. The program was run through Stanford and those professionals donated their time free and everything. We had a circle, we would meet and just talk. They were people whose children had been killed. It helped *me*, but I was single. A lot of people were married, and the husbands wouldn't want them to come. The husbands were the ones who said, "We can manage all our pain."

SUSAN GILBERT

I did not attend any formal support groups for grieving parents. My husband and I saw a psychiatrist jointly for counseling because we knew that there is a high risk of divorce for bereaved parents and we very much wanted to hold onto our relationship. We saw this kind man, sometimes infrequently, for several years and found the counseling very helpful to us.

I also saw a therapist individually shortly after Amanda's death, but this treatment was not always beneficial. Although the psychiatrist I saw truly wanted to be helpful, and I know she felt deeply for my loss, she did not always have the right tools for helping me. For a year following the death, I experienced very severe insomnia. This sleeplessness continued with no effective remedy, exhausting my scarce supply of emotional energy. Additionally, I fell into a deep depression and it continued untreated for months. Unfortunately, I did not feel strong enough at that time to find another doctor so I battled suicidal thoughts and sleepless nights without sufficient help. Finally, after almost a year, the psychiatrist prescribed medication in the wrong dosage for me which made me ill and I lost confidence in her. In retrospect, it would have been better if she had referred me to someone more experienced and competent in treating depression with medication, and I wish that I had been strong enough to force this change earlier.

Ultimately, through some trial and error, I located a psychiatrist/psycho-pharmacologist who is an expert in prescribing psychoactive medications and my depression is adequately treated.

VAN JEPSON

I attended one grief support group two weeks after Ian passed and did not go back. The support group was a big turnoff for me, because I observed everyone just slogging around in the muck of their loss. It was independent of how long their children had been gone, from two weeks in our case, to two months, to two years, to twenty years. Everyone who came just rambled as they shared stories of bottomless grief. Although the benefits of the group approach were confusing, it appeared to me that it was a grief addiction more than a process of letting go. I asked how it affected their relationships with their loved ones on Earth, with their spouses or their living children or family. I saw quickly that the process that they were engaged with was either a choice of staying on the path of contraction and moving ever deeper into the grieving process or moving to a place where there was life in an expanded and opened way. At the time I knew where this other place existed, where life continued and my life was expanded, and I pursued it with all my heart. Because the other choice seemed like no choice at all.

Martin Katz

Although my wife and I recognize the enormous value of support groups for bereavement for most people, we personally did not find them helpful. They seemed to consist of people who were self-indulgent and self-pitying, who were not really trying to recover, and who seemed content to continue mourning. One woman's mother had committed suicide eighteen years ago and the daughter was still attending and refusing to get on with life. I feel that there is need for a separate group for the first one or two years. Then it is time to move on.

Up until Barry's suicide, I did not believe in psychology or counselors. I felt that you had to be personally strong, you had to do it yourself, that I did not need anyone, that I would work it out myself. I never took a tranquilizer. After Barry's suicide, I realized that I was not going to be able to do it alone; that I was a walking Greek Tragedy, and that I needed HELP. I was extremely fortunate to meet a professional counselor whose approach and empathy immediately meshed with my shock, grief, pain, and anger. She helped me go through hell and led me through the stages of recovery and recuperation. I am forever indebted to her.

MICHELE PHUA

[Edited journal entries one year and two years after Ryan's death]

July 25, 2004: We finally got into the grief support group after waiting for one year. Ironically, our first meeting was a few days before Ryan's Ride [a charity event]. Prior to the meeting, I told John that we would check out the meeting, and then probably give others who are on the wait list the opportunity to get in by giving up our spots. Nobody should wait to receive grief support. The moment I entered the room, my heart sank. You know how your heart sinks when you go to a funeral? Mine sank many more folds than that. I was in awe, in shock. I stared at the coffee table filled with photos of children who had died and the candles we were about to light for our children. In the room, these people were like John and me . . . we all belonged in this secluded world. I sat down and tears streamed down uncontrollably. I didn't know I could feel that pain again, so raw and intense even after one year. I just didn't know I had it in me. I fell into a deep well the moment I entered the room. The well was so deep . . . I just didn't anticipate that. All the parents took their turns expressing whatever was on their minds. But I couldn't talk to these strangers, and I thought it would take some time to get accustomed to sharing my feelings with them. I saw the pain these parents had, and I could so relate to those intense emotions. Many of their losses were longer ago than ours. In this room, we were supposed to "unzip" for one-and-a-half-hours, then zip ourselves back up to face the real world for two weeks before coming again. I felt I was stripped naked with my emotions.

At the end of the meeting John and I questioned if we wanted to put ourselves in a situation that brings out our rawest emotions. Why would we want to feel the pain again? Is this just an adjustment, since it is our first time? We thought we had dealt with Ryan's death in the healthiest way, so why would we want to take a few steps back to have those painful emotions that we felt one year ago? If a grief support group is supposed to help, why do we feel worse after the meeting?

September 14, 2005: It has been fourteen months since we started our grief support group. For the longest time I found it a very helpful resource only by absorbing what other bereaved parents were experiencing. Sharing my own experience was more like an obligation. What is powerful behind the closed doors is that these bereaved parents echo how I feel. They can speak on my behalf. Behind the closed doors is my reality, no pretense. I am allowed to express myself freely, and others can relate to what I say. It is a powerful experience.

As grief becomes solitude, support groups give the bereaved the opportunity to talk about their child and their hidden authentic world, which becomes hard to share in "regular" society. After all, it seems unfair to bring others into that dark, intense world. Two years have gone by since Ryan's death and I am afraid to think that it is time to end the support group. I am not ready. I no longer cry hysterically, but I cry. It is one of the few times I let my emotions down and feel authentically. At the end of the session, my emotions are cleansed and I am drained. But I know it is healthy to flush out all the negative energy that is so hidden underneath layers of blankets.

PATTY SHAW

I, surprisingly enough, had two sort of close friends who had lost children. One in a car accident (the car hit a deer) and the other a suicide/overdose. Both were unexpected and devastating, but these friends were of no help because these tragedies happened years ago and they could still not talk about them. One suggested I listen to the religious programs on the radio. I gave careful thought to attending a group for people who had lost children that is held at the local Presbyterian church. A stillborn birth/death, a death due to illness, etc., did not seem to be in the same class as a murder death so I did not go. I did hear of, contacted, and had lunch with a woman whose daughter was killed by her husband just a year ago. That luncheon was of enormous help to both of us and we have one another's names and numbers for contact should we need to share, talk, or cry. (Her daughter's husband strangled her. At least Cathy's death was immediate.)

I think that mothers whom I have met who have lost children still grieve inside every day. They just don't do it on the outside.

LOTTIE SOLOMON
[From an interview]

I went to a grief group once, and my thought was, *Why do I have to come here?* It does not make me feel better at all, it makes me feel worse. I hear other people's troubles, I feel for them too, you know?

I read an interesting article yesterday about *empathy,* how the body responds to the pain of other people—it really was fascinating—they're discovering that when you say, "It really pains me that you have this trouble," that it's true, that you have that reaction. Some people are not pained by anything, I have decided.

But I felt upset because I didn't feel supported; I kept saying to myself, *That's not me, that's not like me,* but that's a fact. There is a difference in the way people feel that should be not a point in causing anger. I really do not know why I didn't want to go back again. It did not help me, I did not feel better.

And, as you see, I don't feel better now. If I mention her name, I cry. If I put on the TV and the building's always going down, every day in every program that building is going down, well, what the heck, am I going to laugh, even smile, at that?

It is the most horrible thing that I could ever see in my life!

MERRYL WEBER

Even though I had a deeply spiritual language for my experiences around Adam's death, I still had many moments, days, and weeks of despair during the last ten years, times when I question why I am still here and he, who was so beautiful and had so much to offer the world, is gone; times when I am not interested in doing anything or seeing anyone. For me surrendering to what I can't understand, what I don't like, i.e., Adam's "early" death, has been a challenge, a challenge I would have preferred not to have faced but one that has definitely changed my way of being in the world.

Which is probably why psychological counseling immediately after Adam's death turned out to be a waste of time and money. This was an experience that defied any kind of normative psychological framework and it felt like I wasn't honoring my self or my true feelings. It was as if the therapist, a good woman whom I had known for many years and who had helped me considerably through other difficult situations, just didn't have the receptors, the language for this most unnatural and incredibly painful experience. She had a language for grief, but it didn't speak to me at my core. I felt like I was trying to fit into her way of looking at it. The more I went, the more I realized that I didn't have the strength or the desire to keep working at trying to be understood. So I stopped going.

I did go to Compassionate Friends for a couple of years on and off, and that was truly helpful though emotionally wrenching each time. At least when I was there I knew everyone understood how I felt, whether they were in the same place or not at any particular moment. Just being heard without judgment was comforting as well as knowing that what I had to say might resonate with, in some small way help, other parents who couldn't put their feelings into words yet. I still call and meet up with one of the women I met there because she more than anyone else I got to know hadn't let her grief overwhelm her sense of humor, her ability to reach out, her compassion for the other parents. She was someone with whom I would both laugh and cry, someone I could be honest with about anything. The freedom of not worrying about being judged harshly for how I was feeling about anything was a weight off me. As we move through the rest of our years, I depend on her to share honestly the continuing experience of having one of your children missing, and the effects of it that keep unwinding in many subtle ways in our lives.

JANE WINSLOW
[From an interview]

When Peter died, it so happened that the husband of a close friend had recently died. We were trying to support each other and found out about this group in Berkeley. It was a marvelous group and we met one day a week. It really helped a lot. The leader helped us to remember all the things our deceased loved ones said to us to make us feel good, and to let those feelings come to us. It was very, very helpful for me.

Responding to Sympathy

There is, of course, nothing that can be done to "fix" our situation, as much as we and those around us would wish to. But there are things people say in sympathy that bridge the distance between us, while other people's well-meant efforts only increase it. You may remember certain acts of kindness that moved you or even got you through a moment or an evening. *What specific gestures of support do you remember as being particularly meaningful, insightful, or courageous? Is there something someone did or said that you'll never forget? Something you'd advise people not to do or say?*

INÉS ASCENCIO
[From an interview]

Sometimes in therapy we ask families, "What was the pregnancy like?" Physically, emotionally, I am very aware of prenatal influences, so with my second child I did not want her to feel depressed. It helped me to have someone to talk to.

My therapist said something that has always stayed with me. I asked the therapist about the impact on my baby of my grieving, because I cried a lot through the grieving process, and I felt bad when I cried a lot. I wondered how much the baby was absorbing the sadness and she said to me, "You know, it is no coincidence that this child has come to you. She knows. She chose to come into your life and at this time." I don't know if I necessarily believe that exactly.

But I had a lot of support. Being a therapist, I have a lot of therapist friends, so I had a lot of great support. One of the things I felt was a gift that our daughter gave to us was to realize how many people were around us. So many times you don't realize how many people are aware, caring for you. The church was filled for the service. She hadn't met any of these people, but just the fact that people came. To me, it was very special.

We also went to a support group, Support After Neonatal Death (SAND). My then-husband's first language is Spanish so he did not feel comfortable in the group, just culturally, so sometimes I went without him; I would go with other women that I met in the group. After my second daughter was born, I started a support group at St. Luke's Hospital in San Francisco for parents who have lost children during pregnancy or after, like SIDS.

SUSAN BENVENISTE

After our daughter Shelly's death, it brought us comfort to have people share their fond memories of her with us. Some notes were from strangers whose paths had crossed Shelly's; in her special way, she had managed to make an impression. Others were from her friends, their parents, teachers, and friends. Whether verbal or written, we embraced these anecdotes with smiles and tears. One letter in particular stands out. It was written by a close family friend of ours, Bill Trevor. With his permission, I would like to share a portion of his letter. His words still offer comfort to us thirteen years later, and we hope will to you as well. In this letter Bill is describing the time he flew Shelly (as copilot) and her father to her summer camp on his plane.

My fondest memory of Shelly is when Ron and I flew her off to camp a couple of years back from Tahoe . . . Anyway, I pushed the throttles forward and we accelerated like a dragster down the runway and rocketed off the end heading right out over Squaw Peak and Tahoe. Shelly was beside herself, this was such a rush! Pushing against her seatbelts and straining to take in the thrill of the speed and as much of the view as possible in what was a totally new experience for her, she was in complete ecstasy . . . I've got this little picture of that flight and her wide grin of pleasure stored in a gold frame in my mind, and I can pull it out whenever I want to, look at it, turn it over and around, and relive that hour as though it happened yesterday, with just as big a smile and just as warm a feeling as I had when it actually happened. And I can do this whenever I want, for the rest of my life. If we all never had Shelly, I'd never have this little gem to carry around and relive every once in a while when I can use a little warmth.

MARY LOU COFFELT

Because I was so pregnant, many people kept referring to the baby in the time immediately following Mattie's death. "This baby will make things better." "God gave you this baby to help you through this." "This baby will help you." As though this second child would replace my dead son! This was very hard to hear, and I had to keep reminding myself that these people probably did not mean it as it sounded.

From others: "I don't know how you can do this." "You are so amazing." Trust me, there was nothing amazing about me. This made me feel like some alien being, and I already felt foreign! I was barely hanging on by my toenails! Lastly and most hated: "You are so strong." This made me feel that I was supposed to live up to some ungodly expectation. It meant that I wasn't allowed to crack, and I knew that that could happen at any given moment.

To this day I think I just did the best that I could and am grateful that God gave me the grace to do it.

SHEILA GEORGE
[From an interview]

What I found that was disheartening to me was that after about a year or so, people wanted me to get over it. You know, just pick the pieces up and get over it, and *that* angered me more than anything else.

Then people wanted me to justify that my son lived, period. Whatever happened, there was no justification, nobody had the right to take my son's life, I don't care what kind of lifestyle he had. That angered me. I don't know if they wanted to blame him, but the question in itself was like I had to justify the mere existence of my son. His death was horrible enough pain for me that I had to justify his life, too. He was mine, nobody had the right to take him.

KEITH GILBERT

Two weeks after our daughter's death, I returned to my job as group president of a large Silicon Valley electronics division. I felt it was time to return. The rituals were over, and even though the numbness was there, I wanted to go on with life. At the same time, I had a dread of how my co-workers would look at me. It was an early experience of feeling like an outcast, a misfit, even a freak because my daughter had died at eighteen in a car accident. There would be no hiding: almost every one of the thousand employees in the Palo Alto plant would know me, and would know what had happened.

Once I returned, there was almost an eerie sense of normality at work. I felt an odd disconnect between the same things going on as three weeks before, even as I knew that things would never be the same again for me. My co-workers treated me very kindly. What I remember most was the "It's really good to see you back." That seemed to me an acceptance by them that it really is hard to carry on, and that maybe I really would not be able to come back.

Two events are clear even after twelve years. A subordinate with three young kids came into my office my first day back. He was a tough young man, who was known for making hard decisions and is now CEO of a technology company. He said, "Keith, I can't imagine how you feel, but if there's anything I can do, just let me know." It was clear he really meant it.

The second encounter didn't feel so good. A manager who had lost his twenty-two-year-old son in an automobile accident two years before came up to me with his condolences. I can't remember what he said, but I do remember that I realized he knew how I felt. And, to my shame, I remembered that when he lost his son, I didn't know what to say to him, and so I had avoided him.

Susan Gilbert

Support came in many forms. Before the policeman who notified us left our house, we asked him to call my sister and brother-in-law who live nearby. They came within an hour and had researched funeral homes, cemeteries, and memorial services. All of the necessities of death. They both took several days off from work and went with us to choose the cemetery plot and helped us choose the church for the memorial, find the singer, and so forth. We will be forever grateful.

Martin Katz

Lee was inconsolable, her grief and anguish were monumental. She and I could not have any peaceful dialogue. Our interactions were traumatic. Friends visited and sat and listened and tried to help her. It was very difficult and I admire and thank them for their persistence. Two people who were not in the closest circle of friends came forward and were most helpful. One was the wife of a colleague whose daughter had recently committed suicide. As for me, not that they did not try, but I cannot remember any friend sitting for any period of time with me or saying anything that was helpful or useful. I think that everyone's efforts were directed toward Lee, and I was glad to be left alone.

ANNE LOGAN

When our daughter died, we experienced an astounding outpouring of sympathy. It was surprising, comforting, overwhelming. Family members, friends, casual acquaintances, individuals who had shared a similar loss, and even many total strangers who read or heard of her death came, telephoned, wrote, sent flowers, brought food, answered the phone, made calls, directed traffic, organized meals, helped empty her apartment at school, drove her car home, dealt with the hospital, the school, the police, the newspapers, the reporters. I was touched by all their efforts, for it is not an easy task to confront someone who is stricken with grief. Our human condition is one that strives to explain, to understand, to fix, to make better. All these intentions are noble, but they have no value to the grieving parent. For there is no way to explain, or to understand why, or to make us feel better.

How often did we hear the well-meaning words, "She's better off now, not suffering any longer." Or, "It's for the best; it could be worse." How could anything ever be worse? "God never gives us more than we can handle. He must love you a lot to have selected you for this burden." Baloney! I don't believe God metes out suffering at all, much less honors those of great faith by selecting them for special personal torture. "It must be God's will." My God is not one who sends suffering, but rather one who stands with us in a world created by him, governed by the laws of nature and subject to our own free will. "There but for the grace of God go I," I remember hearing more than once. To me, that could mean, "If only *I* had had more of God's grace, this wouldn't have happened." In an effort to make sense out of horrible tragedy, we often resort to blaming God, and ourselves. But there is no sense to be made. It is just that: a terrible tragedy.

There were countless memorable and touching acts of kindness. Among the first who came was one of Virginia's elementary school teachers. Now retired and living not too far from our home, she simply said, "I had to come. I'm so very sorry." Not much else. But as we talked, she shared with me some memories of Virginia. I remember wondering how she could talk about these things at such a moment, but gradually I grew to understand that these would be my memories one day. Happy ones which would temper the sadness. There was the very casual acquaintance who knocked at the front door, apologizing profusely for intruding, but saying he felt he just needed to come. And then there was the parent of a close friend who appeared at the back door with a basket of food, tears running down her face. She said nothing, just hugged me, presented the basket, and left. My brothers and sisters arrived. They were rocks to which I clung during those first days after Virginia's death. At the funeral was one of my cousins whose young daughter had been killed in a sledding accident some years earlier. I can only imagine the courage she mustered to come to a service that would revive her own painful memories. I remember her saying, "I'm so sorry. No one should have to bury their child." Amen to that.

In reflecting on all the demonstrations of support and sympathy we received, I came to some conclusions. Some actions were particularly meaningful to me, and I hope I can incorporate these gestures into my own visits to others who have experienced a loss. I remember how comforted, and even honored, I felt when people simply came. I felt as if they were the wagons circling about me. For me, this circle provided protection against the powers of darkness which threatened to pull me into the abyss of mourning. Their coming reassured me that though I felt alone, I was not. The best visitors were those who did not try to explain, or understand why, or try to make me feel better. They said little, just listened. I did not mind being asked, "What happened?" In some ways, it was cathartic to talk about those frightening hours.

Physical contact was therapeutic. A hug was best, even, and perhaps especially, from a stranger. A pat on the shoulder, a squeeze of the hand all spoke volumes, again, that we were not alone. I remember the friend who came to accompany me on a walk. Her brother had died in the tragedy of September 11, only a few weeks before Virginia's death. We said nothing, tears streaming down our faces. Quiet and alone, yet together in our grief. My husband remembers going to the dentist some weeks after Virginia's death. Coming into the examining room, the dentist took his seat, grasped Mark's hand, and said, "I'm so sorry about your daughter. Tell me what happened." His touch and willingness to listen were healing in a way he never imagined.

There are other ways to reach out. Letters, cards, flowers were all appreciated. And the lengthy process of acknowledging such gifts helped to reinforce the caring fellowship of the many who were touched by her death and our sorrow. Most letters simply expressed sympathy, that we were remembered in thoughts and prayers. Some recounted a special memory of Virginia, and the most poignant of these were from her school friends. I received a batch of letters from people I never knew; they had read an article my sister, an author and newspaper columnist, had written. "You don't know me but . . ." How generous and kind to reach out to a stranger.

So if there is something good to be learned from this tragic experience, it is that comfort comes in many guises. The important gesture is the reaching out. I remember every one. May I be as bold and courageous as my comforters were, not avoiding situations that evoke my own painful memories. May my presence bring support and sympathy. May my words be few, my touch healing, my tears ready to share, and my heart open.

MICHELE AND JOHN PHUA
[From an interview]

John: It's hard for the rest of the family. We went home for the holidays for the first time after Ryan's death. Michele said, "Do you want to go?" I said, "Okay, let's just go, because Matthew would love all the attention."

Michele: We went there for Thanksgiving because for the past two years we'd taken the boys back home for Christmas, but we thought, "We can't do Christmas, but let's do Thanksgiving, let's just get it over with. We have to do it sooner or later." And all those relatives! "Hi, how are you, Michele?" as if nothing had ever happened.

John: Yeah, and we knew that that was going to happen, but I think there should have been something said about Ryan. At least something about Ryan's Ride, but that never came up either.

Michele: For Christmas we did what we called an Angel Ryan project. We collected money from each person for two hundred children. I took Matthew to Target to shop for them. We took the gifts over to the Boys and Girls Club. Because our boys' birthday was December 15. So it was, again, my way of redirecting that energy. But actually my Asian friends don't bother to write a check, really, or go buy something.

John: It's not that there isn't caring on their part, but because of their family upbringing, they haven't been given the tools to know how to react. We were not always so great ourselves.

Michele: For me, this was like an open invitation when we said, "Oh, by the way, this is what I need." Many people don't know how to handle it, but I don't understand why some people are too busy to help.

John: I always tell Michele: In our lives now, any disappointment will be enhanced by the loss of Ryan. Because you will always reflect something about it—Ryan's death magnifies it. And yet we want to do the charitable work, and we have to be prepared that we're vulnerable to the hurt.

SUZANNE REDFERN

At one time or another I think each of us is struck by the powerful effect of a single act of kindness. During the darkest days after Mimi's death there was one such gesture from an unexpected source that had a momentous impact on my healing.

After Mimi's service I drove back to my small cottage in Palo Alto to hole up. Every morning I'd force myself to get out of bed and go through the motions. During each interminable day I'd accomplish little beyond writing overly long and detailed thank you notes to everyone who'd helped with the service, everyone who'd donated to her fund, everyone who'd cheered her with cards during her illness. Writing those notes felt like a connection to my girl.

Writing was a survival tool I used consciously. There were six such tools I was mindful of employing every day. Six, because one morning shortly after I holed up, I was sitting at my computer, day-dreaming, when I felt compelled to type out, in boldface, these six commands:

WRITE BREATHE PRAY WALK LISTEN FLOSS

The *floss* one made me laugh even in my depressed state, but I assumed it was a catchall for the tasks implicit in taking care of my physical self. I still don't know where the commands came from— maybe a caring Universe was sending down some much-needed first aid—but I took them to heart. So every day I not only wrote, but I also walked, prayed, purposely slowed my breathing, tried to quiet my monkey-mind by listening to the sounds of nature in my garden, and "flossed"—eating well, resting when I felt tired, keeping myself and my surroundings clean.

The nights were another matter. The approaching winter solstice brought with it afternoon shadows that started creeping up and over my cottage by four o'clock, chilling me in ways that were more about spirit than about climate. As true darkness set in, I waged war against that inner chill by building a roaring fire with the almond wood from an old orchard on the ranch, pouring a glass of zinfan-del, and cooking up something comforting. After a solitary dinner, the hours dragged on as the firelight faded, and the only illumination in my living room became the dead blue flicker of television cook-ing shows bouncing off the walls.

In our sweet old neighborhood of Palo Alto, houses are often cheek to jowl. My easy chair sits only about six feet from my neigh-bors' utility yard. Every time they recycled something by their kitchen window I could hear the clink, so I was pretty sure they were the recipients of a nightly *Son et Lumiere* performance courtesy of the Food Channel—Mario Batali on pork offal, pasta commercial jingles, flashing blue lights. I cringed at the thought, embarrassed by the habit but unable to break it.

I'd met my neighbor only once. A mutual friend had told me the little I knew about her. That her name was Katherine Ellison. That she was married to a journalist named Jack Epstein, and that they had two small boys, Joey and Joshua, four and one. That they were renting the house for a year while she was on a Knight-Ridder fellowship at Stanford, and that she had won the Pulitzer Prize in journalism for an investigative series on Ferdinand and Imelda Marcos's hidden wealth. A *Pulitzer*. And then there was me, chained to my TV and absorbed by pig innards.

One night the phone rang. "Hi," said a female voice, "this is Kathy next door." "Oh, hello," I said, with trepidation. "Listen," she said, "we've just made a bowl of popcorn and we've rented an Italian flick. Please come join us." "No," I blurted, shocked by my own bluntness. "I can't." And I hung up.

Most people at Kathy's end of the line would have been stopped in their tracks by such a rebuff. But a woman without chutzpah doesn't win Pulitzers. A week or so passed, I was again at my blue-light post, and the phone rang. "Hi. It's Kathy next door. I've just pulled out a batch of my mother's amazing brownies. Please come save us from ourselves." This time with a modicum of social grace, I answered, "Gee, thanks, Kathy, but I just can't."

Another try, another refusal, and several more to follow. But one evening during the last days of winter, daylight lingering longer every afternoon and my woodpile dwindling, I picked up the phone to hear Kathy say the words that took my breath away with their audacity and their truth: "Hi, it's me. Look, Josh needs an experienced lap. I know what you're doing, but come love the one you're with."

I fought back tears, swallowed hard, and marched straight out of my house and through the open door of my neighbors—still total strangers—into the indiscriminate affection and obstreperous high spirits of little boys, into the very wet and rather odiferous greeting of a Samoyed named Clea, and into the easy chat of interesting people doing exciting things, all ganging up to give me, despite myself, a kick-start back into life.

Kathy was wise to know it and bold to say it. I couldn't hold Mimi, ever again. But there was Joshua, who needed a lap, and oh, how that lap needed Joshua. Nor could I bring back the days and the nights of which Mimi had been such an integral part. But there was this day, and this night, offering themselves up, asking to be lived. Through Kathy's *nudging* I came to see that if I can't have the one I miss, or enjoy the life I knew, then I must learn to love the one I'm with, and to live the life I'm given. And I have.

A footnote: When I reminded Kathy recently of this period and asked permission to use her family's names, she claimed that it was a "highly improbable sequence of events," gave her okay on the condition that I wouldn't turn her into "some do-gooder that I wish I were but sadly am so not," and insisted that she had kept after me only because she'd thought I was "cool."

PATTY SHAW

My most precious memories of support came from family and friends. Because we had just moved into our house in Toledo and knew so few people, there were no gestures or condolences at all from the neighbors. (Hard to believe, isn't it?) So what I did to hear from those who had known her is this: I took her latest picture, had it duplicated on a hundred sheets of paper, enclosed the newspaper report of the killing, and sent them to all the people on our Christmas card list who had known her from birth until the day she died. I got so many wonderful returns and they all recalled special moments they had shared with Cathy, including many I did not know about.

LOTTIE SOLOMON
[From an interview]

Some people are very disturbed, but they handle disturbance by . . . [whistles] they don't want to hear about it. Bang. You know about it because they change the subject. That's my feeling. It's only my good friends . . . I don't even try to take advantage of them . . . I mean, I don't feel that I have to unburden every time I see someone, but they're conscious of it, you know—what can I say—they *feel* for me, the ones who care, *feel* for me, I mean, it's their *daughters* they feel for, how it possibly could *be*. I always say, "Nobody should know from it, and nobody *can* know from it, until they've lost a child." I mean, I've lost my parents, and I've lost my first cousin this past year, and another cousin . . . you know, people of my age start going, all the family is petering out. It's not the same.

MERRYL WEBER

Though many people surrounded us after Adam's death, most did not know how to respond in a meaningful way and I understood that. Many of our "close" friends fell away because they were unable to face our pain and the fear it engendered in them. I had been on the other side of that equation often enough to know that one really has nothing to "say" that can comfort a grieving parent and yet is uncomfortable not saying something. Most of the time people's hearts were in the right place, and I could overlook the stock things that were said. I remember telling my daughter when we would talk about how silly or stupid or inane some of those comments were to remember that not having experienced this particular form of pain people were just too uncomfortable at the thought of it and felt the need to say "something." People just don't know how to be quiet with someone in pain. My own way of dealing with it was to remember that it takes courage to say anything at all, to want to be there with us or try to comfort us with their presence, so that I could ignore the inanities. Sonya and I would laugh uproariously at some of it, and that helped too. We'd call out to each other, "black humor," and then share the story of the moment.

Some people are able to hold a space for paradoxical behavior of grieving parents, listen to the wide range of conflicting emotions within a short space of time, or stay with a parent who is seemingly acting "normal." Luckily, Rabbi Moshe Rothblum of our synagogue was a tremendous support through those first weeks and months, lovingly and sensitively leading the funeral and memorial services, meeting with us and speaking his truth, compassionate and yet not saccharine or false. In our tradition the community comes to the home for prayers the six days following the funeral. I found comfort in having our home filled each evening with friends and acquaintances, with prayers and stories about Adam, things he had said and done that had touched them. It is no cliché to say that one really doesn't know one's own child and how many lives that child touched.

KATHLEEN WEED

Jenica's sudden death unhinged me from the pattern of existence, which we obliviously weave with the world. And it seemed impossible that anyone except Jenica herself could jury-rig a lifeline powerful enough to reclaim me. But, astonishingly, lovingkindness soothed me in my despair.

Even the food that over-filled our refrigerator, and which for the most part I couldn't eat, comforted me: a fruit basket from the next door neighbor; homemade chicken soup from a co-worker I hardly knew; sushi and poppy seed cake from a friend who inquired after my son Alec's palate; herbal tea from an ex-sister-in-law; and both hydrators filled with Odwalla Superfood Micronutrient Fruit Drink because an ex-stepsister-in-law was alarmed that in less than a week I already looked emaciated. I no longer knew how to eat. Left to my own devices, I would have used a raging flood of adrenaline as my sole source of nourishment. But now I kept an Odwalla close by, and whenever I felt lightheaded I would sip on it.

What I meant to say by writing first about the food was that even kind gestures that seemed so peripheral to my grief mattered. But now I remember a coffeecake, the still-warm blueberry coffeecake that Stefanie Ender, Jenica's pal since grammar school, baked for me and left on my doorstep. I can almost smell the buttery cinnamon aroma, and taste the plump, squishy berries trembling with sweetness on my tongue. Odd that I savored each delicious bite at a time when just about everything seemed inedible.

Here was food made by Jenica's friend. Eating this cake felt sort of like taking communion when I still believed. Does that make sense? It was as though Stefanie's love for Jenica was right there with the blueberries, sustenance for body and soul.

Like most people whose grief is, for a while, public, I encountered a fair share of well-meaning sympathizers who said the wrong thing. Our culture does not instruct us in the communion of grief. Many people stay away because they have no idea what the grieving person needs. They are afraid that they might be intruding, or that they will just make things worse. However much I wish I didn't have to admit it, these are legitimate worries. I didn't always know what I needed from others, so how could I expect them to figure it out?

Even though I told myself the speaker meant well, trite platitudes left me speechless and discouraged: "She's in a better place." "God never gives you more than you can bear." "Only the good die young." "God must have needed her in heaven."

Thoughtless comments were harder to hear. My wounded mind, like a faulty tape recorder, replayed them over and over again: "At least you still have Alec." "Are you better yet?" "Jenica wouldn't want you to be sad." "I hope you will be able to get *over* this." "I know just how you feel because my (mom, sister, aunt, friend, dog) died." "I know just how you feel because I love my daughter the same way you loved Jenica." I rarely retorted, but inside I seethed.

A passing acquaintance grabbed my hands at Jenica's memorial and announced, "You're lucky, you know, because now you can talk to Jenica whenever you want." For months afterward, I pictured this woman's only daughter standing blindfolded before a firing squad, a mere second away from making her mother as happy as I was.

Several times people who didn't know me well—sometimes I didn't even remember their names—would try to pat or hug me on the occasions when I ventured out. I'm that rare person who bristles when people I don't know that well hug me or even simply squeeze my arm. Even trips to the grocery store frightened me. If I were a cat, I would have hissed at these well-meaning consolers.

Here was the dilemma. I didn't want to see anyone. Visits, even from intimate friends, exhausted me. My husband Steven screened my phone calls. "Kathleen probably won't return your call," he would explain. "She just isn't ready for conversation, but letters seem to comfort her. If you want to, write her a little note. I know she'll appreciate it." I had asked him to say this because even as much as I required solitude, I was discovering that the safe comfort of epistolary dialogue assuaged my lonely broken heart.

I lived for the letters. Hundreds of letters, and I devoured every one. Oh, the letters. The letters. I've kept them all. They are piled all around me, spilling out of grocery bags as I write this.

JANE WINSLOW
[From an interview]

I do *not* remember anyone saying anything particularly helpful. Unfortunately, what I do remember is the people who did not ever say *anything* about him dying. If I could get that message out to people, to really say something acknowledging it. Even if you do not know what to say. You can just say, "I'm sorry." There is a person whom I see almost every day, who has a son the same age as Peter. We used to talk about our sons. To this day, he has never acknowledged Peter's death. I have chosen to forgive him, but I cannot forget it.

It is true, of course, that no one goes through what you have gone through. Two women did reach out to me, people that were perhaps twenty years older than I was at the time. I remember their kindness well. I was puzzled, however, at the reactions of my sisters. Through the years, my sisters had been so helpful, taking Peter for extended periods of time, especially after my first husband died. There were times that they took Peter on vacation with them, so they were very close to him. But today my sisters do not mention Peter to me at all. They do not talk about it. I can talk about Peter with my friends who knew him, but my sisters simply do not react when I speak with them. I know that the loss is very hard for them also, very emotional. I know, too, that they feel for me. They are probably afraid . . . do not want to upset the applecart.

There were some special things that people said that touched me deeply and helped me realize that Peter touched so many lives. I am happy and grateful to have these memories. A family friend spoke at the memorial service and he said something I treasure. He had recently seen Peter walking up the street to visit a friend. "There

Peter was, as I recognized him after twenty years or so, head up, striding quickly, buoyantly, expectantly down the street, down our street. My, how we will miss that now."

Consulting with Psychics

Perhaps the most anguished plea of a parent during the first terrible days after a child's death is for reassurance that the loved one still exists somewhere and is all right. We are desperate for concrete evidence that our son or daughter is alive in spirit and isn't afraid or in pain, and until we get that evidence we'll have trouble attending to our own physical and emotional needs and those of the rest of our family. But because the rules of the game don't include those kinds of assurances, some of us seek them via extraordinary means. *Has your grieving process included consulting with a medium or psychic?*

MARY LOU COFFELT

I read *Talking to Heaven* by James Van Praagh. The author is a medium who is very connected to the "other side." I read the book several times. I entertained the idea of contacting him in the hope that he could connect us with our Mattie. I so desperately wanted to hear his voice again, to know that he was okay. I never did anything about it. I am not sure that I felt comfortable with the idea, but if the opportunity had presented itself, I am sure that I would have jumped at it. I think I wondered if it would make me feel better or worse.

SUSAN GILBERT

I have long had an interest in spiritual and transpersonal matters as well as those pertaining to the possibility of life after death; this interest helped me cope in the early years after Amanda's death. I felt strongly that she was *somewhere*, but I definitely wanted reassurance that this was so. More than anything I wanted to know how she was and where she was. I understood the desire of some bereaved parents to follow their children in death so that they could be sure the child was okay. The reassurances of well-meaning friends who pictured her with God or Christ did not help me.

I began combing libraries and websites for information on ghostly apparitions, near-death experiences—anything pertaining to the subject. I subscribed to several single-purpose magazines dealing with these subjects as well. If there was any proof, I wanted to find it. The sheer volume of reports of the near-death experience was compelling, but nothing convinced me to the extent of *proving* survival of the spirit.

I began to consider approaching mediums and researched those who had good reputations. I saw one well-known woman whose office is near me in Northern California. Unfortunately, I did not like her and did not want her near my daughter's spirit. I also found her inaccurate about my life.

Since I had heard of a medium named George Anderson through a variety of sources and through books written about him, I became obsessed with getting an appointment. He is especially sought by those who have lost children and his practice is so busy that one often cannot get through by phone. I ultimately learned that he would be traveling from New York to San Francisco. I persistently phoned his local agent, another bereaved parent, and I got an appointment. I was apprehensive as the day approached for our private appointment with George, and began to have doubts. Should we be doing this? What would it mean if Amanda did not "come through"—would it mean a rejection or that she was angry with me? What if our parents came instead when we were so focused on being in contact with Amanda? I am almost embarrassed to report that as we had tea in a lovely hotel in San Francisco where the meeting was to occur, I asked out loud for our parents to stand back and let Amanda come.

We were led up to a hotel room where the "discernment" (of spirits) was to take place. In fact, nothing was said about our parents, a detail which continues to bemuse me. There was considerable discussion of Amanda's characteristics and how she wanted us to go on with our lives; George, after a few attempts, did present her name correctly and everything he said about her was accurate. He also reported that my deceased brother was present, and he was completely right as to my brother's personality, character, and mode of death.

I am afraid that I was in such an anxious state for the reading that little sank in at the time. Now, when I listen to the audio recording, I can see that George was accurate about most things.

As correct as our reading was, I did not walk away firmly convinced that Amanda came to us in spirit and have decided that absolute proof is just not possible. However, my faith in the survival of the spirit has grown over the years. This is a poem Amanda wrote about a year before she died. It never fails to comfort me in the realm of things we do not understand.

DREAM

I am trying to run
Down a long, dark hall
Candles are flickering all around me
At the end is a light
As bright as the sun
But it doesn't hurt my eyes
All I can feel is goodness
But behind me
They are flying
Trying to stop me and pull me back
I can hear the whisper of the wings
Feel the breeze on my neck
It is getting warmer and warmer
I can no longer feel my legs
Yet I know they are moving
My feet are beginning to feel on fire
Though it doesn't hurt at all
They become transparent

I feel them beginning to be absorbed
Then I stop and think
I am not ready yet
But I can't go back
I'm being pulled in
I can hear wings beating faster
And then their claws are on me
I am being lifted up
And then I am back
Safe
And the light is gone

Van Jepson

My process has not included consulting with a psychic because my direct experience is that I was strongly connected to Ian at the time of his passing and this connection has been ongoing. In this way my heart is opened enough for me to be my own medium or psychic. I know that he is alive and well in Heaven. Whether what I have is a gift or the result of my pursuit of an alternate path to the process of grieving and contraction, I cannot tell. It is a path that I am clearly called to let others know about.

John LeCompte

During Mimi's battle with cancer we looked for answers in alternative methods of healing along with every traditional medical resource. After Mimi died, we looked at nontraditional methods for dealing with our grief. One aspect was paranormal phenomena.

I had been aware of medium George Anderson's work since the mid-1980s. I had been fascinated by his contact with the spirits of departed family members. My intuition was that his work was valid and worth investigating. During Mimi's illness I found a copy of his book, *Our Children Forever.* This book deals particularly with bereaved parents. Appointments with George are difficult to arrange. After a couple of setbacks, arrangements were made to participate in a bereaved parents group. In May 2002, Mimi's mother Sue Redfern and I traveled to upstate New York to participate in a session with George.

Sue and I each had anxiety before the session. Would this be a hoax? Would Mimi be in the room with us? Would there be no contact at all? Even though I had read a number of books containing transcriptions of George's work, I was unsure what to expect.

I will not go into great detail of the actual reading except to say that there was a precision to the information that came from the session: the description of Mimi's illness and her battle with cancer was exact; points of information emerged that confirmed her identity; her personality came through; things were mentioned from dreams and prayers that could not have been known to anyone.

There were ten sets of bereaved parents present on our evening with George Anderson. Hearing the messages of assurance delivered to each of the other sets of parents was a major part of the experience. Each loss had particular circumstances that were specifically addressed. It was an extremely powerful couple of hours.

I felt a great sense of comfort and exhilaration after the session. The experience confirmed my belief that Mimi continues to exist in a very real sense. At the same time, my awareness of her loss and the reality that she is gone remain. The most important awareness to me is this: even with the confidence that Mimi continues, my work processing the grief around her loss is not diminished.

The experience of meeting with George was difficult to share with others. My fear was not that people might consider me strange for contacting Mimi in this way. My fear was that some might trivialize or discount what was for me an extremely important event and awareness. I also felt frustrated because it is difficult to adequately relate the experience. I taped our portion of the session and transcribed it, then shared the information with Mimi's husband, her brothers, and a very small group of her friends.

At the conclusion of *Our Children Forever*, George Anderson responds to a question posed to him by bereavement expert Dr. Therese Random, as follows: "We have a special word for someone whose spouse has died—widow or widower—and a special word for someone whose parents have died—orphan. But we don't have a special word for parents who have lost their child. Any thought on that?" George responds, "Maybe we should think of these parents the way their children who have crossed over do. They call them Mom and Dad."[*]

Considering Suicide

Some people ache so for the company of their children that they'd do almost anything to recover it, including taking their own life in hopes of a reunion in the hereafter. Others consider this desperate act out of a longing to escape from the depths of a clinical depression brought on by their loss. *In the abyss of your sorrow, was suicide ever an option?* What made you choose life?

MARY LOU COFFELT

I had no thoughts of suicide. Thank God. Maybe the small baby in my arms saved me from my despair.

SUSAN GILBERT

I was raised as a Roman Catholic, a church that believes that suicide is a mortal sin against God. Consequently, I never thought it was an acceptable alternative. Perhaps I thought the pull to suicide could never happen to me.

I was therefore shocked and totally dismayed when I began to have suicidal thoughts. For the first few years after Amanda's death, I had great difficulty sleeping. As I fell into a fairly steep depression in the second year, the idea of suicide came unbidden to my mind. I was absolutely shocked at how tenacious the thoughts were and I

---

[*]Joel Martin and Patricia Romanoski, *Our Children Forever* (Berkeley: Berkeley Publishing, 1994), p. 364.

felt as though I had no control over the intrusive feelings. Each night I dreaded going to bed, because I knew that I would spend the night troubled by suicidal thoughts even when I made strong efforts not to entertain them.

At the time I felt that there was nowhere to turn. Although I was seeing a therapist, she seemed not to understand the depth of my despair. I did not want to burden my husband, and so often my friends had the same naive beliefs that I had once had—that one could control the pull. Finally, a second doctor I was seeing realized the straits I was in and insisted on medication. I am glad I could withstand the onslaught for as long as it took. Only my early religious training made it possible to do so.

Today I am adequately treated for depression and I have learned that these thoughts sometimes come to us. I also know that they are a symptom that needs attention and that things will get better.

VAN JEPSON

There were moments when I was stuck in my head and not feeling the heart connection to Ian. In these moments the thought would appear that the fight was too great and that flight was the easy way out. Although rare, when they occurred they were all-encompassing. What I quickly learned was how to extricate myself from that disconnected place and move myself into a position of reconnecting and of choosing life. In time, as my love of life grew, I actually enjoyed life on Earth more than ever before.

MICHELE PHUA

No, suicide never entered my mind. In fact, I never even took any antidepressants to handle my personal grief. I think the best medication is having Matthew, a toddler whose smiles remind me why I still need to live.

MERRYL WEBER

Did I feel suicidal after Adam died? Yes, of course. I had lost a fiancé as a young woman and had been suicidal for many years on and off during that period of grieving. Almost immediately after Adam's death, I remember quite clearly saying to myself, *This time I want to live.* Though I knew that I would feel suicidal at times I was freed somehow knowing that feeling suicidal was one of the panoply of normal responses to the kind of grief I was experiencing, that thinking about it was healthy, a kind of pressure release valve (I can get out of this pain if I really want to). I set my intention right away not to let myself fall into a debilitating illness, to take care of myself physically and emotionally as much as possible, to stay with the pain as it came up so I wouldn't deaden myself in any way. I chose life because before he died I had loved living, was interested in so many different things, had been full of energy, loved him, my daughter, and my husband fiercely. Even though the pain from his death was unfathomable, I knew from experience that it would subside enough so I would want to live my life again. I just didn't know what that would possibly look like, or how long it would take to get there. I still don't know from day to day what it is going to be like, only that living has gotten easier and gentler again.

KATHLEEN WEED

June 10, 2000, day 366, marked the first anniversary of Jenica's death. From that day forward, grief no longer traveled within a single cycle around the sun. I had tethered myself to that cycle, grounded myself in its separate days, as if to live through one year was to live through all that I would ever endure. My small mind had helped me. It could not wrap itself around a bigger number. Now, I faced a loss I could not contain. A feeble asteroid flung from its orbit, I gaped at the wide expanse of my entire remaining life without Jenica. The hollow futility of my continued existence—day after day, waking, sleeping, year upon year—stretched ahead of me.

That summer I daydreamed about my own death. The idea comforted me. I longed for fate to step in—a brief incurable disease, a car accident—I didn't want to be here. And if fate refused to cooperate I could somehow help it along. I stopped wearing my seatbelt when driving alone. I drank two glasses of wine with dinner; maybe the alcohol combined with the estrogen pills I swallowed every morning would give me uterine cancer. Once I had it, I would refuse treatment. Imagining my death was a harmless fantasy, I told myself. It allowed me to pretend that I had some power over my suffering. But I would never complete suicide. How could I inflict grief on my loved ones? I knew its heavy toll.

June became July. I bought a china-blue porcelain box at a local gift shop. "This will be perfect for my pills," I told the saleswoman.

She grabbed my arm. "Do you have cancer?" she asked.

"No. Why would you think that?" She looked embarrassed. "I'm sorry. You mentioned pills, and you have gotten so painfully thin."

I wasn't eating, and the pills were sleeping pills. In my second year without Jenica, I was sinking even deeper than I had in the first, if that were possible. The suicide imaginings became more detailed. Still, I believed that these fantasies helped me rein in my ravaging anguish, and that I was in control. As I spiraled downward, I ignored that the thoughts now arrived unbidden. I denied that they scared me.

But one sunny afternoon in late August, I stood at despair's edge and watched my shadow enter. Some weeks earlier I had begun buying every book I could find that seemed relevant to the death of a child. I spent hours and hours in my bed, reading the books cover to cover. On this particular day, having finished my current inventory, I headed to Kepler's, our local bookstore. There weren't any new titles in the *Death and Dying* section—no surprise—I checked every few days for books I hadn't read yet, always looking over my shoulder because I didn't want anyone I knew to see me.

Disappointed, and wondering for the umpteenth time if I were going crazy, I headed for the *Health* aisle. I went straight to the cancer section. I knew what I wanted. I picked up a book on caring for the terminally ill, and scanned the table of contents. There it was, an entire chapter on how to kill myself: the kinds of pills to stockpile, how to get a doctor to prescribe them, how many pills it took to fatally overdose, and how to get them all down without throwing up or falling asleep first. I read every page. The precise instructions startled me, but more alarming was the realization that I had sought and found them. I put the book back on the shelf.

Our lives are more mysterious than stories, but sometimes we experience pivotal moments that in hindsight seem as carefully crafted for us as the turning points in a flawlessly written plot. *I put the book back on the shelf.* Despair, by its definition, is unbounded. To travel there, one must acknowledge complete loss and relinquish all hope. I understood that if I wandered there, I might not find a road back. I trust that my shadow guided me to the book so that I would honor the depth of my sadness, but also so that I would acknowledge that I valued my life.

In "Love after Love," the poet Derek Walcott writes, "Give back your heart / to itself, to the stranger who has loved you / all your life, whom you ignored / for another, who knows you by heart. . . ." The stranger inside who knows us by heart—to acknowledge the love of this stranger, to receive her help in a time of need—this is a powerful gift.

The fog had moved in and the sun was lower in the sky when I finally left Kepler's Bookstore. There would be many more dark days. There would always be dark days. I would not abandon life, not even in my thoughts.

It's been six years. Have I kept my promise? For the most part. Experts say that people who complete suicide usually do not have a choice. There are conditions of the mind as lethal as the most malignant tumor. On days when my whole body grieves in tearless agitation—when I relive not so much the sadness but the terror of my loss—I feel an affinity with those who have taken their own lives. On those days, I wish I could jump out of my body. Except I want my life—such as it is.

JANE WINSLOW
[From an interview]

I have learned to be resilient because of the experiences in my life. When I was ten, I contracted polio and have needed to wear a brace ever since. Now I have post-polio syndrome and, although I wish I could be normal, I am just wearing out. Before, my body could compensate some, but now it cannot. When I was a child, my parents just treated me normally and we went on with life. I grew up, went to college, married, and had a child. Then my husband died very suddenly but I had to go on because I had a child to raise. I felt fortunate then that I had a job. Then my son died and I just went on. I was fortunate in that my second husband had entered my life shortly before Peter died. I will always have the comfort of knowing that Peter had met my husband and liked him.

While suicide is a draw for those of us who have suffered terrible traumas, I feel you just go on. The alternative has never been appealing to me.

 ## Taking Stock

If you read part 2 in its entirety, you will have been introduced to all of the book's participating parents. This section took us back into our search for assistance as we struggled to reenter everyday life. Every one of us found a question or two in these pages that rang a bell and reminded us of how desperately we needed support in that reentry. As Martin Katz says, "I realized I was not going to be able to do it alone."

It's significant that fifteen of the twenty-two of us answered the question entitled "Responding to Sympathy." A few remembered gestures that were heartwarming and even inspirational, but many more recalled comments that might have been well meaning but were offensively off the mark. You may have noticed, though, that the only unpardonable mistake is not the clumsy or inappropriate remark, but *the failure to make any attempt at all.* The absence of some sort of acknowledgment, the complete slight, cuts to the core. As Jane Winslow says of an acquaintance whom she sees often, but who never mentioned Peter's death, "I have chosen to forgive him, but I cannot forget it." If you are a reader who is afraid of making a blunder when offering sympathy to someone grieving a child, take note. We would all agree with Anne Logan when she says, "Comfort comes in many guises. The important gesture is the reaching out."

The other subject that struck a chord in a number of respondents was "Rethinking Faith." Only a few people say that their faith and religious practice, or lack thereof, were unchanged following their children's deaths. Two others lost faith but continue to observe their traditions, and one abandoned the practices of his religion but maintains a belief in the hereafter in hopes of a reunion with his daughter. However, half of those of us who chose to answer this question report that our spiritual awareness was *transformed* in the crucible of grief. Those transformations generally evolved over time from raging at the God we thought we knew to bowing before the mystery of life and death. Kathryn Lodato writes this about her evolving spirituality: "It has been hard for me to accept that it took the death of my son for me to be open to the gifts of Spirit. But to deny these gifts would compound the tragedy, would, in some odd but very real sense, let Nick down, betray his life and death."

It may be that you are in need of support in your grief. Perhaps you've already tried to get it in some of the places that we did. If you didn't find what you were looking for from those institutions or beliefs or people or programs, we urge you to try again. Like Martin, none of us is able to do it alone.

PART THREE

REDEFINING HOME

Setting Out

At the moment of a child's death, all familial relationships rupture. A seismic shift occurs in the dynamic between partners, between parents and surviving children, and among those siblings and other members of the family as it tries to restructure itself.

Marriages face strains unimagined before the loss. Spouses grieve in their own way, often too consumed with their own emotional survival to lend any support to each other or to their surviving children. Parents often fail to grasp the magnitude of the loss on siblings. It is often only years later that we have enough perspective to realize how deeply our other children were affected.

In part 3, people revisit their own experience in these family matters and in other ones, such as the risk of overprotecting their surviving children out of the fear of losing them, too. This section also looks at the agony of encountering and acknowledging the void that now and forever exists within family units.

We remind you that contributors to this book were free to choose which questions they answered. It would have been easier for them to avoid the ones that plumb such deeply personal areas as one's marriage. We're grateful to those who took on that topic, one that profoundly affects most families in crisis.

Preserving the Marriage

According to some studies, the shock to a couple coming from the loss of a child results in divorce more often than not. Even when the marriage survives, rarely do father and mother react similarly to the insult. However, the upheaval can also shake a formerly complacent union into a more vital, honest one. *How has your lot affected your relationship with your spouse or partner?* Do you agree or differ on such things as how and when to talk about your child, how to memorialize your child, and how much grief is good grief?

INÉS ASCENCIO
[From an interview]

A lot of couples do split up right after. In my work with couples we talk about the importance of respecting each other's process. Some people grieve more openly and others are more reserved.

I think at the point that we lost Angelita I saw my husband's faith grow, and I think we really did support each other well. I don't necessarily think that was the reason we separated and eventually got divorced many years after, but sometimes I wonder if it had any impact. When I was pregnant, I think he started to get anxious, because it was the first child, about how our lives would change, and I think he later wondered if his thinking had caused the death. We always look for reasons—what could I have done, what did I do?

MARY LOU COFFELT

How has this loss affected my relationship with Bob? Oh zowie! We have been affected in more ways than I realized existed. How does a marriage survive such a travesty of life? How do two people connect when all of life is nothing but shreds? Where do I begin?

Early in our loss Bob and I hung on to each other for dear life. It was as though we knew if we let go, one or the other of us would drown. Statistics we kept hearing gave us very little chance to stay together for the long haul. That did not rock us, as we had been in a great marriage for a long time before this happened.

We held each other tight. We built a cocoon around us; we let safe people in, but we always felt that either of us could retreat to the other at any given time. In our favor, unlike some relationships, it was easy for either of us to talk. And talk we did. And cry we did. We were able to say anything to one another. And I am so thankful that blame was truly not even something either of us entertained. Somehow, we managed to allow each other the opportunity to express our grief as we needed, and I think this was critical.

On the night after Mattie's death, we lay in bed like two war-torn victims. I will never forget that night. The pain was unbelievable and yet we were numb. As though symbolic of our intention to hang on to one another and ride out this horror, we made love with one another. It seems an odd time for sex, but it was not about sex. It was about unity, it was about love, it was about need. It was about two people, committed to walking through this battlefield together. I think it helped us through some of the land mines that hit our relationship later.

In our favor was the fact that our marriage prior to Mattie's death was, in our opinion, a lot closer, a lot stronger, than that of many couples that we knew. We had worked as partners in our careers for nineteen years, and relished doing so. We were a team. We had weathered lots of ups and downs (or we *thought* they were downs!). We respected each other, we knew how to talk with each other, and we had learned how to listen. We were so close we could pretty much read each other's minds. For the first years after Mattie's death this worked in our favor. It wasn't really hard to understand the crazy ways we each were going as we tried to figure out how to travel this grief journey. We continued to hang on to our family, desperately at times, hoping it would shelter us from the harsh reality.

But around the fourth year we found we'd ended up at very different places on our road through grief. There were some tough times for us at this stage. I thought I was ready to try to "start anew," whatever that meant. I wanted to let go of some of the baggage grief gives you. I had no idea what I really needed, but I wanted to start feeling good again, to start talking and living more positively. I looked to Bob to jump on board and try to start "enjoying" our life, not just force us both to go through the motions. I really needed to lighten up a bit and, at the same time, let go of some of our protective ways . . . let in life more. Bob wasn't ready. Nothing was the same. Nothing fit. We really were shreds of our old persons, and it really is impossible to drag someone along in a marriage. Add to that the truth that although I wanted to try a bit of happiness in my life, I really had no idea how to go about finding it again.

Somehow, because of our commitment to each other, because we have weathered the worst, because we're committed, because we had so much history, because we love each other, we kept hanging on. We kept hanging in. More time passed and we both kept trying to get there, wherever that might be. Bob worked hard to control his depression, using our thought-changing "exercise" that we had figured out early on and choosing not to let his black attitude completely take over our life. I learned to accept those days that he can't handle life. I've learned to give him the space he needs and not expect him to jump on board at those times. I have learned a bit more patience. He's learned to chase away the demons.

Now, some nine years later, we are at a new juncture. We are beginning to redefine ourselves, our lives. Much still does not fit, and our relationship doesn't sail as easily as it once did, but we are beginning to see that time is giving us another opportunity. That we have weathered the worst and now it is up to us to stoke the fire and focus on the strengths we have acquired post-Mattie, not the struggles. We've learned to value life again. It isn't easy, it happens a little at a time, but we relish it.

VAN JEPSON

My spouse and I have vastly different processes around dealing with the loss of our son. Unfortunately, in our case the individual processes did not enable us to maintain common ground in our relationship. We are currently in a process of divorce that mirrors our process of loss.

ANNE LOGAN

When Virginia died, Mark and I had been married for twenty-six years. We were devoted to each other and to our children, and we shared common goals and interests. I really felt as if we were one entity, for we knew each other's every strength and foible. We respected our individual uniqueness, but gained strength and personal growth through our partnership. We had endured our share of upheavals and emerged stronger. Then our world was shattered. The devastation was abrupt and complete. And we reacted very differently.

News of Virginia's death came early in the morning. Shock and disbelief merged into numbness. Around midday, Mark said, "I have to go." "Go where?" I wondered. "How can you leave me at a time like this? Don't we need to talk or something?" While I was yearning to be held, for his shoulder to cry on, for him to share in my rage against the unfairness of it all, or just to cling to him as my world crumbled—he went for a walk, without so much as a "by your leave." I was hurt, angry, surprised, mystified, sad. I wanted him to join me in the details of planning for the next several days, to greet the visitors at the door and share their hugs and sympathies, to talk together to discover what went wrong, to help know what to do next. At night, we lay in each other's arms, but sleep did not come. I wandered aimlessly about the house; he read the Bible—the story of the death of David's son, and tried to compose some remembrances of Virginia for the priest. The words did not come.

While my nights were spent roaming alone in the dark, my days were filled with the tasks of a death, with planning, arranging, calling, feeding, greeting, thanking. Mark joined me, our son, and our daughter in discussions as we struggled with how to best honor Virginia at her funeral. But mostly he walked. And walked and walked. Looking at the mountains, listening to the sounds of birds, feeling the breezes on his face, smelling the crispness of fall, hearing the gurgle of the stream and the distant, mournful moan of the freight train. While my grief was shared, his was private. I found solace in the fellowship of friends and family. Mark found his in solitude.

There is no right way to grieve. Nor does grief progress in any orderly way. After some time, Mark and I understood that while we felt the same loss, we grieved in different fashions. In our culture, men are expected to be providers, doers, to be strong, to fix what is broken. Women are perceived as emotional, nurturing, social. Mark could not bear to see me weeping; he felt helpless. There was no way to "fix" my sadness. I believe that he also feared becoming swept away by his own emotions, to lose control, to fall into the abyss of sadness and never emerge. On the other hand, I knew he had no answers; I just wanted him to cry with me, to rail at the stars. So I felt abandoned.

We got through those early days and weeks. And as the months passed, we found we were able to talk about Virginia, about ourselves, about our son and daughter. We learned not to expect too much of each other, or ourselves. We forgave ourselves for real or imagined weakness. We had allowed each other to mourn our loss individually, and now we were ready to proceed with "What next?" Mark talked about his visit with Virginia at college, only two weeks before her death. I was jealous that he had that time with her, for I had not seen her since September. I worried about our older daughter, only two years older than Virginia, who seemed to be floundering and ready to abandon college. Our granddaughter had nightmares and often retreated to her room in sadness. We began an effort to focus on life, not death. I was amazed that the day arrived when my first waking thoughts were not of Virginia's death. And together Mark and I forged forward. We started going out, traveling, making commitments to causes and activities that had lost our interest. Having a strong relationship prior to the tragedy of Virginia's death, we were able to build on that foundation of trust and love to survive the devastation of grief.

The sadness is still there. The empty space remains forever unfilled. A part of us is gone. There is no cure. Mark still goes on walks, and I have tea with my friends. Our paths are different, but parallel, and we meet on the common road where our son and daughter and granddaughter and family and friends all reside.

JOHN AND MICHELE PHUA
[From an interview]

John: At that point, when Ryan died, we were so busy with Matthew . . . he needed us so much more . . . but now that he's older and more independent, things begin to shift. We were talking about it. In normal times, when one is strong, the other counters. When one is ill, the other one is there. But when something's happened like the loss of a child, there's no energy to help each other. So you go on with your own individual process.

Today, because there is Matthew, we're finding our own space within that process, but we're not necessarily supporting each other. It's a kind of tradeoff. I think you unconsciously offer support, but you're mostly just finding your own space.

Michele: I think it is true that when I saw John coming home, that guy who used to think he could do anything, who would fish, and—"I'm going to catch a fish!"—when I saw that attitude lost for the past two years, I'd be taking care of Matthew and I'd think, *I wish I could see more of that old John back.* Because I just didn't want my family to be written off in society, I didn't want to be that victim. So maybe I did try to balance John's loss of optimism by being stronger, because he wasn't there yet. But now I see him coming home and I say, "John, you're getting some of that strength back," and then I know that I've got to relax more.

LOTTIE SOLOMON
[From an interview]

I have never been certain if my husband Herb was aware of Naomi's death. Through all this, he suffered from Parkinson's, which has become so severe that he is unable to do anything for himself. The life he lives now! Unreal, unreal. But I think he knows.

When a shot of the tower going down appears, I can see a tiny tear rolling down from the corner of his eye.

MERRYL WEBER

Steve and I grieved very differently those first years, as men and women often do, handled our anger and sadness differently, were estranged by our grief in some hard ways.

We had always talked about pretty much everything, but it seemed to me that there were just places we couldn't go with each other once Adam died. We were often angry at each other for a variety of reasons, anger that masked our pain at Adam's death. Yet underneath it all we knew, and verbalized to each other, that no one else would ever understand how we felt; no one else would ever "get" Adam, his life or his death, the way we did. While we never formalized times to speak about Adam, the rhythm of our religious life provided us with some formal times, and of course there are all those days when one normally feels more acutely the child's loss—holidays, birthdays, Mother's Day and Father's Day, graduations. We talked about him, and we would grieve together, crying in each other's arms. We talked about our feelings, not often, not daily, but enough to keep us together. We went to Compassionate Friends together. We were aware of how precious life is, ours and our daughter's, and it deepened our connections. That alone got us through the turmoil of everyday living with all its emotional fissures during the years we were reconfiguring as a family of three living, one dead.

Involving Siblings

In the turmoil immediately after a death in the family, surviving sisters and brothers are often shuttled to the corners, protected from the physical facts of death, and not consulted about the arrangements. As time passes and their parents are absorbed in simply getting through each day, these siblings frequently are left to fend for themselves emotionally. *How available do you feel you are/were to nurture your surviving children? What did you do well? What would you have done differently? Are you generous about forgiving yourself for your omissions? Have you talked with your surviving children about that period? Are you able to speak with them at all about your common loss, and they with you?*

STATHI AFENDOULIS

One of the reasons I went into therapy after Lainie died was for my two surviving daughters. Samantha, who is now fifteen, and Alexandra, now ten, suffered loss that was clearly different from my own, and I needed to understand how they felt.

One night, it became frighteningly clear to me how incapable I was of dealing with their loss without first dealing with mine. Samantha was in her room, upset about something and longing for a sympathetic ear. She began to tell me her problem and I dismissed it immediately as being trivial. I admonished her to go to sleep, that it was a small matter upsetting her and would work itself out. As I turned to leave her room, she burst into tears, begging me not to leave her, but I simply *could not stay.* The burden of my loss had left me helpless to offer her comfort. I went to my room, the sound of her sobs filling my head, and wept with a sadness I had never known before. I knew in that instant, I had reached a defining moment. In order to save my sobbing child from greater despair, I had to change. I had to be there for her. I could not lose another child.

In the ensuing months and years following Lainie's death, Samantha and I have found solace and comfort in each other's company. I have asked her to forgive me for not being there and shared with her my deepest feelings and fears. I have also empowered her to help me recover by asking for her help. By sharing my grief with her, I have gained her love and understanding, and more important, her trust in the knowledge that I will always be there for her. Five years later, we continue to build a relationship based on shared experiences, laughing and crying together, about our lives with Lainie.

SUSAN BENVENISTE

Recently our son Josh gave us a book he wanted us to read. It is titled *The Empty Room* by Elizabeth DeVita-Raeburn. Reading it was a jolt to the stomach for me.

Our daughter Shelly died in a car accident on July 17, 1991. She was seventeen and one of two children. Our loss and grief were indescribable. In one split life-altering second, we had to learn to become a family of three. Josh, at nineteen, was leaving in two weeks for his second year at Arizona and my husband and I wanted his life to remain as normal as possible. We sent him off to school and his friends whom he loved, arranged for counseling there, and hoped for the best. Meanwhile, we trudged through our days just trying to comprehend *our* loss.

So—back to the book. DeVita-Raeburn writes about sibling loss. Her brother died of a long-term, rare disease. It wasn't until she was grown that she realized her grief had really never been acknowledged, or as she terms it, "owned." It is almost second nature for well-meaning people to say, "Oh, your poor parents" or "How are your parents doing?" without recognizing that the surviving sibling is going through the same pain. In the midst of our grief and trying to shield our only child, we neglected to recognize that Josh was feeling totally alone. DeVita-Raeburn calls it being an "emotional amputee." Ron and I had each other. Josh had lost his sibling. As he put it to me, "I lost my sidekick, Mom."

Hearing those words brought a flood of flashback memories to me: the plays they would put on for us, the first time they experienced seeing snow and building a little snowman together, Josh bringing breakfast (a still half-frozen pastry) to Shelly's crib where they proceeded to have a picnic, Josh waking Shelly at 5:00 a.m. Christmas morning to sneak a peak at Santa's gifts before we woke up, leaving for summer camp together, the four of us out for Sunday dinners in restaurants, and then, as teenagers, exchanging knowing glances at an inside joke, probably about us! I realized that with Shelly's death Josh would never have that bond again. He, too, only has his memories.

In our pain and desire to protect our son, we had excluded him from decisions that he felt we should have done as a family . . . not just parents. For example, we selected Shelly's coffin and plot location, shielding him from that devastating task. Recently we had her stone removed and polished, mentioning it to him after the fact. We set up several grants in Shelly's name. It never occurred to us to consult Josh in these decisions. As a result, he felt left out. Causing him further pain was and is the last thing on our minds. My advice to anyone going through this experience is try to include your child(ren) as much as possible in decisions involving their deceased sibling. Recognize they might feel "alone" in social situations that you attend as a family, especially if other families are there. And, as Josh says, realize they lost their sidekick.

Mary Lou Coffelt

When Mattie died I was eight months pregnant. Life instantly shifted from the euphoria of expecting our second child, a new and welcomed life, to the empty and horrid darkness of death. Twenty-nine days later, as I was whirling deeper into the abyss of death and grief, I delivered Joseph, our second, but—then—only surviving son. I cannot begin to identify the whirlwind of emotions that I experienced. I don't think I had any idea, truly, of what I felt. It was all too mixed up. One second I was in despair, the next second I would be holding our child in my arms and crying tears of joy. It was crazy. But through it all, God's love, the love of this precious baby, sustained me. I vividly remember sitting stunned, holding my newborn, nursing him, staring at him, with tears streaming down my face, missing Mattie. Bob and I used to worry and wonder if this child would turn out normal, because we were so messed up. To our credit, this child probably got the most holding! Neither of us would let him go. As though laying him down might make him disappear.

As he grew, he watched us fall to pieces at the drop of a hat. Before he could even begin to understand, we would talk to him about his older brother, sharing with him wonderful stories of Mattie's life and being open about his death. Somehow, I think he understood. We began to believe that he was sent . . . he seemed to know what we needed.

I vividly remember us sitting at our dinner table, a place where, it seemed, one or the other of us was regularly reduced to tears. Joe was still a toddler, not yet a year old. Bob began to sob, and Joe, who was sitting on my lap, leaned toward his father and reached out his hand and placed it on his father's cheek. It was eerily amazing. We were stunned! The healing was enormous. Of course, we both ended up in tears, but they were filled with grace. This child seemed to find ways to walk us through our pain. The three of us shared our Mattie experience. Joe embraced it lovingly and willingly. Today, our Joe is a healthy, active nine-year-old, very aware and proud of his brother Mattie. We don't see the scars of our craziness from the time in his life when we were in the throes of grief. He is a kind, caring young man . . . maybe a better person for having lived through such an ordeal. We can only hope.

VAN JEPSON

My surviving son was my top priority in the earthly world and was included in all conversations and projects during and after Ian's death. Calvin witnessed the accident and was there as I did CPR, and he was with me when the chaplain told us the bad news. He continued to participate in the discussions about the memorial service and worked on projects for the cremation. I spent two hours in meditation and prayer every morning for my own process to grow the heart connection to Ian, and two hours with my spouse, and three hours with my son.

I suggested projects for us to work on that allowed us to be quiet together, while we were busy with our hands and hearts and minds. I talked to his teachers and his counselor at school to ensure that we had eyes and ears alert during his day when I was not with him. I learned of the material he was studying in his classes and got extra involved in ensuring his connection to school did not break. I talked with his history class teacher and chose a project to build a Trojan horse with him. The other project I suggested was to build a radio-controlled airplane. It was a way for us to grow our heart connection and for me to be a reference behavior that continued to move through each day.

These projects were a very nourishing time for me to connect with my living son. They also allowed a variety of conversations to take place at different depths. For very short periods of time at first and later at greater lengths, we were able to talk about Ian and what we liked, how we missed him, how we wanted him back, and how the accident happened. However, the spiritual connections that we each had with Ian were the hardest, and still to this day are an unbridgeable gap.

ANNE LOGAN

Our children and grandchild are truly remarkable, for it was they who supported and nurtured me through the difficult early days and weeks. Emotionally, I was unavailable, for all my energy was usurped by the wrenching loss, the details of death, and the overwhelming sense of guilt. In planning Virginia's funeral service, our priest asked us to all write down something about Virginia. Words would not come to me, or her father. But Bret, her stepbrother, created the most wonderful remembrances, truly inspired and eloquent, which he shared with the family and friends assembled at her memorial service. This is some of what he said:

"For me, it all started a little over two decades ago, with a note taped to my dorm room door. The scribbled message on a ripped page: '6:53 a.m., girl, 8 lbs, 2 oz, Virginia—call Dad at office.' I had a sister . . . And sure enough, from so many pounds and so many ounces came a person who touched my soul. A person whose time on this Earth added so much love and meaning in my life, and continues to now, even when away . . . Virginia's beauty and complexity defy my words. Her loyalty was legendary, and extended to those she encountered in her short life as naturally and indiscriminately as she breathed. Her humor was immense and powerful—even when she could be so shy that only a handful of people really got to know it. Her love of life—all life—was intense, and any creature, human or otherwise, that required care or nurturing she felt was her responsibility. Her ability to be unflinchingly true to her own character amazed me, inspired me. Virginia was always exactly who she was, uncovered, unqualified, with no excuses."

As the house became filled with family and friends, and flowers and food began to arrive, it was Catherine who took charge. Greeting friends at the front door, answering the phone, making sure that I ate something, locating air beds for the cousins and friends staying at the house, getting up early to make coffee, giving directions, explaining what had happened . . . she handled it all. And was comfortable to let me and her father become absent for a while, both physically and emotionally. We drew strength from her, and her brother, and still do.

As time has passed it has become easier to talk about Virginia with her brother, sister, and niece. I think we avoided these conversations in the days and early weeks following her death. It was just too painful, and the memories were sad and hurtful. Tears took over, and it was impossible to keep them from coming. But now, we find ourselves often reminded of Virginia with the sight of a special tree, or when holding a fuzzy worm in our hands, or while watching reruns of *Serial Mom*. And we enjoy that remembering, and speculating about what she might think about Catherine's new puppy, or Audrey's lacrosse expertise, or Bret's new band. And what she might say when her father wears brown socks with his shorts, or when I activate the smoke alarm at dinner.

MERRYL WEBER

Our daughter suffered, without a doubt. She was only seventeen when Adam died. She was just about to graduate from high school, in the middle of her own tumultuous adolescent changes. His death created a storm that wiped away our interest in the normal things in life. What had mattered before was completely submerged in our grief. Her life was turned upside down. She had to grow up overnight. She had to deal with our irrational fears for her as well as her own pain and confusion. I was heartbroken for her and the normality of family life that was lost.

I kept cooking meals, inviting people over for dinners, reaching out so that we wouldn't be isolated, or isolate ourselves. In my own way I felt it was necessary so we would survive as a family and not each go off into our own little corners to lick our wounds separately. I made a point of going to bat for Sonya to make sure she graduated. I contacted her teachers and counselors and talked to them about giving her as wide a berth as possible, and most of them were helpful. I encouraged her to give them enough so they could graduate her, and to her credit, she did. With the mother of her dearest friend we made a graduation party for them.

Many people tried to make her feel responsible for Steve and me, counseled her to "take care of us" because our son had died and it was "so much worse" for us. I encouraged her to ignore this advice. I didn't want her sense of responsibility for us to keep her from her own grieving. Inevitably, she had to take care of us in some ways because it is different for the sibling, and she did feel more responsible for us whether I wanted her to or not. Yet I didn't want her to feel her grief was somehow not as important as ours. From my point of view it is impossible to compare grief in terms of who is more hurt. There are as many ways of grieving as there are human beings. Each loss is unique.

Yet I'll never forget one thing she told me after many years had gone by. "I didn't just lose my brother but my parents; you were never the same after that. You got old." That is absolutely the naked truth. Our home was broken in a way that could never be fixed or returned to the normal it was when Adam was alive. Gray hairs popped out where there hadn't been any before. No matter how hard we all tried to be present with each other, the grief irrevocably created emotional chasms. Moments of closeness faded into the walls of pain we each had around us. Adam's absence was huge. It was the elephant in the room that we couldn't talk about enough. Yes, we talked about Adam. Yes, we talked about pretty much everything we were feeling. We remembered things differently, but that didn't matter. We learned to live with this feeling of being so close and yet often so far away at the same time. I think of it as having been on a lifeboat in the middle of uncharted territory, wondering if we were ever going to make it back to dry land.

Overprotecting Surviving Children

Having lost one child, it wouldn't be surprising if we were terrified of losing another. *Do you find that you are overprotective of your surviving children?* Are you more attentive to them in general? Do you put more pressure on them? Treasure them more?

MARY LOU COFFELT

Am I overprotective? I don't think so. I believe that there is a plan . . . our job is to trust. But I would not be honest if I didn't say that at any given moment in my life I have the thought, the memory, of the accident in the back of my mind, wondering, worrying if something so hideous could happen again. Somehow I have let it go, allowed our children to fly through life without the false protection of my own fears. But I carry the picture in my mind and feel a sense of gratitude and appreciation each time I watch my children "safely" at play.

ANNE LOGAN

Of course, yes. I think it is impossible not to be. How desperately we want to protect ourselves from losing another child. It is an almost unbearable thought. And we don't want to make the same mistakes, perceived or real, that we believe we have made in the past.

But what has been helpful for me, and I hope for my children, is recognizing that feeling, facing the fear, and discussing the ramifications with them. Particularly with my daughter Catherine, two years older than Virginia. They were inseparable growing up, and while they often were at each other's throats, when push came to shove, no two were closer. I used to dress them in "match alike" outfits, especially as toddlers. They went to the same schools, Virginia often not thrilled at being Catherine's little sister. They rode ponies, then horses together, often competing in the same classes at the horse shows. Virginia always had very definite opinions about Catherine's boyfriends, which she was not hesitant about expressing. And Catherine loved her sister and wrestled with how to help her when she struggled with depression and drugs.

Shortly after Virginia died, I remember sitting at dinner with Catherine. She had become engaged. I had a zillion questions, most of which presumed that she not only had no sense, but that what she did have was defective. Have you really thought about that? Where are you going to live? How will you support yourselves? What is his family like? Have you met them all? They live where? She answered my questions politely and patiently. And then I followed with a litany of "shoulds and shouldn'ts" of which any overbearing mother would be proud. I suppose my voice became higher and shriller, and no doubt more strident and tremulous at the same time. Finally, while I was trying to catch my breath, Catherine said, "Mother, I'm going to be okay. And so are you." A light bulb went on in my head, and Catherine and I both laughed. A bit tearfully, I confessed my fears for her, and for myself. We talked about her, and about her feelings of loss, regret, and sorrow. And I learned that we shared something in common. Just as I was trying to protect her, she was trying to protect me. She is okay, and I'm working on it.

Bret, already an adult with his own family when Virginia died, faced his own anxieties as he thought of his own daughter and the difficulties she would face as she grew up. And I think he would tell you that it has been and is very stressful to understand the depths of his loss and his worries for his child. To me, he has been enormously supportive, reassuring me of our excellence as parents at a time when we felt anything but. And he and his wife work hard at keeping communications open with Audrey, letting her know that all feelings are valid and any conversations are allowed. But they do keep a tight rein on activities and behavior, fueled in part by their experiences with loss.

SUZANNE REDFERN

When Mimi died, Peter and David were thirty and twenty-seven—grown men, really. You'd think that my protective maternal juices would have dried up a little by then. But when John, their father and my former husband, decided the following summer to take them, along with Peter's girlfriend (now wife) Melia and Mimi's husband Brett, on a bear-watching expedition in Alaska, I lost it. This was no Seabourne cruise, mind you. Transportation means included single-engine planes, small boats, and kayaks. They would be spending several days on the water without radio contact. Weather was a highly volatile element during that season of the year. And people had been attacked and mauled by bears on similar expeditions. Even the propaganda put out by the tour company described the danger level as significant.

Why, I wondered, *would John have chosen that particular trip out of all of the possible vacation destinations on the planet?* I took it personally and imagined him scheming to place everything that was dear to me in risky situations without electronic communication. I envisioned him staying up late, poring through catalogues with names like *Dare-Devil Expeditions* or *Near-Death Adventures.* It may seem funny now, but my terror was real and all consuming. Had the prospect of such a group adventure surfaced before Mimi died I might have grumbled and spent a sleepless night or two. With my loss still so fresh, it set off a fear and a fury that had no bounds. I remember shrieking at John on the phone like a fishwife, something I'd never done in our marriage. Wisely, he kept his cool, muttering in shock and confusion something like, "I'm sorry you feel that way." I sent him a blistering note in which I promised to take the whole bunch of them the following year on a trip of *my* choosing, like a cruise on a nuclear Russian sub.

The trip happened despite my protestations, and everyone survived, though an angry storm stranded them for a couple of days. John's and my congenial relationship has been restored. But the experience was a lesson for me that, no matter how old they may be, our kids are always our kids and that having lost one of them, I will forever fiercely protect the two that remain.

MERRYL WEBER

After Adam died, Steve withdrew into himself a great deal of the time. He became overprotective of Sonya in ways he hadn't been when she was young, yelling at her not to cross a street in the middle, not to ride her bike, stuff that a parent would have been fearful about for a young child. We both were more demanding about her telling us where she was going and exactly what time she would be home. I was on the verge of tears all the time. So Sonya, as any adolescent kid would have, made herself pretty scarce. She left for college three weeks earlier than she needed to just to get away from home, from us. I was angry a good deal of the time at having my family torn apart like that. Adam had been so alive, so full of passion for life. He always had a lot of kids with him when he was home, playing music, hanging around the house talking and eating with us. When other kids weren't around, we would hang out and read each other poetry, talk about politics; he would help me cook. When he died I really missed every nuance of what had been our lives together, even the music that I had so often put in earplugs to mute! It was all too quiet for me.

Encountering the Void

When a member of one's nuclear family is ripped from the core, the entire dynamic is altered. To us it feels as if we've lost a wheel and are always tilting and spinning off-center. This imbalance manifests itself in a million places. Some are in-your-face, like the first time we tried to limp through a holiday. Others, no less wrenching, are more nuanced, such as family discussions that unravel because they lack the dependable thread of irreverence or humor that the child once interwove into the conversational fabric. *Describe some of the ways you most profoundly encounter the void in your midst, both individually and within your family dynamic.*

STATHI AFENDOULIS

I was speaking with one of my counselor friends recently and she shed some light on a situation with my daughter Samantha. Sammi is two years younger than Lainie and was always content being the younger sister. Lainie was a very pragmatic child and was able to help Sammi sort out her fears and answer her questions. Sammi very rarely came to her mom or me for advice, but sought out Lainie for explanations on life as a kid. And Lainie was a good mentor, giving guidance and support that was right on, at least for an eleven-year-old.

I used to call Lainie daughter #1 and Sammi daughter #2. When Lainie died, our youngest, Alexandra (daughter #3), looked to Sammi for companionship and support. Sammi is five years older than Alex and, unlike Lainie, did not have the capacity or the desire to be "the older sister." She even told us that that was Lainie's job and she did not want it! Of course, being parents, we told her she didn't have much of a choice, but this revelation explained why Sammi always signs her cards and letters to us as "always #2." She just didn't want to have to fill Lainie's shoes, and we didn't ask her to.

However, as time went on, we realized that this stance was not good for any of us, especially Alex, who really loves Sammi and wants to share all her experiences. As an emerging teenager, Sammi is now experiencing all the normal things she should be, and so is Alex! Unlike Lainie, who might have shielded her baby sister from the vagaries of the early teenage years, Samantha sees no problem in sharing what she knows with Alex. It's during these times we all feel the loss of Lainie's presence, especially Samantha.

Lainie was perfectly suited to responsible, levelheaded thinking. It wasn't just Sammi who turned to her for this reason, but her friends at school as well. Many of them have told us how they turned to Lainie for help and she delivered clear solutions to all their questions. In the five years since her death, Sammi has struggled to become the older sister and, by her own admission, doesn't love the job. She is full of emotion and volatility, two qualities that don't always lead to clear thinking and decisive actions. I am certain, in times of difficulty, confusion, or I-just-don't-want-to-be-bothered, Sammi, and all of us, wish Lainie were around to tell us what to do.

Van Jepson

Although I felt that the joint projects we were doing together were healthy and flowing for my son, the greatest loss that couldn't be described or openly discussed was the shift from a vibrant family of four to a sad and different family of three. This in hindsight was the hardest thing to understand how to describe. Because when each of us turned to the other to ask, "Are you there for me?" we discovered that the other person was in a different place from before. These constantly shifting relationships and family landscape naturally isolate the family unit into a group of individuals living under the same roof. And although the daily routine appeared the same (work, school, shopping, etc.), the emotional routine was very different and disorienting. Maybe this was unique to our situation because we (son, wife, and I) had not had previous dialogues at this level of emotional engagement, and we found ourselves trying to put our awareness into the emotional level, then trying to put our emotions into words, and finally trying to open communication links between each person. This, at first, reduced the common ground and it was only with the heartfelt discussions that occurred during projects that my son and I shared, and flexibility on both our parts, that we overcame this awkwardness and moved together in a new way.

Unfortunately, even with the projects that my wife and I worked on, the common ground shrank and slowly disappeared.

SUZANNE REDFERN

Ours is a game-playing family. It's a tradition. I grew up with games, passing many a hot Central Valley summer evening shuffling two decks together and dealing out canasta hands to my mother and me. My father loved games, too. At our mountain cabin we still have dice cups and dog-eared poker chips he and his cronies played with in the 1940s.

When my children came along, I started them on games very young. During our long summers at the cabin, where *television* was a bad word, games were our major recreation. Mimi was hooked on Hi Ho Cherry-O at three. Both she and her two little brothers seemed to have been hard-wired with a fierce competitiveness where games were concerned. Peter brought the other two to tears for longer than I like to think by overturning a board game whenever he was in danger of losing. As they grew, so did the stack of game boxes in the bookcase: Monopoly, Clue, Trivial Pursuit, Boggle, Scrabble. We taught each other backgammon, cribbage, and hearts.

As, one by one, they grew up and left home, whole summers together in the mountains became a thing of the past. But when we *were* able to extricate ourselves from our studies and our jobs and our complications and meet for a few days at the cabin, we'd unload the food and make a beeline for the porch and the games table. It wasn't until the four of us were seated at our positions that the get-together was officially kicked off. That first shuffle was as much a rite and as full of gratitude as a grace.

Mimi died on December 6. Christmas loomed in all of our hearts. We couldn't contemplate trotting out any of the trappings of the season, but decided to come together on Christmas Day for a simple meal at Peter's converted barn. It was icy that December, and Pete's barn was drafty and dark. When David and I arrived we hugged Pete and then stood around awkwardly. There was nothing to say. Mimi's absence was everywhere.

Finally, David half-heartedly suggested, "How about a game of hearts?" We shrugged and started toward Pete's plank table. Then all three of us stopped cold, struck in the same instant by the realization that—once and forever—we'd lost our fourth hand. That moment has become for me a metaphor of how our remaining little gang has had to try to carry on without Mimi. Her place at the games table, and in our family, will always be a gaping void. As any real card player will tell you, three-handed hearts is an entirely different game—less interesting, less challenging, less fun. Altogether an inferior game.

 ## Taking Stock

In part 3, you were invited into the private lives of some of us as we described the crumbling foundations of family units in the aftershocks of our children's deaths. In no quarter does that shakeup cause greater turmoil than in the relationship between husband and wife.

Within each partnership, you saw two individuals reverting to their own instinctive nature as a survival mechanism. Rarely are those mechanisms similarly geared. Merryl Weber says, "Steve and I grieved very differently those first years, as men and women often do, handled our anger and sadness differently, were estranged by our grief in some hard ways." Anne Logan was comforted by company, her husband Mark by solitude. Van Jepson and his wife took such divergent grief paths that they were unable to find any common ground, and eventually divorced. John Phua sums up the disconnect: "In normal times, when one is strong, the other counters. When one is ill, the other one is there. But when something's happened like the loss of a child, there's no energy to help each other. So you go on with your own individual process."

Even when couples hold fast during the early days, fissures often appear later, as when Mary Lou Coffelt was ready to start "enjoying" life again, and Bob wasn't. As she says, "Nothing was the same. Nothing fit. We really were shreds of our old persons, and it really is impossible to drag someone along in a marriage."

It's as if the intricate network of connective wiring that transmits communication within the family unit has been violently severed, and we don't have the tools to mend it. With time, people find new ways to move forward, separately and together. As Merryl Weber puts it, "We learned to live with this feeling of being so close and yet often so far away at the same time." Ann Logan sums up her re-formed partnership this way: "Mark still goes on walks, and I have tea with my friends. Our paths are different, but parallel, and we meet on the common road where our son and daughter and granddaughter and family and friends all reside."

PART FOUR

LOOKING WITHIN

Setting Out

As you've moved through the previous parts of the book, you may have noticed an orderly progression that seems to follow a loosely framed timeline of grief. We don't mean to suggest that grieving is either orderly or on a timeline. However, there are challenges that every bereaved parent will encounter at one time or another, or all at once. To help you navigate through the book, we've put them in an order. First, we explored the early days and months when we were in shock. Next, we recalled the various places where we sought support and whether we found it there. Then we considered our relationships with our mates and our surviving children.

Now we move into a more introspective realm, in which we talk about our changing relationships with *ourselves:* how we moved through the inevitable despair of early loss, how we redefined ourselves, how we continue to process the guilt that seems to be universal, and how we deal with anger.

With the loss of a child, our pain reaches into such deep recesses of the psyche that we often become what feels like a different person. The effects of that fundamental change are as varied as the people who undergo it. Some experienced new wells of life-enhancing feeling, such as Nancy Emro, who felt more empathy for others, and Van Jepson, whose entire worldview became what he describes as *heart-centered* rather than *head-centered.* Many others say that the careers that used to drive them became meaningless. Sheila George left a lucrative life insurance sales position to found a residential center for at-risk adolescents. Kathryn Lodato, Susan Gilbert, Van Jepson, and Michele Phua all took new career paths.

Personal change is hard. When we're already struggling with terrible emotional distress, bearing the weight of both upheavals becomes almost unbearable at times. As you read our words you may discover whether the hard work of personal transformation, especially at such a difficult time, was worth the effort.

Fighting Despair

Some time after our children died we remember despairing that nothing in our lives would ever again approach normal. We were sure that we would never feel joy and that each small part of our day would always be permeated, as it was then, with the stain of our loss. We wondered if sleep would ever be uninterrupted by terror. It's our guess that all parents fear for their futures. If you are presently despairing of ever finding meaning in your life, talk about your feelings. If you remember such despair, describe it and then reflect on what your life is like today. *How does your awareness of your loss weave in and out of your consciousness? Are you sleeping normally? How often do you weep? Do you experience joy? What creates it? Are you hopeful? How engaged are you in your life?*

NANCY EMRO
[Written less than two years after Sean's death]

My emotions since Sean's death nearly two years ago have been uneven, to say the least. The first three months I was in shock. I just could not take in any other emotions, or deal with the emotions of others. Then I was terribly, terribly sad for probably six months, the worst, most despairing I have ever felt in my life. But especially during this time, I also felt a depth of emotion I had never before felt. I was able to truly relate to people and to empathize with them, like I never had been able to before. I was very sensitive emotionally and was devastated by reading newspaper articles about children who had been abused or injured. But at the same time, I was able to enjoy a sunset or the laughter of children. I think because I knew how fleeting life could be I appreciated these special moments that we usually take for granted all the more.

However enjoyable these moments are, they are fleeting and they do not constitute true happiness. I feel as if I will never truly be happy again and that the only "happiness" I will feel is tied up in those few moments at sunset or an hour spent with someone else's kids. It is conditional and does not last. It's not the kind of happiness and contentment that one feels from having lived a good full life, from being content with your achievements in your career, from having the unconditional love of a spouse or a child. I do feel I have had a good life, despite losing two people who were very close to me—my mother when I was only thirteen, and my son before he turned eighteen. My career does not carry much meaning for me anymore, and I cannot get excited over my achievements; they pale in comparison to anything I did with or for my son. And although I have a very loving family of origin, my dad and five brothers and sisters, it does not fully compensate for the loss of my son. And because of my ever-present loss, I do not ever truly feel happy. I feel better than I did a year ago, but its not quite up to feeling unconditionally happy about life in general, which I had always felt before. Sean, and the fact that he is not here to live out his life in adulthood, is always just beneath the surface of my consciousness.

In the past, I have always had a passion in my life. Rock climbing, folk dancing, playing soccer, my accounting career. After Sean died, I lost all my passion in life. I have often asked my bereavement counselor, "How long does it take to find something you feel passionately about?" A passion for anything, I don't even care what it is. For her, the passions have not come back; she feels that she has been changed forever by death. The more I read of what others have written about death, the more I think this may be more the exception than the rule. I have given up looking for passion in my life. My interests are now more even keeled and well paced. I invest less in them and perhaps because of that I enjoy new things instead of feeling wildly passionate about them.

For me, I now have "interests." I am still an accountant, but I no longer have the old enthusiasm about my work. I no longer work weekends or take work home with me. I am no longer excited about reading about some new accounting pronouncement. I still like my job, it's interesting work, but I am not passionate about it anymore. I still folk dance, and I still garden and hike. I have taken a new interest in music, but I'm not obsessed with it, like I used to be when I would take up a new interest in something.

I have occasionally found contentment, but this feeling has been incredibly rare. Spending a few hours at a deserted beach in the late afternoon with a good friend is the only instance that even comes to mind. And I wonder if I will ever feel this sense of contentment again.

I do enjoy some things more often than I used to—I take more time to spend with my friends, my family, the children in my life. Reading, writing, hiking, rollerblading, swimming, gardening— these things are still enjoyable to me. And I would love to re-create that feeling of deep-seated contentment and peace which I felt that day at the beach. I felt it once; I know I could at least occasionally feel this way again.

[Update: Written more than five years after Sean's death]

Things have changed. It's been almost six years since Sean died and four years since I answered this exact same question. In a way I hate to say this, as I feel as if I'm betraying my son in some way, but I feel pretty normal in ways I did not two years after Sean's death. I am happy. I still feel sad around his birthday and the anniversary of his death, but sad feelings are the exception in my life now rather than the rule. The fact that my son has died is no longer just below the surface of my consciousness, as I wrote four years ago. I no longer have gut-wrenching dreams about my son.

Two years ago, I moved from the condo Sean and I shared together and bought a house in a nearby town, one of the hardest things I've done since he died. I gave up Sean's old bedroom but I keep Sean's things on a wall in the family room, where I can see them if I need to but where they don't dominate the house. I've changed jobs twice and learned new skills. I am more interested in my work than I was several years ago, but am no longer willing to work the long hours I used to, realizing the most important thing we have is time with family and friends. And, I have found a passion in life—for the past three years, I have sung in a community chorus, something that so lifts my soul that when I am there I forget about everything else going on in my life. I promote railroad safety by giving presentations at local high schools, so that the same tragedy that befell my son does not happen to some other youth. And I am very much connected to honoring my son's passion in life—technical theater at the high school level—by offering an annual scholarship, going to the high school theater productions, and getting to know the high school theater students.

I remember my son every day, in some small way, but usually only for a moment and then . . . I move on with living my life, enjoying my life. My son would not want me to be eternally sad. He would just want me to remember him, which I do, each and every day.

SUSAN GILBERT

Even as I write this, thirteen years after Amanda's death, I must admit to moments of despair. I am better able to cope now than I was a few years ago, and life is worth living, but occasionally desolation strikes.

Keith and I are both family-oriented people and having neither children nor grandchildren is difficult for us. The entire focus of some friends seems directed toward their families, especially their grandchildren, and they often speak of little else. I am certainly interested in their children and grandchildren and inquire about them, but when it is the ONLY topic of conversation for long periods of time, I feel overwhelmed with sadness. There is a hole for us where family should be, and I feel isolated when that fact is not acknowledged by people we know.

We try to find people and activities to fill the void, but have not yet fully succeeded. I have been on two civic boards, one relating to the elderly and the other helping the homeless. As much as I care about these issues, the primary function of a board is to raise money so participating in these organizations does little to assuage the empty feelings. I also work with at-risk children, both tutoring and mentoring; I love being with children, but they go home to their families.

My challenge for the rest of my life will be seeking ways to make life meaningful. I will continue to try to be of service to others, since I have found that it helps to focus outward. But I have learned that I must be realistic. There are many enjoyable moments in my life and many people I like to be with; I like to garden, cook, read, go to the theater and movies, entertain friends. But nothing takes the place of my child and I will miss her and sometimes feel bereft until I die.

VAN JEPSON

It has been twenty months since my son Ian died. On the pragmatic activity side, my life had meaning before, during, and now after the loss of my son. Before he passed on, I was a marketing executive, now I am a writer. The person I am is the same, the things that I do in my life are different, and the way I do them is different and the things I have are different. I responded to this huge loss by learning my lesson (notice I did not say *the* lesson). That I am not to be consumed by what now is gone, but that all on Earth is temporary, and I am not entitled to anything merely by having it the previous moment. Sure, some of life does go on following this continuity, and there are earthly laws that attempt to ensure it. Yet, much more of life ends silently and abruptly, and sometimes violently, every day, then continues on. On the feeling, emotional side I am transformed. I am more sensitive, not in a fragile way, but in being able to read people's emotional states and heart- versus head-centered choices. Recalling the loss of my son or experiencing a present moment loss, I am quicker to recognize it and release it in emotional terms that include weeping. This has lightened my life considerably and has allowed joy to move back in. Joy for me comes from experiencing what is in the present moment fully. Without the colored view of past experiences. This is a vivid intensity that makes life a thrilling adventure, and draws me to people with similar intensities. I'm more engaged in life now than I ever was, yet in very different ways.

MARTIN KATZ

In retrospect, I began to observe what I felt was a proverbial and biblical seven-year cycle in the aftermath of Barry's suicide. It seemed to take the first seven years to be able to recover and come back to the world with some degree of normalcy; the next seven to recuperate and handle the functions of everyday living without a perpetual cloud hanging over every event; and the third seven years to say that you are healed and ready and able to handle living with an extra dimension of growth, awareness, and perception. Perhaps this is best exemplified by how you answer what is a most distressing question from a stranger soon after the death, namely: How many children do you have? Our patterned responses tended to be the following. Years 1–7: "We have two daughters." It was too painful to mention our son and it was very hard not to cry. Years 7–14: "We have two daughters and grandchildren" with an occasional allusion to our son under uniquely private or personal encounters. Pain felt and self-control needed. Years 14–21: "We have two daughters and a son who died. We also have four lovely grandchildren." An accompanying ache. Years 21+: As above, but more of a possibility of saying "suicide" than before.

YEARS 1–7: People avoid you: You see people crossing the street or ducking down another supermarket aisle to avoid seeing you and having to make conversation. People avoid the subject: They think that by not mentioning the death, you won't think about it. During the first years, it is the most prominent thought in your mind at all times. You avoid people: I did not want to see anyone. I disliked visitors because the subject might come up. When our friends visited, it was particularly painful to see or hear about Barry's friends and contemporaries. Career: I moved like a Zombie, trying to carry out research and executive activities in a recently changed career responsibility. I worked very hard. The stress and strain of home, family, and career were awesome. Should I have taken a sabbatical and not worried about what job I might find when I returned to work?

YEARS 7–14: I learned that shutting down to family or friends was wrong, that every day that you live should be filled with as much enthusiasm and accomplishment and interaction as possible, that I could laugh and cry and joke again and enjoy life. I learned that when you see a friend or acquaintance who has lost a loved one, bring it up immediately, talk about it, get it out of the way. When something happened to any of my colleagues or people who worked for me, I was out of my office, down the hall to put an arm around them and talk to them about it as soon as they came back to work. Say, "I'm sorry, I heard about it, what happened?" My therapist would arrange for me to take recently bereaved fathers out for dinner and I would try to help them.

YEARS 14–21: My life became very busy and fulfilling. I was and still am a part-time consultant in the pharmaceutical and cosmetic industry, became an accomplished semiprofessional sculptor, have several opera, ballet, and theater subscriptions, travel, play tennis, ski, and have fun with my grandchildren.

YEARS 21+: We can now talk about Barry every once in a while with family or close friends and refer to some past event or experience. It is still not all that easy. I recently went skiing with one of Barry's closest and dearest friends. We skied all day. Then she and I sat up long into the night talking, reminiscing, crying, laughing, and remembering many wonderful moments and how deeply we had both loved him.

I cannot possibly describe the devastating, never-ending pain and suffering of his mother. Her recovery and recuperation were slow and painful. It is a great tribute that she has returned to a very full and active life. She is the CEO of our entire family, the CFO of our estate, director of all social activities, wife, mother, grand-mother, and friend and advisor for so many people on both personal and financial matters. The death of a child is horrendous, death by suicide is an order of magnitude greater, and a mother's anguish must be another order of magnitude greater than the father's.

JOHN LECOMPTE

The loss of our daughter Mimi left an enormous hole in each of our lives. I never imagined I could experience the level of pain and depth of confusion that came with her passing. I was as angry with God as I would have been at a person who had taken her life. I grasped for meaning or reason and none came. My anguish deepened with time. I had no vocabulary to express my feelings.

I looked to traditional support systems in my life, expecting them to take the pain away. I felt they were ineffective because they could not meet my expectations and quickly remove these feelings. Ultimately, I had to find a new path and deal directly with my situation, on my own terms, in my own time.

In the five years since Mimi's death I have been with parents who have just lost a child. I have been able to put my arms around them and say, "I understand." I do not have answers, quick or otherwise. I cannot take their pain away. But there is something special and pro-found in saying, "I know what losing a child is like." No prologue is required, no explanation necessary. There are times when the great-est gift is simply to be present and witness another's desperation.

LOTTIE SOLOMON
[From an interview]

I do not feel any better now. Time has gone by since September 11, 2001. I feel worse. I feel the loss worse. Naomi was very atten-tive to us. And she was a single herself, and although she lived three thousand miles away, she was here at least every three weeks. And she was here holidays, and she was here whenever she could be. And

I think if she lived right here I might not see her more, you know—the feeling that she was just ever attentive and omnipresent.

I never pictured myself being around for her *demise,* so to speak. There is no burial; there is no finality. We tried to find anything—we submitted stuff for DNA testing, and they never located a bone of hers. So I assume she disintegrated. All my friends said, "Don't think about it. It was over for her in a minute. 'Cause there was such heat in that room," they said, "she died quickly." Well, I do not know about that. You see, I sit and surmise other things. I sit—you saw the pictures of people jumping out the window? And I think of her hitting on the . . . Well, she was on floor 106, which was Windows on the World. They were having coffee, pre-meeting, and what happened was she called down—apparently she was in charge of arranging something, I'm sure the audiovisual part of it—she called down to the office on the floor to send up a screen or whatever was needed. The person came up and he never lived to go down. The plane hit just then, and he was dead, too. So that is the only thing we had. They had a record of her phone call—I didn't have it, but my son who handled . . . my older boy, who is her trustee and unfortunately I can't go anywhere anyway, and he's been doing it all. They were very close. The boys and she were like this. [Lottie holds up three fingers pressed together.] They talked . . . they had these conference calls, at least once a week, sometimes I was in on them. Every week, they covered each other, they were so close. She had no other family . . . we had two grandchildren, her niece and nephew were her little pets, because that's what we had at the time; we've since got two more boys. So we are a boys' family, I guess.

MERRYL WEBER

When Adam died I lost my own passion for living. I didn't realize it then. I thought it would come back the way it had been. For a long time after he died I felt an invisible shield of love around me that sustained me through those first years, as if I were being held by some mysterious force. I saw it as a kind of teaching about surrendering to something larger than my small self, its dramas and needs and desires.

For many years I threw myself into this way of living and learning. Besides writing, I lost interest in almost everything that had held my interest before his death. I couldn't read anything but nonfiction and hardly that. I had never enjoyed small talk much, and after Adam's death, I couldn't tolerate it at all. Music hardly touched me. Occasionally I would be drawn to a piece of art or music and it would open itself to my senses in the old way, but it didn't happen often. I painted or drew sporadically. Socializing became painfully awkward and to be avoided as much as possible. I needed time alone or at least a lot of quiet time. I didn't speak about Adam much when I was with people who hadn't known him unless they asked me directly. What was going on was too personal to share lightly.

Pondering Your Identity

How has your loss altered the way you view yourself? Consider this question from various viewpoints, such as your attitude toward your own mortality, whether you have a right to have survived your own child, or whether you feel a greater responsibility to live your own life more fully. Have you had to redefine yourself and your role on the planet?

INÉS ASCENCIO
[From an interview]

Angelita came into my life and she changed my understanding of life. I think that the bond begins before you give birth to the child. I had never experienced that much love, maternal love, before. Such a strong love for a person. I love a lot of people in my life, but she was my first child, she made me a mother. The only time I got to sign as her mother was her death certificate. When I had to write on the line "relationship" and I wrote "mother," I thought, *this was not exactly what I had in mind.*

SUSAN GILBERT

Before Amanda died, I was a mother, a wife, a published author, a business executive, and a person who felt she had a bright and hopeful future. I planned to retire when Amanda finished her education. I saw myself as a pioneer, one of the women who pushed ahead in the corporate world and smashed through the glass ceiling. I was proud of having successfully raised a wonderful daughter when society was still coming to terms with whether or not women could handle both work and family responsibilities; there was still much criticism for this path. I identified with each of these roles strongly and gave speeches at conferences of women in business to encourage other women. That identification may not have been the healthiest thing for my wellbeing, but it is who I was at the time. My identity became what I did rather than what I now prefer, *who* I was and am.

All of the above lost meaning when Amanda died. I left work within a few months and went to graduate school so that I could stay busy with something that would hold my interest, at least in part. My primary functions were gone: I no longer had a child or a career or any of the activities that went with those two roles. While I still consider myself a mother and always will, there is no living child to whom I can give my love, care, and concern. I do volunteer work with people and care very much about them, but it is simply not the same.

The major difference now is that I consider myself a human being rather than a "human doing." Or, at least I try to do so. I fail often and find myself tongue-tied sometimes at social events when someone asks what I do. When I am feeling strong I like to smile enigmatically and say something arch like "whatever I want." But that is not always true. I simply do the best I can to capture some meaning and happiness in each day.

Monica Jones

Bronwyn set a shining example for redefining my life. She loved to watch Mr. Rogers and even spoke to him on the phone. He had asked her to send him a tape about what it was like to be handicapped, and shortly before her death she made an outline of what she wanted to tell him:

FOR MR. ROGERS

1. What it feels like to be handicapped:
   a. Need help from others
   b. Be patient
   c. Take naps, can stay up later at night
   d. Have more time to think and listen
   e. Have to do exercises
   f. Can sympathize with others with problems

2. What a handicapped person needs to know about life:
   a. Can use mind to entertain yourself
   b. If you can't change something, it doesn't do any good to worry about it
   c. If you can change something, then do it
   d. If people are learning how to take care of you, be patient and don't give up

3. What others need to know about the handicapped:
   a. They are people just like you except they have some problem(s)
   b. People should treat the handicapped as normally as possible
   c. Please tell us if you can't understand what we say, because we want people to understand us
   d. Like you, we like friends and like to be included in groups

The fact that my totally paralyzed nine-year-old daughter, who knew she would die soon, could write that helped me to keep my own life in perspective. I had long before come to the realization that we can't ask for our problems in life. Even if we could, I wouldn't have known what to ask for, as we had come to love and care for Bronwyn as she was.

After her death I reckoned that if she could keep smiling, so could I even though it wasn't always easy in the beginning. I realized that many parents had lost children during much more difficult times, such as wars or natural disasters. With time I knew and could tell others with assurance that a parent such as myself can not only survive the death of a child, but can also continue to live each day to the fullest with the awareness that one's life has been immeasurably enriched by having had this child, even if the child did not live to adulthood.

MICHELE AND JOHN PHUA
[From an interview]

John: I'm dreamy, philosophical, too idealistic. Has that changed? Unfortunately, yes. I say unfortunately, but it's fortunate, too. Unfortunate in the sense that it's the negativity—things just won't work out—I never would have thought that before. However, I'm even more hopeful and positive in the sense that, if you have hope, it takes time—you have to endure pain of some sort—but whatever you're dealing with, in time you can do it, you can walk through it. I don't know what it is, but there is hope of something, some meaning. I'm just not as idealistic.

Michele: I changed a lot. I hate to tell you, but I don't spend time anymore with my Asian friends. Which is sad because I have a lot of Asian friends, but when I share my innermost feelings with them they do not respond, and what's the use of sharing? My dad wasn't a private person, which is unusual for Chinese men. I don't know— he shared his stories, and maybe I picked it up because I'm a very open person, and when I open my heart to my non-Chinese friends, they then reach back to me.

Suzanne Redfern

In an odd way, Mimi's death gave me a passport to the human race. Throughout my whole life I'd felt different. I grew up a child of privilege in a small farming town. We had a big house with a pool and three Cadillacs at any one time. I spent summers at our mountain cabin on a river. My mother was beautiful, intelligent, and widely loved. My father—an ambitious, visionary, and principled farmer—was amiable and content at home. They were older parents, and I their only child.

While I didn't feel resentment from my classmates for my embarrassment of riches, there was a gap between us that I hated. Not that I didn't enjoy the bounty, especially that pool, but a kid wants to be like everyone else. I realize it's a tough sell, drumming up sympathy for a privileged childhood, but in my case it hampered me as a human being. I didn't know trouble, couldn't relate to pain, so I was afraid of it and ran from it. Believe me, I cared deeply, probably too deeply, about other kids' problems—raw poverty the most common—but I had no tools with which to approach them.

That era's particular form of political correctness didn't help. I grew up in the 1940s and 1950s, when talking about one's problems was considered airing dirty laundry. The vocabulary of trouble was a foreign tongue in most households, certainly in mine. People didn't divorce, they separated. They weren't institutionalized, they took a rest cure. They didn't die, they passed on. Believe it or not, doctors sometimes didn't tell their patients that they had cancer.

Such taboos further compounded my fears of confronting reality. Those fetters were hard to shake as I matured, preventing me from seeing my own personal problems and interfering with the forging of meaningful relationships. Lasting bonds are hard to maintain under the strain of perfection.

In one stroke, Mimi's death dissolved all of those barriers. Now I knew pain. I *was* pain. My pain was like everyone else's, and everyone else's like mine. Overnight my fear evaporated and I found I could not only approach others in distress, but I felt drawn to them. Today, in all but the most superficial of situations, I tell people about Mimi. It's who I am as much as any other aspect of my being: I am the mother of an adult daughter who died of cancer. I find that that fact, and the suffering it implies, has given me a lifetime passport to people's trust, no matter what their situation. We are inhabitants of the same country.

Mine is a hard-won evolution, one I had to lose Mimi to gain. That's why I often remind myself to use it fully and to thank her for it.

PATTY SHAW

I believe that I consider myself more aware of my remaining children and do not take lightly what they say and the time that we can spend together. Yes, I feel a greater responsibility to live more fully. Lord knows that is what Cathy would have wanted and she did urge me to live fully those long forty-two years.

Feeling Indifferent to Life

Many report that the activities that used to engage them are no longer interesting since their loss, that what once turned them on now seems trite. Some note with sadness that they no longer find common ground with people they once were close to. *Do you find that your interests have shifted, or the people you choose to spend time with? In what aspect of your own person—behaviorally or attitudinally—has the biggest change occurred as a direct result of your loss?*

SHEILA GEORGE
[From an interview]

I had to go back to work. They all thought I could handle it, but . . . he died in November and I went back to work in January and blew it. I sold life insurance—I was the top agent in the country at one time—and no longer did I want to do that. I went to work and just lost it. I wasn't ready to go back. I realized that was no longer what I wanted to do. I worked for a year and my job suffered. I knew after about the third month that that wasn't what I wanted to do.

In the interim, I started taking care of kids and this is what saved my life. I always wanted to do this. Not *this,* the Teen Center, but I just wanted to take care of kids that were disenfranchised. Who didn't have anybody to sit with them and talk with them. All my life kids have gravitated to talk with me, and I would keep their secrets.

So I knew my desire was to help kids—that's what was there first—and it turned from there to this, the Teen Center, with something small to something large.

I really am living my dreams. This is not a job—I love doing it— I would do it if nobody gave me a dollar, if I could pay my bills, you know what I mean. And I always say when I speak—because I speak sometimes—that if it wasn't for my son's death, I don't know where this business would be. Because we just go on about our own lives and we don't touch other people's lives unless something traumatic has happened. Then you want to reach out and touch other people's lives, *really* touch, and I'm not talking about just fitting in, I'm talking about really being a force for change. I have two girls' homes and one boys' home. Kids from all over Santa Clara, Alameda, and San Francisco counties. From twelve to eighteen years, and the one girls' home is from eighteen to nineteen to help them transition into the world.

My relationship with the community is better now, because I'm involved in it. See, I wasn't involved in the community before, but that has pushed me into this. So my relation with the community as a whole is a lot different now because I'd lift a blind eye to what was going on because it didn't affect me. But when it affected my kids, then I had to get involved to see actually what was going on and see if I could make a difference. I didn't know whether I could or not. I think I've made a vast difference since I've got involved with the community and the kids.

KEITH GILBERT

As far as my functioning in my executive position, I think I did okay and made some good decisions. But my priorities were different. Business travel seemed much less important than being with my wife. While I could concentrate well for short periods, I thought of Amanda every hour of every day.

I'm not sure what to say about my career after our daughter's death. The results were okay, but not great, and I didn't satisfy my boss in moving rapidly in shifting the focus of our group away from the defense market and into the booming commercial telecommunications market. Two years later I was fired, but later rehired, and subsequently selected as CEO of a spin-out company.

What I can say, without a doubt, is that none of the corporate wins and losses seemed to matter as much after Amanda died. There were now much more important things in life. Maybe the difference was that now I insisted that the requirements of the job match the priorities of my life. After experiencing how quickly a loss can happen, that would seem a much better way to live.

VAN JEPSON

Some of my interests outside of work have stayed the same while others have shifted. I have continued to enjoy flying airplanes and participating in triathlons, yet my desire to work full-time in high-tech has given way to a desire to write and work part-time. The people I've been drawn to have changed considerably. There are some people in my life that I was very close to that I now am distant from. And others, especially those with the ability to be strongly in the present moment and have unobstructed access to their joy, I am drawn toward. The best way to say it is that I am closest to those people who are connected with their hearts, have agile minds, and are interested in participating in the present moment.

I do more to let people know who I am. This includes being more sensitive and taking more action about what I perceive people's behavior is around me. Not by getting stuck on their behavior or trying to change them in any way, but being clear about how to express exactly what is going on inside me.

KATHRYN LODATO

I was at a party the other evening, the sort of party where I only knew the hosts. For years after Nick died I couldn't tolerate such events, but I can put my party face on now, and can even enjoy myself. I was talking to two young couples and noticed that both members of one couple were wearing the yellow Lance Armstrong bands. Lance had just won his seventh Tour de France, and I made some comment about him. The young man smiled and told me that he had a real affinity with Lance. They both liked to ride, he said, and they are both cancer survivors. We spoke briefly about that, but there were other people around and soon the conversation drifted. Later in the evening, I sought out the young woman with the yellow armband. I just wanted to connect, let her know that I acknowledged the strength and courage it took to face what they were facing. Amid all the cocktail party chatter, we had a real talk. She told me about her husband's treatment, the recent recurrence of the cancer, the little girl who was born during remission. I told her about Nick. We told each other about how important it is to live each day as it comes, to be aware of and thankful for the small blessings in our lives. Since Nick died, I've had many such small, moving encounters. Before he died, I do not remember any. I don't think the number of people I meet who have poignant stories has changed, but I know my ability to hear them, to be present for them, has radically changed.

In the years since Nick died, I've regained the ability to be a "regular" person. I can go to parties, make small talk (to a limited degree, I was never good at that), laugh at jokes, discuss politics. But I find that there often remains a certain veil between me and the rest of the world. I was at a presentation recently at which a young gay man described what it was like to be gay in a straight-dominated world. He described little exchanges with his dentist, with a checkout clerk at the grocery store where people just assumed he was straight and his ongoing dilemma: Do I say something? Or just let it ride? He described the instant calculation and the breath-held gauging of the response when he did take the risk to talk about it. It sounded so familiar to me. There is no word for a person who has lost a child. There should be, because I feel that in many ways it is the most central thing about who I am. So when I meet people, how do I tell them? If it's just someone casual, I don't. But if someone is going to be in my life, that person needs to know this about me. And it pains me to admit it, but if someone's reaction reveals an inability to take in what it means to be the mother of a child who has died, then I don't really want to bother to be close to that person. I wish I could say that I am a big enough person that I can overlook that, but I can't. So it is always a risk to tell people. My heart pounds each time I have to speak those words: "I have two sons, one is dead." I feel exposed, vulnerable. And I feel that I have exposed Nick and that I need to protect him. One way to protect him is to not spend time with people who I feel don't understand.

The veil between me and the world exists not only with people I'm just meeting, but also with many people who I've known for years, who knew Nick. Many of the people who I thought were my closest friends before Nick died, I just don't see anymore. That's particularly true for friends we had as a couple. It's sad, another loss. When Nick died, they didn't know how to be with us, and we didn't have the strength to tell them. I'm not sure we even would have known what to tell them, but the implicit pressure I felt from them to be the same, to continue to be able to laugh at the same things, have the same conversations, relate in the same way, was intolerable. I miss their friendship, but when we run into each other it's uncomfortable, awkward, even painful. After spending years together as friends, watching each other's kids grow up, we suddenly have nothing in common, nothing to talk about. Other people, people we knew only casually, reached out to us, showed us in small but important ways that they acknowledged the enormity of our loss. It's amazing how freeing that acknowledgment can be. It frees me to have light, casual fun, laugh at jokes, all the things I used to do with our old friends but can't do anymore. And I've made new friends in the years since Nick died, friends with whom I feel I can connect,

open my heart. In many ways I feel that I have more friends, and friendships that are closer and deeper, than I did before. I count that as another gift from Nick. When Nick died, I was still a lawyer, although not actually practicing. Instead, I was very involved in environmental politics, an advocate for an environmental group, actively exploring ways to become more involved in that small, intense world. I was passionate about politics, even ambitious in a way. I found long meetings with a roomful of lobbyists to be challenging, exciting, even fun. When Nick died, I knew almost immediately that I simply couldn't do that. I didn't know if that was a temporary or permanent condition, but I knew there was no way, in the short term, I could continue. After about a year-and-a-half I made a halfhearted attempt to go back to that world. But it failed. Impassioned arguments, intense strategizing, detailed research, and exacting reporting—I couldn't do any of it. It still seemed important, but in a distant, vague way.

What increasingly seemed crucially important was finding a sense of meaning in life. More and more I felt I could find that only through connecting to individual hearts and individual lives, rather than in larger, abstract ways. I became a peer grief counselor, which was enormously meaningful and enriching to me. I decided to see if I could make a new career out of that sort of work, and recently obtained a master's degree in counseling psychology and am working toward becoming a marriage and family therapist. It feels like the right thing to be doing. As I type out this brief history it sounds as though my interests have completely changed since I lost Nick, but I realize that is only part of the truth. My career has changed, the way I spend my time has changed, but in many ways I am just becoming more fully who I am. I still love many of the things I have always loved: hiking, nature, birds, reading, the list goes on. But my interest in things has grown more specific, more in touch with the heartbreaking beauty of the individual instance of each particular flower, each particular bird, each particular story of how a fellow human being is making her way in the world. I'm working toward finding ways to connect my affinity with the specifics in life to larger questions of peace and the future of our lovely little planet. But this time, approaching larger issues feels more grounded, less abstract, since it grows out of my deeper awareness of life and death. In many ways, Nick's death freed me, gave me an almost frightening liberty. In the midst of the unspeakable shock of his death, all of the things that used to matter didn't matter anymore. But to live—and I owe it to Nick to live—I had to find things to care about. As I am rebuilding my life, I have the freedom, and even the obligation, to build it out of things that really, deeply matter to me. Things that speak to my soul, not things that I think I should do. In walking this path of finding meaningful work and connecting with people, I continue to become more fully myself. And again, it is another gift from Nick.

MICHELE AND JOHN PHUA
[From an interview]

Michele: We were at our therapy session and I told my therapist, "Okay, so I don't know what it is, but now, at this point, my life has become so routine. Is this it, John, is this how our new life is going to be?" Because when there's stimulation it means you're living. Colors in your life, or stimulation. I feel that experiences can be very tragic, but there's just so much color in them, whether it's positive or negative.

John: When a person goes through tragedy and allows himself to feel that tragedy, like anything else, you sensitize. Like when you've first mastered some skill. It's an excitement. So when you've experienced something that's just so hard in the soul, when you come back to the daily life of everything else, it's just not that exciting. So you push yourselves to add that color, the sensitivity to those extremes, and you get pretty tired, but you need it—that stimulation.

Michele: Another thing that's really different for me personally is that before I was a mother I had a big-time job, a really big career. The people I work with are really wonderful. Now the work itself is just a way to get to the office—it's not demanding, it's easy work for me. It's a gift, for me. If I were in a really high-profile position, how I was before, that demanding, there's no way. I would probably quit. I'm in a very unusual situation. We're all contributing, but they're not demanding a lot of me. But I just don't have the energy to be spending, to be trying . . . I just need to take care of myself. Just because someone used to be my friend, but now I don't connect with her on the same level, I just can't give any more to her, so I find other people to give to. I don't want to waste that time anymore.

John: It's unfortunate, but it's healthy, too. It's good for her, but again that idea—like everything else—you just don't have the energy anymore. I have learned not to expect anything from my men friends. And that's part of it—the effort. That was the hard part: not to expect anything of others. It's part of the acceptance. Let's face it, if I can sit in a room now and not have to go into any aspect of my emotions—that's part of the loss of ideals—and just be okay with it, just allow myself that disconnection, that's nice for most men, it's comfortable for them.

MERRYL WEBER

Being of service to others became an obsession of sorts. It was the only thing that made any sense to me, using what time I had left to be of service to others. I pursued my interest in learning about all kinds of healing processes even though the mental fog I was in a lot of the time kept me from being able to retain "information." I deepened my contemplative practice. At Metivta, I found myself in a community of like-minded people for the first time in my life, people who were open to the profoundly unknown and unknowable aspects of existence, who were struggling to find a language and a way of living that reflected this way of being in the world, who wanted to be of service, each in their own way, to others. I fought off the despair that came to visit me by staying present with the pain, the grief that came welling up at any given moment. I wept and wrote, I studied and prayed. I reached out to others who were mirrors for me, who could "get through" the anger and pain with me and give me some perspective. By doing this I had moments of incredible clarity, of gratefulness for everyone around me who gently helped me stay aware when I was despairing, angry, unable to get out of my own drama.

I never recovered that sense of passion, that boundless energy I had before his death. My life became subterranean, more ruled by the subtle, the almost invisible undercurrents of living, even while I kept on doing many of things I had before without much attachment to them. The outdoors called to me and I was nurtured in it, by it. I spent many hours just sitting outside, day and night, in a way that I had done as a child.

Battling Guilt

Studies on grieving parents agree that we are more consumed by guilt than any other group—guilt over the lapses in our parenting, guilt for not having somehow prevented our children's deaths, survivor's guilt. *Describe your guilt and how you cope.*

INÉS ASCENCIO
[From an interview]

The only thing I remember is having a dream about the baby's death two weeks before. I thought about telling the doctor. I did tell some people in my life but everyone thought, you know, that's crazy. So, I thought, *Why tell my doctor?* So sometimes I think, *Well, what if I had told her? Perhaps we would have caught it.* But it is not like I put myself down or anything because I think that when it is our time to go, it is our time to go. We all have our own mission and purpose in life. The lesson in that is that we are all a little bit intuitive and psychic. So I find it is important to listen to my intuition and I tell people in my support groups, especially when it is a subsequent pregnancy, it does raise that anxiety, especially if they did not believe, or put it aside. We tell them to listen to their maternal instinct and speak to their doctors.

NANCY EMRO
[Written less than two years after Sean's death]

How I handle guilt. Not very well. I have dreams about guilt all the time. I think my dreams express my feelings best. I feel guilty for having survived my son, for not having been a better parent. What do I do about feeling guilty? Not enough. Expressing my guilt in dreams is at least a way of expressing my feelings. I guess that is a first step.

Guilt has also made me feel very responsible for people I am close to. I have had dreams about people I am close to dying or getting sick or engaging in risky behavior; it's all about the same thing—guilt. After such a dream, I have called up a close friend and berated her for not checking out her symptoms with her doctor. I never would have done this before. Now I feel responsible for people I am close to, really responsible.

When I am feeling really guilty, it helps to write it all down. That gets it out of my system so I don't keep going over it and over it in my head. Secondly, then I can look at my feelings on paper and actually then it doesn't seem so bad. I don't really "do" anything else about my feelings at this point.

I am volunteering as an advocate for a child in the Juvenile Dependency systems, and while doing this helps me to concentrate on someone else rather than on myself, it also sometimes causes my guilt feelings to rise to the surface, because I am doing for someone else's son what I could not do for my own. I haven't figured out how to deal with these feelings yet, except to express them in writing. That seems to help me move on with my volunteer work.

Here is an excerpt from my dream journal—my guilt dreams. I suppose they are probably pretty normal for someone who has survived the death of her son. These could be pared down to a couple of examples:

December 4, 2000: I dreamed while dozing in the doctor's exam room, waiting for the doctor to arrive. I dreamt a young child was asking me, his mother, if he could go and play with the big kids, who were standing next to him, three of them, teenagers I guess because of their tall, lanky size, but I only saw them from the back. And my heart just broke. The child was Sean and I had to tell him, no, he couldn't go and play with his friends because he was dead. (I just realized Sean was dressed in white and his friends were all dressed in black, just like theater techs.) But I didn't have the heart to tell him; he didn't know he was dead. I knew I had to tell him but I just couldn't. I was so sad. And this is how I feel. I am so sorry that Sean cannot go out and play with his friends.

I am really sorry, Janny and Jen and Cassie, that Sean cannot play with you anymore. I am really sorry, Jeremy, Matt, and Elvin.

I am really, really sorry, Sean.

January 22, 2001: Very strong emotions woke me up at 3:00 a.m. from this dream. Sean was in jail and due to be executed for something. I had pleaded and done everything I could for a stay of execution, spent a lot of my time presenting his case in court. But failed. The execution was scheduled for Sunday and today was Saturday. I went to see Sean, to say goodbye. When I got to the jail, the jailer said Sean was gone, had already been executed. I was totally distraught—there are no words for my feelings. I said, "But he was not supposed to be executed until Sunday! How could you do this?!" And the jailer said, "What difference did it make if it was Saturday or Sunday, he had exhausted his pleas, he was going to die anyway." And I said, "But I didn't get to say goodbye to him! I didn't get to tell him how much I loved him!" I am heartbroken. I am heartsick. My son, my beautiful boy, gone and I didn't even get to say goodbye.

I don't think this dream needs much explanation. *As a parent, I failed to save him.* And I didn't get to say goodbye.

June 30, 2001: Dreamt Sean was going off to college, I was taking him to his college dorm. He had suitcases and was in the back of the elevator. He looked about fourteen years old. And there were other people in the elevator, it was very crowded and for some reason, I didn't get in the elevator with him, somehow the doors closed without me on the elevator. He was going to the fourth floor of this hundred-floor building. And I thought, no big deal, I'll just run up the stairs and meet him there, he's old enough to figure out where he should get off. So I ran up the stairs and waited for him, but no Sean. And I started to worry that he would know where to get off, and how would I find him if he got off on the wrong floor.

I felt that I let him go too soon, that I let him make decisions for himself before he was really ready. Like walking home from school by himself, even though he was seventeen.

[Written five years later:]

Over the past five years my dreams have changed. I had two dreams about Sean recently, within two days of each other, after not dreaming about him for months. One a guilt dream, about not being a good enough parent, and then a second dream the next day about making sure Sean is okay, and realizing that I am not part of his "world" any longer, and he is no longer part of mine. My subconscious always reminding me that it's time to move on.

SUSAN GILBERT

The first year after Amanda's death I was often consumed with guilt. I did not sleep much, but when I did I was presented with horrible dreams. I felt so aware that Amanda was a treasure, a wonderful person, and I felt inadequate and unworthy to have been her mother. I chastised myself that I was not a good enough mother, that I had not been a good enough wife and presented her with a perfect home. I was too moody and sometimes depressed. I made her play soccer because I thought a girl must learn to be on a team when she did not like soccer and so on and on went the litany of self-criticisms.

The week before the fatal accident, Amanda and some of the other debaters from UCLA came to our home for a competition at Stanford. It was the end of February and the weather was horrible: rainy and windy. I called Amanda and begged her not to travel north that weekend since I was so concerned about an accident. In typical teenage fashion, Amanda said, "Mom, you worry too much." They did arrive safely but I continued to worry about the frequent highway travel this group did. They were all responsible and did not drink and drive, but I worried.

Later, after the accident, I castigated myself for not being more convincing. There were so many things I felt I should have done.

A year or two later, when other symptoms became more obvious to me, I realized that unreasonable and excessive guilt is a symptom of depression. After the depression began to be addressed, although not fully, I came to see all the guilt for what it was.

I also realized that whatever my failings and faults as a human being and a mother, I must have been good enough. Amanda was a terrific person, and surely I had done many things sufficiently right.

I had a dream a few years after Amanda's death and I thought that she literally had come to talk to me. In the dream, I was frantically packing for a trip and Amanda was calmly lying on the bed, reading. I was worrying, fretting, chastising myself. Amanda looked over at me with total acceptance and said, "You'll be alright, Mom, I'll always be with you." I remembered then that she had told me shortly before her death that I did not need to be perfect. The dream felt like a gift to me, reminding me that in Amanda's eyes I was always good enough.

VAN JEPSON

I'm clear that the small amount of guilt that I do have is contained in my mind as a way to cope with the question, "Who was responsible for this action?" Then, as I move into my heart, I'm clear that I am forgiven and that there is no blame or corresponding guilt. I call it more than a coping mechanism, it is my way of living. By living in my heart I am connected to the love, compassion, and forgiveness that reside there.

MONICA JONES

The more ill a person becomes, the smaller the margin of error, and Bronwyn came close to dying many times because I didn't know what I should do or because I had made a mistake. However, my pediatrician was very reassuring, telling me that we had made the right decision to care for her at home rather than hospitalize her, for, in his words, "Life's not worth living if you are stuck full of tubes." He often told us we could only do our best, but since we knew Bronwyn so well, the chances of making fatal errors at home were much smaller than they would be in a hospital. Ultimately, Bronwyn stopped breathing when her oxygen tank ran out on my watch. Although I got her breathing again, I realized that we were keeping her alive by artificial means and that it was time for us to let her go with no regrets. After Bronwyn died, the challenge was to honor her life with the way I lived mine, attempting to be cheerful, kind, and helpful to others.

Martin Katz

Barry was a sensitive, charming individual with a great sense of humor. Although friendly and with several good friends, he seemed to keep somewhat apart from groups. He was a good student in his early years and exhibited an aptitude for music. He was not particularly athletic but did participate in some sports. He skied with me until he could beat me and then stopped.

Barry was our youngest child. We have two daughters and he got along with them very well. He used his charm and great sense of humor to help settle family squabbles.

During the last part of high school and his freshman college year, Barry began to drift and act strangely. He cut classes, went on abstinence diets, and became ill. When communication stopped, we went to see him and found him in a terribly debilitated state. The university said they were not allowed to inform us of his deteriorating condition!

Like his older sister and then his cousin, Barry decided to go to Israel and work on a kibbutz. He seemed to fit in well and have a good time and made rapid strides in learning to speak Hebrew. We were so proud of him then.

Barry told us that he had passed the entrance exams and had decided to enroll at the University of Jerusalem with a goal of becoming a rabbi. I was very happy with this idea. So we made all the necessary arrangements for him to live and study there.

On his first flight home, Barry told us at the airport that he was quitting and not going back, with no explanation. After that, he was totally adrift. He had no goals, no aspirations. I tried to make him get a job, move, do something, to no avail. Finally, he got a job at the Stanford Book Store, which seemed suitable.

But the disintegration continued. His mother had some intimation of danger and was very fearful. I didn't understand, psychology was never my thing, I felt useless. I could not believe that he was ultimately going to commit suicide. I was also too busy with my career. I was senior VP of research at a major pharmaceutical company. Where were all the wonder drugs that my colleagues were creating? Why didn't they work? We sent him to counselors, therapists, psychiatrists. This was their profession, their specialty! Why didn't they see it coming? They all *failed!*

Some of the events of the very last days remain vividly in my memory, mainly because I now berate myself for not having recognized them as possible trouble signs. The guilt trip never ends. We went to the Stanford Book Store one night to buy some items. While walking back to the car, Barry would not walk with me or near me but stayed apart. I tried to link arms, but he pushed me away. One evening, while I was working at my desk, he suddenly interrupted me and told me that he wanted me to listen to him play the piano (which he had not done for some time). To this day, I start crying when I hear the classic Beethoven "Für Elise" or Scott Joplin's famous piano rags. Another evening, he looked for one of my favorite recordings, Stravinsky's *The Rite of Spring,* and asked me to sit and listen to it with him. In the middle, he abruptly stood up, turned it off, and left the room. What dark and guilt-laden thoughts come to my mind each time I hear the opening chords. I have already mentioned the extra long farewell hug when we left for the airport. A last chance missed?

What did I do wrong? "You can't punish yourself enough." What did I say to him that made him do it? Maybe I was too harsh with him in that last year in trying to get him to find some purpose in life. What a lousy burden to bear that is! Maybe I was too wrapped up in my successful career and should have spent more time with him. Another lousy burden to bear! I saw this sign, that sign. Why didn't I recognize or realize what was going on? In retrospect, one can dredge up dozens of indicators. Why was I so stupid and blind?

ANNE LOGAN

Guilt. Even saying the word generates a depressing effect. Looking at it on the page evokes sadness and anger. An overworked motivation for many of our actions, its corollaries can be heard whenever we say, "I should have . . . You should have . . . I ought to . . . You ought to . . . If only I had . . . If only she hadn't . . ." Its destructive powers are legion, its burden unbearable. And yet there is no emotion that so overwhelms a parent upon the death of her child. From the moment of our child's first cry we are mobilized as caregivers, teachers, comforters, guardians, disciplinarians, providers, mentors, models. Our purpose becomes one of nurturing, of responsibility, of protection. When death comes to our child in untimely and tragic fashion, immediate responses resound which lay blame on the parent. "What did I do wrong? Why couldn't I have prevented this from happening? She's my child; I'm supposed to protect her!" Whether we direct these thoughts toward ourselves, or whether they come in the often heard refrain, "How could that happen to her? She has such wonderful parents!" the wound is equally deep.

Nor does it ultimately matter what caused the death. Accident, illness, suicide, overdose, crime, war—in all cases parents feel that somehow they should have been able to prevent their child's death. "I shouldn't have let him drive home that stormy night." "If only she hadn't gone on that trip she might not have gotten sick." "I should have put her in the hospital." "I should have seen it coming." "We ought to have moved from this neighborhood." "I wish I had persuaded him not to enlist." We will deny the forces of nature, the unfair curse of disease to strike without regard to merit. "Why does it always happen to the nicest people?" Particularly with adolescents, we expect that our love and the efforts of the overworked angels that ride on their shoulders will keep them from harm. That their risky behaviors will not result in life-altering consequences. Whatever the situation, we will find a way to point the finger at ourselves, mired in guilt, assuming responsibility for events neither of our doing nor within our control.

An exuberant young child with a perpetual smile, happy attitude, generous sense of humor, and caring heart, Virginia began to sink into depression during high school. She was unhappy in school, struggled with an eating disorder, and her personality began to change. Throughout these years, she saw counselors and psychiatrists who treated her with a variety of therapies and medications, none of which seemed to provide her the stability she craved. She self-medicated with alcohol and street drugs, and sought the company of those who supported her behavior without question. My grieving for her started long before her death, for she seemed to be on a downward spiral that could not be averted. She was a gifted artist and found ways to express herself on canvas. She loved to paint trees, abstractly, but with roots firmly in the earth and crowns lifted to the sky. Her college professors were amazed at her gift and predicted great success for her. And she seemed to be happy, to be excited about her courses, and to have a close group of wonderful and caring friends. But she could not escape the demons that troubled her, and died as a result of methadone toxicity. "If only we had been stricter, stronger, less trusting, more understanding, less permissive, more perceptive, found better doctors . . ." She was dead. We had failed.

The guilt we felt was wrenching and tenacious. It was exacerbated by society's belief that bad outcomes from mental illness are always preventable. If someone dies from heart disease, it is because of the disease. If someone dies from psychiatric illness, it is because she didn't get the right help. So our hearts were doubly burdened, both with the blame we piled on ourselves and with the onus of societal expectations. Even though we intellectually know that these views are false, we cannot keep the feelings from coming into our hearts. I wallowed in that for months. Going about the motions of normal existence, I felt the enormous weight in my soul. I struggled to find gladness in anything; I didn't deserve to be happy.

There were two encounters that helped me turn around. I went to see a psychiatrist. An insightful physician and longtime friend, he knew our family well. "I'm stuck," I said. "I can't get over the guilt. I know in my mind that I'm not at fault, but I can't seem to get my heart to believe that." "Yes, these emotions, they're always the problem, aren't they?" We talked for a while about what I was experiencing. "I fall asleep at the drop of a hat, but in a couple of hours I'm awake, mind racing. I remember the times when I might have done something differently, or said something else, and could have made a difference. I become tearful at least once a day. I can still function and I don't have bad dreams or nightmares, but I just can't get over feeling responsible. I should have been able to do something." And then we got to the heart of the matter.

We are very arrogant, we parents. We so often see our children as mirrors of ourselves, as personifications of our goals and values. We believe that we exert control over the decisions they take and the choices they make. We do, for a while. But the time comes when our children decide for themselves the path they will take. While we hope and pray they make sensible and wise choices, they often do not. Adolescence is replete with bad choices and risky behavior. I was unable to prevent Virginia's death, and so was the mental health profession. We were not in control, nor probably was she. Her disease was. Understanding this fact and accepting it to be true are different tasks. We were not bad parents. We did everything we knew to do. We explored every avenue of therapy. Our efforts were not in vain, they just didn't work.

About a year-and-a-half after Virginia died, I took my older daughter Catherine for a week at The Golden Door, a luxurious retreat that nurtures both body and mind. We indulged ourselves in the pampering it provided. But the most remarkable encounter was not with my trainer, or masseuse, or beautician, or tai chi instructor, but with another guest. In swim suits and robes, we sat by the pool, truant from our aerobics class, and talked about Virginia. A remarkably perceptive and insightful woman, she seemed to understand just what Virginia was about. "What courage she must have had," she said, "to have tried to handle her problems on her own." I had never thought of it that way. "And furthermore, I think Catherine is tired of seeing you beat yourself up over Virginia's death!" I hadn't thought of that either. She saw that my pleasant affect was a front, that under it all was sadness, grief, and guilt. It showed. "Virginia wouldn't want to see you so miserable."

So with the help and insight provided by these two remarkable individuals, I am letting go of the guilt, the blame, the regrets. I can't erase these emotions. Rather, I acknowledge those feelings, then move on. I remember the happy times. And I see Virginia's spirit in the towering trees of the Blue Ridge Mountains.

MICHELE PHUA
[The following is an edited journal entry]

October 25, 2005: That night when I found out Ryan was dead, I had checked on him every one to one-and-a-half hours. It is impossible to be awake with a child twenty-four hours. Sometimes I feel guilty that I didn't check on him during the one-and-a-half hours, and I explore the what-ifs—if I could have saved him. He died of unexplained death, not something I could have prevented. My anger is directed to "air" . . . unfortunately, there is just no suspect who caused his death.

PATTY SHAW

There is one thing that I feel guilty about, though when I logically think about it I am not sure that I would do anything differently. Cathy had made up her mind concerning getting a divorce; she had also met an attractive man who was vigorously pursuing her. (This was easy to do since Cathy's husband was gone about twenty-five days of every month.) It was during her last telephone conversation with me that I urged her not to sleep with this man before she had officially separated from her husband, or had at least filed her papers for divorce. I told her nobody cares what a single woman does or a separated wife does but they do care what a married woman does, especially if she has any children living at home, living within dropping-in distance as she did. She told me that I did not understand. I again scolded and implored her not to get intimate, and if she was already, then to stop until legally she was free. She should consider what her sons would think of her. Her response was, "Oh, Mother, you don't understand," and she hung up. That was the last time I heard her voice. I regret that I was scolding her the last time we talked, but I still feel that if she had not been sleeping with that guy that perhaps she would still be alive. Who knows? I will never know, so no need to beat myself up since nothing can be done or changed now.

LOTTIE SOLOMON
[From an interview]

I do feel guilty sometimes. I think of the very strict work ethics we imposed, my husband was that way, too, we were two of a kind—hard workers, you know. While I did not have a job, I worked every single day of my life; I had three children, I ran a big house—everybody in the world was in my house, was entertained in my house. I worked in charity, I did many things. I was on the Juvenile Justice Commission of Santa Clara County and subsequently I chaired it. I did various things, worked in the Jewish world. I did music, I played in the symphonies around here, all this at the same time, I mean, this is what Naomi saw.

One time we were talking and I said, "Naomi, maybe you shouldn't work so hard, and try to, try to . . ." and she said, "A fine person to tell me that. Somebody who never stopped working a minute." If I was not cooking, I was baking. Two o'clock in the morning. I had to read a book a week, every week. And the last thing we talked about she said, "Mother, I remember the night we stayed up and we made 950 hors d'oeuvres, and I went to sleep at 4 o'clock in the morning, you and I were making hors d'oeuvres 'til 4 in the morning." She helped me, and she said, "I've never forgotten that."

I said, "Well, you should, don't do it, it's really dumb." Except in those days we couldn't spend so much money, so we made them.

So I said don't work so hard, she said, "Who's my model? Who should I look at for not working?" And all my boys worked very hard. My daughters-in-law work too. They work and they have children, they have full-time jobs. So that is the way our lives go. [Sighs]

The other thing I thought of, what is the influence? So I think we were hard taskmasters over her, she was child number one; child number one always takes a bit of a beating. So nothing is ever good enough, you know. She was valedictorian in her high school. There is this girl—she is one out of a bright class—number one—she gave the valedictorian speech—and I think to myself, *Why don't I even remember it?* Today, if a grandchild is good in kindergarten there is a whole fuss. And she was doing that, and she was a pianist, so she played for all the plays, she was just across the board an able girl, and a pretty, pretty girl—and then . . . But never had a good opinion of herself, I think that may have been a bit of a problem.

We talked about that once, only—she was very uncomfortable about it, so I never brought it up to her again. I didn't bring it up—but she'd say, she's not *this*, she's not *that*. Once I said, "Are you *kidding?*" And the reason she said that is that her father and I were very tough on her, we were *very* different to our sons. They were also very able, very capable, but I think we praised them, I think they had a better image. I don't know—we were bad as image-makers. It's a funny thing: If you're very honest and straightforward as a parent, that's not such a good trait, you have to know how to temper that. My husband and I were tough in a sense, you know? "You bring home five A's, why didn't you get the sixth A?" That is being pretty tough, you know.

MERRYL WEBER

I was never able to shake the guilt I felt as having failed him as a parent, of not having been able to protect him from harm, of having actually bought the plane ticket that sent him to his death. On top of that, I had also had many premonitions about Adam, too many to count or recount, and I hadn't shared them with him. I thought that maybe if I had, maybe if I had looked to other traditions or cultures, I might have been able to do something so he wouldn't have died so young. I knew in my heart this wasn't true but I couldn't stop the thoughts from rising up. Though I believe, and have believed from my experiences since my early twenties, that everything born will die when its time is up, no matter where or what is happening in life, the vague sense of having failed him haunted me. I knew Adam's life and his death had nothing to do with anything I did or didn't do, at least not in the ways I was thinking about it. Yet I couldn't shake the guilty feelings. I had failed at my "job" as a mother.

What finally shook me loose of the guilt was the realization that some aspect of not being able to forgive myself was keeping me from living more fully. I had no idea what that really meant practically speaking, and called for help from the Universe. I opened myself to find an answer and it came within a couple of days in the form of a man I have known for many years who has become a spontaneous healer. We were together for a few hours one day doing some business and as we talked he shared what was going on in his life. He began to talk about forgiveness in all its manifestations, how it is predicated on being able to surrender to the mysterious love that is all around us, that we keep ourselves away in destructive patterns by our belief that we do not deserve to be loved, to be forgiven. I began weeping, for there it was, verbalized so simply. I did not believe I deserved to be forgiven. I had let my child down. I had let him die. That belief was keeping my heart shut. As soon as I recognized that was what was holding me back, when my whole being resonated with that understanding, love began flowing around me. I heard and felt Adam close by. His presence was reassuring. What a relief after so many years.

JANE WINSLOW
[From an interview]

Peter did not want to go to college, and for the first time ever in our relationship, I asked him to do something because I wanted it.

So, he went. Sometimes I think about that and feel a little guilty, but then I remember that he was such a happy person that there were no negative repercussions.

Working with Anger

What feelings of anger, bitterness, or blame do you hold toward another person or toward God/fate as a result of your child's death? Have you felt the need to forgive anyone for your child's death?

STATHI AFENDOULIS

A friend of mine once told me that anger was a "secondary emotion," one that came as a reaction to some other feeling. Unlike happiness or sadness, which are considered primary emotions, anger seems to always stem from something else. Take, for instance, the parent whose child wanders in a department store or public place. If you have ever been a mom or dad who has lost track of a little one, you know the feeling. It is fear and panic at its deepest level. Until, by some miracle, your little one is restored to you by the store manager or park ranger. Your loving embrace and sense of relief are soon followed by an overwhelming anger. If your child is old enough, you say, in no uncertain terms, "Don't you ever scare me like that again." If looks could kill! Your kid, most often, gets the point.

On the night that Lainie died, she was home with us for a few hours before her body was removed by the funeral directors. During this time, all the family and many friends came to say goodbye. To kiss her one more time or sit with her, hold her hand, or stroke her hair. Many whispered personal secrets or parting words meant only for her to hear. Our parish priest was one of the many supporters who came that evening, and when everyone had retired to the family room, we were alone with Lainie, preparing her for her final journey from home. The funeral director was there with the gurney and that horrible black bag. I lifted her up one last time, holding her in my arms as I had done so many times before. I lifted her body while her mother supported her head. We placed her onto the gurney and watched while they zippered the remains of our oldest daughter. Father Jim and I walked out the front door of our home, hands laid gently on the rolling gurney to the awaiting hearse. As they placed her gently in the hearse and offered their condolences to me, I began to experience the overwhelming anger that the parent of a lost child feels. The hearse pulled out of my driveway, and as its lights proceeded into the darkness, my anger grew.

When your child dies, anger is one of the greatest emotions you experience. You look for something or someone to direct your anger toward, but except for the usual suspects—doctors, nurses, therapists, indifferent medical assistants—you have no one to blame. Father Jim told me, "Be angry at God, he's there for you." And that made sense in a way. When your child dies of cancer, there is really no one to blame but God. Why not put it on him? So why, then, do so many of us carry this anger for so long without any clear resolution? The answer has not been an easy one to find, but for me, it became obvious that the person I was most angry with was myself.

As the hearse that bore Lainie into the night faded from view, the reality of my failure to save her settled in like the darkness around us. Father Jim telling me to be angry at God was good advice, but why should I blame him? It was me who failed Lainie. If I had only been more aggressive; if I had only demanded more of the doctors and the health care workers; if only I had been more vigilant when she was young. If only, if only, if only. Anger burned my soul like a fire burns a forest.

It's easy to forgive someone who has done you wrong. You can look over the facts of the matter, mete out the punishment, and then choose, in a spirit of benevolence, to forgive the transgressor. Simple enough. But what happens when you must sit in judgment of yourself? When you must reveal to yourself your own shortcomings? When you must judge for yourself your own failures?

It was not until someone said to me, "Let Lainie help you make your decisions," that my road to forgiveness became apparent. The more I kept Lainie out of my life, as a victim of my own inability to save her, the more angry I became. Through luck, love, and a great therapist, I started to learn that Lainie was not really gone from me. I could still grab on to her, heart and soul, and ask the hard questions that every parent yearns to ask. Did I do the right thing? Do you still love me, even though I couldn't save you?

In the past six years, I have learned to forgive myself, for every transgression, both real and imagined. I know now that, if Lainie and I could talk, she would tell me there is no need for forgiveness. The time for that has passed and now we must live. You in your place, and me in mine, until we are together again.

SHEILA GEORGE
[From an interview]

I waged anger for a while—I waged anger for years. I remember maybe a year after my son had died and I was trying to pick up the pieces and they had caught the guy that killed him, but because they didn't have a weapon they let him go. They had a police informant who had seen everything and he went over there and they picked the guy up but they let him go. So I was cleaning up my yard one day and this guy walked by my house, just walking by. I was in the yard, and I had the strangest feeling that came over me, and then my daughter came walking up to the backyard and she said, "Mom, do you know who that is?" She said, "That's the guy that killed Ronnie!" And I like froze, okay? I got in my car and I went back to this guy—I don't know what I thought I was gonna do—and then I met up with him in a park—it was right where my son got killed! I got out of the car and I said, "They tell me you're the person who killed my son." He was walking toward me—I don't know what I thought I'd do 'cause he was furious. I'll never forget the look on his face, but then I didn't care about death or dying at that time, I was so angry—I had just seen the guy who they said had killed my son. So then I got a restraining order so he couldn't even come down my block.

So the anger? I lived in East Palo Alto, I put my house up for sale, it wouldn't sell and I just think God didn't want me to go anywhere because this was where my business was, in the community. I blamed the community at large because of everything that was going on here and the black-on-black violence. I just blamed everything on them. But my house wouldn't sell, so I know God intended me to stay here, 'cause houses were selling at that time, and my house wouldn't sell, and I have a nice house. He just kept me here. But by dealing with United Mothers Against Drugs I had to deal with the community and I had to deal with the police department. And I dealt with them and they didn't like me at all, because I was bad in the mouth trying to find my son's killer. They said, "Stop trying to play detective." I said, "Well, you're not doing it!"

So we went on like that. Anger? Yes, a lot of anger, and for years, I think about four or five years, then I decided I can't live in that space. I need to do something with my life. I still have anger when I think about it. They still haven't done anything.

MARTIN KATZ

A typical gambit of professional counselors is to ask, "If you could talk to your son, what would you say?" It's a tough question. First, I would tell him how much I loved and missed him! But, would I tell him this: that I cannot conceive or understand the depths of despair that would lead him to do this selfish, uncaring act; all the wonderful things that he and his family missed; how much pain and anguish he caused; how angry I still am. I don't know. Grandparents: Having lived such unusual lives, having raised families and given them an education in spite of many hardships, having each already lost a daughter, having loved Barry so much, how could he inflict so much pain? They were all wonderful, almost to their last days, and he had so much to both give and take from them. Sisters, nephews, and nieces: His sisters loved and cared for him. They each now have a son and daughter who never met and enjoyed Barry. He would have enjoyed watching their growth as unique individuals. They would all have had such a good time together! Other people:

He was intellectually good, musically talented, a good and kind friend. What would these assets have developed into and for what humanitarian use? What the world lost will never be known. He lost everything!

I cannot and probably never will understand that Barry's life was so distressed and that he was in such despair that he would willfully commit suicide and inflict so much pain, anguish, and suffering on his entire family. Did he not know how terrible the loss of our two sisters had been on his grandparents and parents? How could he equate any of his problems to those of the Holocaust survivors? How could he be so selfish?

You pour a lifetime of work, study, and accomplishment into creating a beautiful family in a wonderful home. Unlike your parents, you can now provide so many things, so many opportunities, so many advantages. All this love and care and effort and hopes and dreams are *rejected* by one you loved so much.

MICHELE PHUA
[From an interview]

I don't know what I'm mad at, but I'm still mad.

LOTTIE SOLOMON
[From an interview]

Of course, I am angry, I am so angry, you can hear! I am angry because I think terrorism was not tended the right way. I think there was nobody at the helm who was clever enough to take note of any warnings. I think it was negligence, clear negligence. I am sure. And this group that works—you know there is a whole unit, it is called Survivors of 9/11—and they are really mad, they are really angry. You know that they have no money to even put up the building, let alone a memorial, that is the newest thing, but most of all they don't like the memorial. They sent me all the pictures to ask if I have any comment. Well, I have a mile of comments, but I did not write anything. Nobody is listening to them. What they want to do is not what I want.

I think it should be a memorial. Never mind all these fancy fountains; I do not think that's necessary. You want a memorial, you want just to read a name—that's what will hang on—people don't care about the fountains floating, not the surviving families. I went to Ground Zero this past year where Naomi died and it almost did me in; there were no answers there and I cannot make peace with what happened.

JANE WINSLOW
[From an interview]

Peter died in a traffic accident as a result of another driver's carelessness. There was a trial, and the driver had his license taken away for a year. It was his second or third moving violation, and I felt so impotent that I lost so much and yet he suffered so little. Yet, I did not want to sue or do anything otherwise damaging to the driver.

I wanted to say something to the driver at the courthouse, so I practiced with my husband and with a friend. Yet, when it was over, there was really nothing I felt I could say that would make any difference. So, I just went up to him and said, "Please be careful." It seemed so inane, yet I could not verbalize anything more. What could I say? Be ashamed of yourself? What do you say? But, I must say I do not feel any resentment. The driver may have said something inane as well, like "I'm sorry." In the end, punishing the driver would not accomplish anything.

Taking Stock

Nowhere in this book does the element of time play a larger role than it does in part 4 and its look at the emotional challenges we struggled with after our losses. With the benefit of hindsight we now appreciate that while our internal path ran uphill for what seemed an eternity, eventually the grade evened out and the going got easier.

Despair, for instance, waxes and wanes over time. In the fresh throes of grief, we wondered if we would ever feel joy again. Some of us answered the question on despair while still deeply depressed. Nancy Emro did. Then, five years later, she felt such a renewed zest for living that she added an update.

Guilt, too, diminishes with most of us. We've all felt it, however irrationally. Guilt for not being good enough parents, caring for sick children imperfectly, not taking action to prevent an accident, not seeing the severity of a depression or the possibility of a murderous rage, not acting on what now seems a premonition. Ultimately, we resolve most of our guilt by coming to forgive ourselves and recognizing that we don't have total control and that no one can be a perfect parent.

Anger is another consuming emotion that eventually fades. At first we are angry with God, with those who deliberately or accidentally caused the death of our children, with people who don't understand the depth of our sorrow, with a government that didn't prevent a terrorist attack. We're angry with our children if they took their own lives. We're angry with ourselves. And sometimes we're just angry. As Michele Phua says, "I don't know what I'm mad at, but I'm still mad."

If you're despairing of ever finding meaning or pleasure in your life, you may take heart from what you just read. If you're burdened by guilt, or plagued by anger, be assured that while time may not cure all ills, it does relieve their most debilitating symptoms. Like us, one day you will look back and feel empathy for that struggling self you once were.

PART FIVE

GRASPING THE SILVER CORD

Setting Out

Even though death has claimed our children, we parents want to feel them near. Regardless of how few or how many years they were a part of our lives, it's inconceivable to imagine an existence devoid of their presence. If your child has recently died, it may be comforting to know that—even if you wanted to—you couldn't sever the connection between you. We call this ongoing relationship, the ethereal tie that links parent to child in life and beyond death, the *silver cord*.

Although we may sense the existence of that bond, our experience of it is highly individual. In part 5 we explore the various ways some of us connect with the children we loved, and love still.

Some have virtually felt or seen the spirits of their children. Susan Benveniste saw Shelly reclining on the couch days after her accident. Inés Ascencio received vital and otherwise unknown information from Angelita. Van Jepson experienced Ian's presence so vividly that it has transformed the way he looks at life.

Others of us continue to talk to our children, like Patty Shaw, who converses with Cathy on her daily walks, and Suzanne Redfern, whose casual "chats" with Mimi keep their relationship vibrant. Some see our children's spirits in nature. And while Lottie Solomon may not speak of sensing Naomi's spiritual presence, Naomi's life and legacy have taken on a greater meaning for Lottie and given her a sense of continuity.

In our search for ways to preserve the silver cord, some of us choose to honor our children with charitable acts, such as the Phuas' annual sponsorship of Ryan's Ride and Anne Logan's creation of a studio for young artists at Virginia's college. You'll also learn that many of us fan the flame of our children's memory by incorporating aspects of their personalities into our own.

If you're hoping to maintain a connection with a deceased child, or wishing to honor one, we're confident that you'll discover your own way—one that will be appropriate within your traditions, your belief structure, and your makeup. But perhaps some of our practices and inventions will serve as food for thought.

Continuing the Connection

Even if our children are physically out of our lives, our connections with them will always remain. However, like our relationships with those in the temporal world, our bonds with our departed sons and daughters are organic, rarely remaining static over time. Often even our vision of them changes. *Please describe your continuing relationship with your child.* When brought to mind, how does your child appear—what is the strongest recurring physical image? Has it altered since your child's death? Do you sense growth in either of you?

INÉS ASCENCIO
[From an interview]

My daughters, who never met Angelita, talk about her. So they have a relationship with her, too. My daughter Camila has a really strong connection to Angelita. Recently I was showing a friend a whole bunch of pictures and there was a card that Camila had written when she was younger, and in it she talked about her connection to her sister. I have heard that so often from parents—that the next child is somehow so attuned.

[Inés recalls three incidents involving Angelita]

My family's from Cuba and I wanted to go there . . . I wasn't born there, but I wanted to go. One my clients had a Cuban boy that they were going to send back to live with his father and so I was going to take the child. I couldn't find my passport and I was really frustrated and didn't know where it could be, so when I went to bed I prayed to all the angels that when I woke up I would know where it was. And when I woke up, I remembered. My kids weren't with me that day, they were with their father. The next day we were having dinner and my daughter Camila said, "Mommy, there she is. I see Angelita." And I said, "Really?" And she said, "Yeah, she says she found your passport." So I said, "Tell her 'Thank you.'" My daughter went on, "Angelita said to tell you she loves you a lot." And then she started laughing and said that Angelita wanted some pancakes.

I was engaged and I was considering breaking it off and I was praying, not just to Angelita but to God. My fiancé didn't believe in that stuff, but he said that as he drove my kids to school one day he heard a voice say, "Pull over." So he pulled over and then he said my daughter was in the car. He said this young girl was in the car, and he described her. I mean, the age she would be now. She appeared to him and was asking him all these questions. He said, "If anyone saw us, they would think I was crazy." She was asking all these really deep questions. He said, "I never believed in apparitions before, but I am sure it was her."

My fiancé and I had a joint phone plan, and I told him, "I'm not going to turn the phone on, so check the voice mail." One night I was awakened and I got a feeling of Angelita's presence saying, "Turn on that phone." I did get up and turn on the phone . . . it was about three in the morning. At six in the morning the phone rang and it was this woman who was asking, "Where is he?" She was really angry and then she said she was pregnant. There was more evidence, concrete things. It was this really weird person he got hooked up with. She could have come with her brother and his gun to my house because he had shown her my house. I just think it was really a protective thing; I look at it like divine intervention. There's no other explanation. Why was I awakened? I really didn't care who was calling, it was just going to bring me more grief. Finally, it was so much that I broke it off. So I do feel like Angelita got back to me on the question I asked about my fiancé.

VAN JEPSON

Ian and I are in constant communication, which started with me when I was meditating early after his death, and has evolved into a spontaneous dialogue through our hearts, not through our ears or voices. Within days after his passing his spirit came to me and said, "You'll learn more from me now that I'm gone than you did while I was on Earth." This has been true because he and I have been on a journey of growth and expansion since the moment of his passing. Although his earthly body was eight when it died, his spirit showed itself to me as a young child for only a short time, before it showed me the vast magnificence of itself. I tracked his growth and transformation daily in my journal, and always found him in a different place and with expanded skills. His skills expanded at an incredible rate as he shifted from the constructs and challenges of Earth into the constructs and challenges of the world he moved into.

KATHRYN LODATO

Nick was on the cusp of manhood when he died, just a month after his twenty-first birthday. He was away at school, and I remember looking at him, drinking in the sight of him, when he was home for that last Christmas. He was still my Nick—tall and gangly, busy and funny—but he was growing into himself, and I had a sense of a new young man emerging, a young man with whom I'd have a different relationship. For a long time I felt that we'd never get a chance, now, to have that relationship. It was one of the many things I mourned. And I continue to mourn it, but in an odd way I also feel that our relationship has continued to grow and develop since Nick died.

For the first months, or maybe a year, after Nick died, the two images of Nick that came to my mind most often were both so sad, so terrible, that I felt like I was falling into the abyss all the time. The first image: Nick dead. In the funeral parlor, lying so still and pale on a table, draped in a green cloth. Jim had told the funeral director that he wanted, needed, to see Nick's hands. The director, a sweet man, had told us that Nick looked "good," that he never knew what hit him, that he had arranged Nick's body for us to see with one hand visible, outside of the draping. But he made us promise not to lift or move the cloth in any way. For months I'd close my eyes and see Nick's face, his hand, both so still, so pale, and torture myself with imagining his poor broken body under the cloth.

The second image was almost as painful. About five years before he died, when he was about sixteen, Nick and his brother and cousin had an accident on Thanksgiving Day when a three-wheeler motorcycle they were riding tipped over. Nick was the only one hurt. It wasn't serious, but we didn't know it at the time. The three-wheeler had landed on his face, cracked his jaw, and he was bloodied and scared and in pain. He was lying on the couch at my mom's house when I got to him. Jim was calling emergency rooms. I went to him. His big eyes were filled with tears. He looked at me, scared and hurt, and let me mother him. My tall little boy, six foot four, almost all grown up, but he needed me. After he died, I kept seeing him on that couch—hurt and afraid and needing me—and I wasn't there. I'd see him like that during the day. And at night I'd dream of him lying hurt, needing me, and I couldn't get to him. Six years later I can still close my eyes and see those images, and they are still so painful that I am crying as I write this.

But they aren't the images I live with anymore. Often my mind's eye sees Nick as he is in favorite pictures we have around the house. That's almost as bad—to only see Nick frozen, in those few moments. I consciously work on seeing him at other times, laughing, moving, talking, kidding me. I see us making pizza together and Nick teasing me with slices of salami—a food I despise and don't even like to touch. Nick would slice the salami for his side of the pizza and wave it under my nose as I'd recoil in exaggerated disgust. I see him lounging on the couch with the cat draped over him. I see him poring over topographical maps of the hills outside of Santa Barbara, tracing the trails where he rode his mountain bike, telling me of trips he'd taken, trips he was planning. But those scenes also become set pieces, as I run them through my mind again and again. The vitality leaches out. I fear to lose the real Nick, so full of life and plans, so fully himself, so fun and unexpected. All the scenes are in the past, there's no future. I carry him with me, but those remembered scenes are such a pale substitute for my living son and his open future.

I have another image of Nick. My sister, who is an artist, painted a picture of Nick the first spring after he died and gave it to me that first terrible Mother's Day. It is a watercolor painted from my sister's favorite picture of Nick. Nick at about nineteen, home from college for Thanksgiving. His dark hair is longish, tucked behind his ears. He's holding Mickey, our black cat, like a baby, their two faces nestled together. Those two pairs of eyes—Nick's dark blue, Mickey's yellow—gaze out levelly from the painting. Nick isn't smiling, but he isn't not smiling. "Nick was with me the whole time I was painting this," Peggy told me when she gave me the painting, "I could feel him." I too can feel him in the picture. It hangs above and a little to the left of the place I sit when I write. I pause often and look at it, look at Nick.

Several years ago, about two years after Nick's death, I went through a long period—at least six months—when I couldn't look at the picture. Nick looked so sad, so unspeakably sad, that I just couldn't stand to look into his eyes. And I was so sad, so unspeakably sad. The shock of his death had mostly worn off, and I was left with what felt like a bottomless despair. I was stuck, unmoored, hopeless. I spent many afternoons doing little more than staring at the ceiling. Before that period I had been working on developing a meditation practice, but the despair had worn me down and I had given up. One warm summer day, for some reason I cannot name, I lit my candle and sat down and closed my eyes and followed my breath and tried to meditate. I sat for fifteen or twenty minutes, nothing momentous happened, but the next day I lit the candle again, and the day after.

After about a week I opened my eyes after meditation and looked at Nick's picture. His eyes met mine, as they always do, but the look of unutterable sadness was gone. He was almost smiling, on the verge. I felt like he was saying, "All right, Mom!" I could feel his love, his encouragement. I felt like he was saying, "Yeah, this is one damned sad situation we have here. But that's not all. There's more." I felt our relationship shift. And most important, since then, I've felt that our relationship has continued, has developed and grown. Nick will always be my little boy, my dear son. And I will miss his physical presence in my life, miss it terribly, every day, until the day that I die. But he is also, in some very real sense, the competent, strong, wise man that he was on the verge of growing into. I ask him for help when I'm most sad and most lonely. I ask him to help his brother, who misses him so much and has such a hard time talking about it. I ask him to look after his dad. I don't profess to know or understand where Nick is or in what form, but I believe—I know— that he exists, that he is safe, that he loves us still.

SUZANNE REDFERN

From the moment I closed Mimi's eyelids on December 6, 1999, until today, six-and-a-half years later, I have talked to her in the same way I did during the thirty-two years of her life—easily and often. In the first few months after her death she was so vividly present to me that it would have been impossible not to carry on this running dialogue. It came about so naturally that I sometimes spoke aloud, especially with the agonized question, "Where *are* you?" As that particular terror faded, the subject of my conversation largely concerned my efforts to live more courageously, a challenge Mimi had put to me during one long hospitalization. I'd report in whenever I managed to conquer a particular fear and be more out there in life, as I'd promised her I would try to do.

These days I still report in on my progress, but also find myself casually chatting with her on a variety of subjects that would have interested her: Barry Bonds's joyless pursuit of Hank Aaron's home run record; my search for the best tulip bulbs for fall planting; the appropriateness of her toddler niece Chloe's taking title to the section and a half of good farmland that used to be Mimi's. Because we spent so much time together throughout her life and during her illness, and because she was an open book—her husband Brett used to joke that she *had* no inner life—I can intuit her responses to my thoughts. Sometimes they come in the form of actual words; more often I just *feel* her reaction. The exchange is, in an ineffable way, satisfying. It flows effortlessly and is unclouded by the need to decide absolutely whether or not Mimi's spirit really *is* somewhere, ever accessible and up for a chat. It's enough that I enjoy the experience and that I'm usually calmed—and occasionally inspired—by what I receive from it.

As I think back on this ongoing habit of mine and note the gradual shift in subject matter and tone, I remember that there's also been a shift in the way Mimi appears to me during our talks. For years she came as an invalid. Thin, pale, and bald, confined to bed. My heart broke again each time I saw her that way. My grief over her death was overlaid with memories of the pain of her long dying. My stomach would wrench once more with the fear, the panicky need to *fix* it, a compulsion that had been my constant companion during the nine months of her illness. Along with Mimi's husband, father, and brothers, I had paid sorrowful witness to every intimate detail of her physical deterioration and the incapacities it produced. We watched helplessly as, one by one, the activities that gave meaning and pleasure to her life became impossible for her to attempt. Tennis. Gardening. Cooking. Showering. Rising from her bed. Laughing. And, finally—when the flow of air through her riddled lungs became drastically restricted—even hugging. My beautiful, strapping, athletic daughter had become a terminally ill cancer patient.

It was, of course, unthinkable to us all that Mimi should be so afflicted. Unthinkable and also unforgettable, for it was as a cancer patient that she appeared to my mind's eye for a very long time. Then about a year ago she came to me in a dream. There was no physical setting, no context, and no dialogue to that dream, only the thrilling vision of Mimi's old vibrant self, bounding in great joyful leaps across a blank landscape. I awoke to find tears on my cheeks at her liberation. Since that dream I find that I talk to a young woman who is in abundant good health, with glowing skin, rounded breasts and hips, and lustrous auburn hair. Her smile is as gorgeous and as ready as ever. Ready, that is, except once in a while, when I'm taking a hard look at the way I'm living my life, and I sense that she's a bit cross with me, *peeved* because I've not done my best to live with courage, to be of use, to fully engage myself. Though I take Mimi's "scoldings" seriously, I'm grateful that they're delivered by a vision of health and vitality.

I'm also grateful for this abiding conversational habit I developed early on and have maintained. It gives me a bridge over what would otherwise be an imponderable divide. It's just the sort of device Mimi herself would have dreamed up for us to keep in touch. During one of her many hospitalizations I went along as she was wheeled through the bowels of the UC Davis Medical Center for still one more invasive and frightening diagnostic procedure. Waiting in an adjoining room while the test was done, I was drawn to a small, framed picture on one wall—a snapshot of another smiling young woman, one who had worked in the lab before her death. Under her picture was an imperative on this very subject, an appeal for us to maintain our relationships with those who precede us in death. I jotted it down, finding it remarkable in its unconventionality, considering the period and the position of its author. We put it under Mimi's picture in her memorial service program, knowing she would approve.

> Death is nothing at all. I have only slipped away into the next room. I am I, and you are you. Whatever we were to each other, we still are. Call me by my old familiar name, speak to me in the easy way which you always used. Put no difference in your tone, wear no forced air of solemnity or sorrow. Laugh as we always laughed at the little jokes we enjoyed together. Pray, smile, think of me, pray for me.
>
> Let my name be ever the household word that it always was, let it be spoken without effect, without the trace of a shadow on it.
>
> Life means all that it ever meant. It is the same as it ever was; there is unbroken continuity. Why should I be out of mind because I am out of sight? I am waiting for you, for an interval, somewhere very near, just around the corner. All is well.

—Henry Scott Holland (1847–1918), canon of St. Paul's Cathedral, London

PATTY SHAW

I think that I am continuing to be Cathy's mother through my talks with her during my walks in the morning. As I walk, many pictures flash through my mind when I think of her at different stages of her life—from crawling to walking down the aisle at her wedding, to welcoming her new sister-in-law into the family when Debbie was so very shy and timid. I think that both of them discovered that they were soul sisters and they took every opportunity to be together. Their love for each other was joy to see. And because of the love Debbie has for Cathy, we (Debbie and I) can talk and talk about her and always come away rejuvenated. Sad, too, in a way, as she is no longer physically here, but so very much alive in our thoughts, prayers, and dreams. For instance, the other day during my morning walk, I was walking along the shore of a large pond that is bordered by tall reeds and grasses. The sun was almost to the horizon on my left so that the sky was the most glorious peach and apricot which shed that same magnificent light on the pond's surface to my right. Then, the heavens be praised, a red-winged blackbird landed on one of the tallest grasses which swayed with its weight and he just sang his heart out. It was a breathtaking experience . . . the beauty difficult to describe. Now, that is something which I would have either called Cathy or e-mailed her about but now I have Debbie to share that with since we three thought and felt the same way about things like that. I still have someone to share with and both Debbie and I feel that Cathy is right there with us. How lucky can I be?

LOTTIE SOLOMON
[From an interview]

They are no longer with you . . . that is the philosophical point of view . . . then you remember all these wonderful oddities about them. In Naomi's case, she was so interested in so many things. She wrote this magnificent report that went all through the World Bank on river blindness. She wrote a paper assembling all the information on river blindness, and she was so moved, she said, "Gee, I'd love to go to French West Africa and really have a look at what this is about now that I wrote about it."

Something that has changed for me is that Naomi's *life* has become more evident to me . . . I get more meaning out of it. There are books of information, pictures, testimonials. When she died there were many cards, letters about her, notes, I put it all into folders. This was what her friends did, they had a little party, memorial really, and they gave me a lovely memorial book. When it came, which was November of that year, I didn't look at it, and it's been on the shelf, and you know what? I just took it off for the first time, and I read a lot of it, and now I want to read it all. I couldn't, you know what I'm saying?

What I did was put cards and everything . . . cards, stamps, everything into those folders, and it's all . . . I guess so that my grandchildren will know who she is. In our foyer there's a flag for her and a memorial at Congress for her, because our congress-woman, Anna Eshoo, came to the memorial service for Naomi after she had read it into the record in Congress. Then they brought me a flag that hung in her memory at half mast, and I have it in the foyer, framed. No, I don't see hiding away from it . . . it doesn't help to hide away.

Sensing the Presence

Although we're reticent to talk about them, some of us enjoy moments in which we sense the presence of our children. Most often these moments occur in the first days after their passing, but a few people continue to experience such visitations. *Do you sometimes feel the spirit of your child to be vividly present?* How does this presence manifest itself? Are you awake or asleep? Do you converse? Do you sense being responded to? Are you able to call up that presence, or does it appear of its own accord?

Inés Ascencio
[From an interview]

In the Latin cultures, when people have lost a loved one they say the person comes to them, especially right when they are dying. When people told me that before my daughter died, I just could not relate to it. I can now.

Susan Benveniste

It's a few days since Shelly's death and I'm sitting downstairs late at night unable to sleep. My husband and son are sleeping upstairs. I'm on the landing of the open doorway leading to the patio and lagoon beyond. The sky is clear—lots of stars and moonlight shining on the water. The quiet is a brief but welcome respite from the chaos of these past few days. The outpouring of support and embracing by friends and acquaintances has been amazing, and yet, knowing Shelly and her connection to others, not surprising.

I'm looking to the stars for answers—Is she up there? Is she okay? Can she see us? As a parent, the urge to protect my daughter is still with me. Oh, how I miss her and her flashing dark brown eyes and abounding energy. Looking at the stars, I am reminded of my father's remarks after he had digested the news of Shelly's accident. "When you need to be close to Shelly, look at the sky, pick out the brightest star—that will be Shelly, working the room!" Through grief and tears, this manages to make me smile. We all loved to watch Shelly interact in a crowd, with poise beyond her seventeen years. To use an expression, "She could fill a room with her very presence," a trait inherited from her dad, my husband Ron.

Closing the sliding door against the chill of the night, I still am not ready to go upstairs. The family room is illuminated only by moonlight. I sit in a chair by the window and am suddenly aware of a "presence." In the darkness I can barely make out a figure across the room, stretched out on the couch. (As I write about this almost twelve years later, it still seems real and like yesterday.) I'm afraid to move or go closer. I *know* it's Shelly. If I approach, I'm afraid she'll disappear. Oh, how I want this experience to be real! I sit quietly rocking, holding my arms around me, which has become my pose these past days. It's as if I may crumble if I unwrap them. Tears are streaming down my face and all I can utter is, "I love you, I love you," over and over. I just want to soak up this moment. We sit like that for what must be ten to fifteen minutes, until I quietly ascend the stairs not quite sure what has just occurred. I now welcome sleep.

In my heart, even today, I know it was our daughter assuring me that she was all right. That moment was the beginning of knowing I would survive this loss.

Susan Gilbert

I am now convinced that I knew Amanda was gone from the moment of her death. I was sitting in a meeting with a colleague on Monday, March 1, and at about 2:20 I was suddenly overtaken with a deep sense of disturbance and depression. I turned white (according to my colleague), excused myself, and went home. I attributed this episode to illness until the knock at the door the next morning.

For the first few years after Amanda's death, I was almost obsessed with receiving reassurance that in some way her spirit survived. I read everything I could find concerning the spirit's survival of death and found some credible and many not-so-credible sources. Some studies of near-death experiences and sightings of ghosts are persuasive, although scoffed at by skeptics. Finally, it was my own personal experiences that helped me hope that there is, indeed, the possibility of continuation of life.

A few months after Amanda's death, I was compelled by waves of sleepiness to go back to bed at 11 in the morning, an unusual occurrence for me. I had a most vivid dream in which Amanda came to me on a beach. There were no words spoken, but I had a very real sense that she was there. Her eyes sparkled and she seemed so pleased with herself, as though she had pulled off a wonderful surprise for me. Although she is a frequent figure in my dreams, the experience of her presence seemed exceptional and very real in this case.

VAN JEPSON

Do I sometimes feel the spirit of my child to be vividly present? Yes, and it has persisted. I've made it through some bumpy times with my earthly body screaming in denial of the ability I have to hear him and converse with him. I have weathered those obstacles in awareness and have shifted myself to maintain contact with his spirit in my daily meditations, when I call and ask him questions, or open myself to his comments and advice, or just play with him. In the beginning, for the first several months, he was able to press his spirit through my sadness at any time of day or night to communicate and make his insights known. His analogy to me was that viewing Earth from where he was, was like watching TV because those people on Earth who have their hearts closed would do destructive things and hurt each other because they couldn't hear from their friends in Heaven. When the people's hearts on Earth were open, it appeared to him like a video game where he could communicate and make them do things that he wanted. He still presses through on a regular basis when he desires, not only in response to my calls during my meditations. And there are times during my meditations that he cannot pick up the phone. We call it the heart phone.

MERRYL WEBER

Sometimes I feel like I am hearing Adam speak to me or that he is just there watching us. This happens especially at times when I, or we as a family, are happy yet missing his presence, at a holiday, a birthday, a celebration of some sort. Sometimes my daughter and I, or my husband and I, will sense his presence together and we will acknowledge it as a matter of fact. But it happens at other times too, when I am listening to a piece of music I associate with him, or I am with one of his friends, or I am in an emotional space that is constricted around his death. I mostly feel him without seeing him, though every once in a while his little boy self comes roaring back to me with an intensity that reduces me to tears with my heart breaking open. The overwhelming love that I feel for him and have felt since I knew a little being was growing inside me comes pouring over me, flooding me with memories of his childhood. Once in a while, I feel the young man near, the musician, the rebel with the long hair, all dressed in black, gently chiding me to get on with my life, to do the things that I have always wanted to do and not hold back.

I know in my heart that we are both very different beings than we were before he died, that the shift from being embodied to not being embodied changes everything in a way that cannot be known by me. I still speak to him every day, whether I feel his presence or don't. I have no idea if he hears me, how it works, whether there is some objective reality to all this or not. There are times when I haven't felt him around for a long time and feel the need to sense him. I do call upon him to let me know he is okay and, inevitably, I either have a dream about him or someone else lets me know that he has shown up and spoken to them in a dream. Every once in a while it is someone I had no idea had a deep connection with him. I am fascinated by that phenomenon.

Kathleen Weed

I know a grandmother whose dead grandson hides her car keys, and then plops them right in front of her favorite chair. A friend of mine's dead daughter arranged perfect weather for her sister's wedding, even though the newscaster had predicted rain. Another mother described the spirit of her child as so vivid and constant that she feels like she is "parenting in two worlds."

Occasionally, on clear moonless nights, I stand alone on the deck of our country house, bundled in Jenica's old blue ski jacket, beseeching her to flash me a shooting star. The night sky is startlingly magnificent. My head tilts backward, and my eyes bore into this vast black dome festooned with numberless garlands of scintillating stars. If I stand there long enough, I imagine that even in the darkest edges of the firmament faint stars are struggling to show themselves to me. Often, I give up before I see a shooting star.

Sometimes two, even three, will whiz by if I wait long enough. I hate that it's all so far away.

Others say that Jenica visits them. I admit that I am sometimes skeptical of their accounts. "Why is Jenica visiting her fifth-grade basketball coach?" I will ask my husband. "She didn't even like basketball that much." I live the profoundness of Jenica's absence. I want to be grateful when people tell me they sense her presence. Mostly, I envy them.

Even though I don't experience Jenica as a spirit, hanging around and keeping me company, she is rooted in my heart. I will say that once in a while I feel unaccountable soothing warmth on my shoulder—my right shoulder—the one with the muscles all in knots. Once I thought I caught a glimpse of Jenica while looking in a mirror at my own green eyes. And when I find myself walking on my tiptoes—we shared this quirky habit—Jenica balances with me for a moment.

She lives in me. That's what I'm trying to say. And her indwelling exists with embedment not attributable to mere memory. My daughter who lives in me has been freed to present herself, with strikingly equal clarity, as a pink-cheeked baby, a third-grader who smiles through her braces, or the young woman who was my best friend. Since Jenica's death, she is no longer just one age. The timeline has disappeared too.

I did get a message from Jenica a month or so after she died. My daily housebound wanderings that first summer included opening the door at the end of the hall. This wasn't Jenica's shell-pink bedroom overlooking a rose garden. It wasn't her childhood bedroom. Steven and I bought this house the summer before her freshman year at Dartmouth, and so Jenica had only spent school vacations here. Even so, each day the room drew me in. Maybe I would touch her things. Or I might just sit on her old brass bed while time floated out the screen door.

On this particular morning, I noticed that the bottom drawer of her tall pine bureau wasn't properly shut. I tugged on it, but it was so overloaded that it jammed. I tugged again, harder. Suddenly, the whole drawer slipped off its rollers and landed on the carpet. Old spiral notebooks, schoolwork, and miscellaneous papers spilled out.

I sat down to sort through the mess I'd made, and that's when I found it, a single page divided into three passages written by Jenica. She called it *Home Story*. I had never read it before, so I'm not even sure when she wrote it.

In the first verse Jenica describes a dream that I dreamt when I was eight months pregnant with her.

The woman's mother held the baby girl, and called her Jenica. The woman didn't know that name, and asked her mother where the name originated. The mother responded, "like the child, the name began in you."

Even though I had not been told the sex of my baby and had never heard the name Jenica, I sensed that this had truly been a naming dream. When I awoke, I understood that very soon I would give birth to my firstborn, Jenica.

In the middle verse Jenica writes about a night I cared for her when she became ill a few weeks after her birth.

She kept the child near to her all night. She prayed for the child and sang to it.

Jenica had suffered from infantile diarrhea, and as a result became severely dehydrated. I remember sitting in a big oak rocking chair with her cradled in my arms. She nursed at my breast all night. When the sun rose, we slept and she was better. But no one held her the night she died. Oh, how I wish that I could have been near to Jenica on that terrible night. Instead, she died hooked up to machines in a faraway ICU. Instead, she died among strangers. Dartmouth Hitchcock Medical Center sent me the medical report, a thick manila envelope. I tell myself that one day I'll read it.

It is the last verse of Jenica's *Home Story* that takes my breath away. When I finished reading it that first time, I sank to my knees on Jenica's rug, with the paper clutched in my hand. It may seem a little thing, but at that moment I wondered if the Universe had pitied me in my wretchedness and delivered me a gift, a message from my daughter.

My mother walks on the wings of the universe, moving with a magic that stirs all around her. There is an acute nearness of her when she speaks. Sometimes, when I call her, she knows it is me even before I say hello. "Jenica, I've missed you," she will say. She always knows how to comfort me, as if silken strands of understanding were spun through her mind. Her soul is like a beam of light refracted by her tongue into a thousand words of wisdom. Even when I am far from my mother, I am near. She is an eternal moment happening inside me.

Darling Jenica,

Thank you for *Home Story*. Yes, when you were away, I always missed you. Sometimes I even missed you when you were in your bedroom. I'm trying to live by the wisdom in your words. Even though you are far from me, you are near. You are an eternal moment happening inside me. I love you with all my heart, Sweetie.

Mommy

Losing the Intimacy

One metaphor for grief is the ocean. For a time we're wading in shallow, clear water, placing our feet with some confidence on a fairly solid surface, then a tidal wave out of nowhere tosses and tumbles and bruises us all over again. Over time, the extremes begin to disappear from the screen, particularly the insupportable pain of earlier days. However, what feels like relief to many of us is tangled up with the worry that diminishing agony implies a diminishing connection with our beloved. *As your grief changes over time, do you fear losing a sense of intimacy with your child? Do you feel bad about feeling better? Do you resist letting go a bit, fearing to lose too much?*

Van Jepson

No. There are two parts to this answer, one from an earthly perspective and one from a heavenly perspective. From an earthly perspective, and from the beginning, I never connected the thought that getting better was reducing the intimacy with my son. The intimate relationship I had with my son's body was severed permanently at the time of cremation. From the heavenly perspective, and because I was connected to him through my open heart, the intimate relationship that I had with his spirit continued. Although the first time that I got a busy signal on his end or he didn't pick up, I thought I'd lost him in the world he was in. It was only because he was in such a rapid state of change or busy doing something essential to that moment or because I was too obstructed by my earthly activities that I did not hear his response. It was then that I became concerned and thought I had lost him forever. I have put my focus and energy into maintaining and expanding the intimate relationship I have with his spirit so I will never lose him.

Patty Shaw

No, I cannot imagine that. It hasn't happened yet. I hope it never does. She was my firstborn and not wanted by her father because she wasn't a boy, so I always tried extra hard with her and encouraged her to be proud that she was a girl and would be a fine woman someday. As a consequence, our bond was always very close. Sure, there were rough patches, but we got through them.

Merryl Weber

For a long time I was aware that not being able to call up his face, or not feeling too much pain in any given moment, made me feel like I was losing him again. Yet the very awareness of it kept the fear of losing him at bay. I knew he had never been "mine" to begin with and would remind myself that people cannot lose what is not theirs.

This is not to in any way imply that on an emotional level I wasn't experiencing a sense of acute loss, only that while I was experiencing this emotional upheaval there was a concomitant awareness of the infinite nature of all things, of the complex relationships between souls as they move in and out of corporeality, and that this awareness was soothing at the same time.

Fanning the Spark

If there is one thing all of us would wish to do—besides bringing back our children—it would be to keep their spirits alive. That impulse may be followed in a number of ways. Some are more formal, such as establishing an award in his honor for something he loved; some are more personal, such as talking about her with her friends, keeping flowers in the house because she did, or setting a place at the table for her at Thanksgiving; and some are more metaphysical, such as invoking his energy into a situation, or consciously carrying on your life as if you were living for both of you. *What ways have you found to keep burning the unique spark of life that was your child?*

Susan Benveniste

Shelly wasn't known for neatness. Personally she was well groomed; it was her surroundings that were untidy—specifically, her room and car. Like most seventeen-year-olds, activities and friends held more allure than being tidy. Thus, I knew cleaning out her room would hold many surprises. But never did I expect to uncover something that would comfort us and identify her forever.

On a day that I was feeling strong, I gathered up Tammy, my cocker spaniel and constant companion, and began to tackle a very difficult task, one that I dreaded, but knew had to be done.

Shelly had left for camp in Bass Lake to serve as a junior counselor one month before. It was a place she and her brother Josh loved, returning each year as campers. Shelly had finally gotten old enough to start staffing. None of us ever dreamed her life would be cut short that summer as a passenger in a senseless car accident.

I started on her dresser. Memories flowed. Through tears there was laughter—discovering lavender cable knee socks from the fifth grade, shoved to the back of her drawer; finding a very petrified peanut butter and jelly sandwich, hiding between t-shirts (fortunately in a baggie!); and, of course, the expected empty chip and cookie bags shoved under the bed! Going through Shelly's things was like a visit with my daughter, forgotten memories flooding to the forefront. But I also was having feelings of guilt, intruding into her privacy.

Saving the closet for another day, I decided to clean out her bulging backpack leaning in the corner. A pile of unorganized papers came flooding out—math, biology, English, but one caught my eye. It was folded in half and I could only see what appeared to be a dark semicircle drawn inside. Unfolding it, I could hardly believe my eyes. The dark outline was that of a cemetery marker with the mimeographed letters R.I.P. at the bottom. Shelly's handwriting filled in the rest:

Shelly Benveniste
1974–1991
Though short, her life was a masterpiece of pleasure; she
expressed Herself out of happiness to all those around her.

I could hardly breathe. Tears were pouring down my face, Tammy trying to lick away the pain. I couldn't get to the phone fast enough to call my husband Ron. Shelly had been buried weeks before. In the Jewish faith, a headstone is not placed for a year, thus we hadn't even thought ahead that far as to what it would say. Little did we know Shelly would provide the words for us. It gives us comfort to this day, almost twelve years later, that she felt so positively about her life.

A masterpiece of pleasure, indeed!

Postscript: We later found out that the above was part of an English assignment. The teacher told me Shelly was the only one that placed her death in the present. The rest of the students projected themselves into their seventies or eighties. It was an assignment the teacher said she would never give again.

MARY LOU COFFELT

On the anniversary of Mattie's fifth birthday, a little over one year after his death, we had an orchard-planting party. The idea grew from the months before his death, when he and I had made plans to plant an orchard next to our house—a dream Mattie and I were unable to accomplish together, but that Bob and I carried out with the help of a multitude of friends. It was a cold and rainy day and probably a hundred people gathered. Some brought food, all brought love.

Despite the weather, we dug holes and planted a variety of fruit trees in memory of Mattie. We prayed together in the wind and the rain. By day's end, there were rows and rows of little trees honoring our little son. A flagstone plaque given us from a dear friend was placed at the entrance to our orchard:

> *Mattie's Orchard*
> *Planted with Love*
> *In Memory of an Angel*

The picture below the inscription was a little boy in a cowboy hat pulling a wagon. This orchard has been with us through our grief journey—it has grown with us. It has been a sanctuary for us. It has been a symbol of our son and of the love of the community. In the years past, I used it as a gauge of my husband's emotional well-being—the more he struggled with our loss, the more time he spent in the orchard. I would watch him walk and stand in the middle of the trees and live with his loss. I think the orchard provided peace.

Today, for our two active boys, the orchard has become *their* sanctuary. The few neighboring homes all have their own orchards, but all the neighbors' children, and ours, choose Mattie's Orchard to play and eat in. It has become difficult to harvest any fruit because the children gobble up each fruit as it comes into season. Mattie would be proud.

NANCY EMRO

What I do to honor my son:

- Give blood, because Sean gave blood and thought it was a cool thing to do and no big deal

- Volunteer as a child advocate (being an advocate for kids in the juvenile justice system, kids who were taken away from their parents due to neglect or abuse)

- Volunteer for Operation Lifesaver, a railroad safety education program

- Set up a memorial scholarship fund at my son's high school for kids who want to continue in theater past high school

- Give a donation to the theater department for scholarships so kids who couldn't otherwise afford it can go to the annual weekend Thespian Festival

- Spend more time with my nieces and nephew

- Put something Sean wrote about life and living it to the fullest on a plaque on a bench the kids made in his honor, which overlooks the valley where we spread his ashes

- Bring stuffed animals to the Children's Shelter on holidays so children won't feel so alone in the world after being taken away from their parents

- Light a candle at the dinner table, in a special candle-holder, right next to my framed picture of him at sixteen with his goatee

- Keep his room the way it was when he was alive and spend a few minutes each day in his room to remember him, to tell him I love him

- Donate money to a charity Sean supported through volunteer work, Habitat for Humanity

- Laugh more often, because Sean always wanted me not to take life so seriously.

SHEILA GEORGE
[From an interview]

Ronnie had a son, not long before he died. The baby was about two years old. When anybody saw him, they saw the baby. So he was called a Mister Mom, and he didn't care; the baby really changed his life. At one point he got on drugs, and he had changed his life around and went into a rehab program. So he'd gotten *out* of that life, and he was working as a roofer. He was twenty-two when he died.

Ronnie Jr. looks just like his father. I mean, the mother has nothing to do with him; he looks so much like *him*. But he doesn't act like him. My son was mild-mannered, this other one is not mild-mannered. But it's like I never lost Ronnie at all; physically, he looks exactly like him. He's twenty now.

He was having a difficult time with his father's death as he got older. His mom had other kids and they'd say, "Well, at least my daddy ain't dead," and it would just tear him up! And so he ended up really doing badly at school. So his mother said, "I've done every-thing. Do you think you could try? Will you try?" So I said, "Well, I'll try." He said he wouldn't come, but I wouldn't take that for an answer. And so he came down here, graduated out of high school, and enrolled in college. He wants to be a policeman, so he's going to a police academy now. He was doing so bad until he got with me, but I said, "Why do you want to be with me when you know I holler and scream when the house is not clean and you haven't done this, and . . ." But he went from D's and F's to graduating out of high school with A's and B's.

He's doing good, he's doing good. But if you'd seen my son, and if my grandson was walking here, you'd . . . [she gasps]

VAN JEPSON

My child's spirit lives on. His spirit lives on not because I make it so every day, but because he and other spirits *do* live on. I'm clear that I am not the only one responsible for the care and feeding of his spirit, as I was the care and feeding of his earthly body. Now he is in a heavenly body, and he is safe. I choose to remember him in my daily meditations and writings, my daily journey with him in an ever-expanded state of mutual awareness.

MARTIN KATZ

We have established two charitable trusts in Barry's memory. They are at the Peninsula Community Foundation and the Jewish Welfare Federation. We use these for many local, national, and inter-national charities. After our deaths, the responsibility for overseeing these trusts goes to our daughters for them to continue the remem-brance by helping those in need.

Just a few years after Barry's suicide, Lee became very active in the National Suicide Prevention Organization and made frequent trips to Sacramento and Washington. Unfortunately, no program seems to be especially successful. Sixty thousand Americans commit suicide each year, twice as many as die from AIDS. Four to five thousand are between ten and twenty-four years old. Eighty-five percent of those are male.

In my continuing attempts to return to the world, I decided to fulfill a long-suppressed desire to do sculpture. For the first time, I took a week off from work by myself and enrolled in a class. The experience was therapeutic, supportive, and very gratifying, and I continued to take occasional classes. When I retired from full-time work about twelve years ago, I was able to devote more time to this avocation. I found the work exhilarating, and learning and mastering the various skills and technology involved provided challenge and accomplishment. I work in ceramics, bronze, wood, and stone, have had shows and sales, and am now a serious semiprofessional.

One year, right after a "Yahrzeit" memorial weekend for Barry, I participated in a one-week Scottsdale sculpture workshop. On the third day, the teacher approached and asked, "What's going on here?" Without realizing it, I had created a composition of grief, two seated figures, heads bowed, and one twisted standing female figure above them. I had obviously poured my sorrow of the weekend into the composition. I titled it *Yizkor,* the Hebrew word meaning "remembrance of the souls." In 2002, a special sculpture exhibition "In Remembrance, September 11" was held as part of the New York City commemorative services. I was honored to have *Yizkor* selected for the exhibit as one of twenty from almost two hundred submissions. "Three figures locked in grief, the emotion of the piece so raw and universal it would in 2002 serve as a symbol for an entire nation."[*]

KATHRYN LODATO

Since Nick's death I have been wearing my watch. Before Nick died, I wore my watch only to work. It would bug me otherwise. I would take it off literally the very first thing on arriving home, and I never wore it on weekends.

Nick was the only one in the family who wore a watch. We gave Avery, Nick's older brother, a watch for his birthday when he was

[*]Lisa Eunson, *Stanford Business,* February 2003, p. 14.

about seven or eight. He had requested it and was happy to receive it. But it clearly bothered him on his arm. For a week or two he walked around supporting his watch-bearing wrist with his other hand. Then he took it off for good. When he graduated from high school, we gave him another watch, a nice one. I figured there would be times he would need a watch. He wore it some when he was in school and even wore it initially when he started working. But after Nick died, he admitted that its battery had run down a year or so earlier and he had never bothered to replace it.

In the thirty years that I've known Jim, Nick's dad, I think I've seen him wear a watch maybe twice. He doesn't even own a watch, although he disputed that when I mentioned it the other day. "Yes, I do," he said, "I think I have a couple of watches in the desk drawer." "But do any of them have bands on them or working batteries?" I asked. He had to acknowledge that, no, probably not.

But Nick always wore a watch, ever since he was a little boy. His first watch was a plastic number that played the game Simon. A clever game, it consisted of four differently colored buttons that could light up. The watch would light one light, and you had to match it, then the watch would light the first light plus another, and again you would have to match it, and it would progress until the player missed. So—it would light green, red, green, blue, blue. If you successfully re-created that, it would light green, red, green, blue, blue, yellow, etc. Nick loved that watch and was an extremely accomplished Simon player even at age eight or so. Nick always had an exceptional memory for detail, and Simon played right into that.

When we were talking about this a couple of months after Nick died, Avery reminded me that the Simon watch was an early casualty of our Europe trip in 1984. After a very long and tiring flight on an overpacked cut-rate charter flight from Seattle to Amsterdam (during which we played a thousand games of Simon), we collapsed into a hotel room. We didn't know it at the time, but we were all in the early phases of some sort of flu that made the first week of our trip into a pretty miserable experience. At the time, we just thought we were exhausted. The room was simple, but it had a deep, inviting tub in the bathroom. We filled it up and Nick climbed in, forgetting to take off the Simon watch. Disaster. We knew it wasn't waterproof, and Nick had always been so careful about it. It never worked again.

All of Nick's subsequent watches were waterproof. He went through a Swatch phase in junior high and early high school before settling into the basic black plastic diver's watch. He wore it always. I can close my eyes and picture it on his wrist. I have a wonderful picture of him poised in midair as he was jumping into the American River. It looks like he's flying. His arms are out, his body is turned towards the camera. On his outstretched left wrist is his watch.

In the days right after his death, just a month after his twenty-first birthday, I constantly felt like I needed to do something, that I had important things that needed to be done, even though I could never think of what they were. I needed to know the time, at all times. I've since learned that such restlessness is a typical symptom of stress and shock. The dry mouth, the unbearably tight chest, the feeling of not being able to sit still, the inability to concentrate—all very typical.

I got into the habit of wearing my watch. And in the weeks that followed, as the shock turned to deep grief and depression and the restlessness turned to lethargy, I wore my watch. And I wear one still, six years later. Right after I brush my teeth in the morning, I put on my watch. I wear it on the weekends, I wear it on hikes. In the spring and summer I develop a faint mark from the watch where the rest of my arm is tan from short-sleeved hikes and gardening.

It is comforting. Seeing the watch on my arm, feeling its slight weight, always reminds me of Nick. Shortly after Nick died, a friend, who had lost his sister when she was only eighteen, told me that one way to honor and love and keep our loved ones who have died is to incorporate some of their qualities into us. To, in a small sense, become them. When I first started wearing my watch, I didn't really think about it. I didn't do it consciously to invoke Nick—I just needed, for no good reason, to know the time. But about six months after Nick died, my watch broke. I was unreasonably disturbed, disconsolate really, and would have a pang of real anguish each time I looked at my naked wrist. That watch was temporarily fixed. Two months later, on my birthday, Jim and Avery and I went and picked out a new watch for me. That watch I put on consciously, as a symbol of trying to not only remember Nick, but of incorporating some of him into me. Truly incorporating part of Nick into me is hard work, much harder than just putting on a watch. It requires me to become a better person, to honor Nick by living my life well, with courage and love. This watch on my wrist helps me remember that, and to not give up.

ANNE LOGAN

When grief is new, its sadness overwhelms, and the mind latches onto the loss and yearns to turn back the clock. But with the passage of time, it is easier to remember happy days and celebrate memories that will make us smile, or even laugh. My husband and I were at an antique car show and came upon a 1955 Chevrolet, Pepto-Bismol pink with turquoise-trimmed white leather seats, wide whitewall tires, and the requisite tail fins with chrome polished to a mirrored sheen. Seeing the car made us smile, and we both looked at each other and almost simultaneously remarked, "Virginia would have loved this car." It came slowly, that allowing ourselves to bring Virginia back into the present, talking about what she would have thought about us, or that car. And since then we have found ourselves often seeing the world as she might have seen it, and remembering her perception and humor.

On special occasions—her birthday, the anniversary of her death, Christmas, Easter—we continue the more traditional remembrances. Having a birthday party, serving her favorite meal and chocolate-chocolate cake with lots of icing, hanging up her stocking on Christmas Eve, putting and planting flowers on her grave in the churchyard. This, of course, is for us and gives us an opportunity to remember the Christmas of her first pony, or the bowling birthday party, or the holiday trip to New York where she broke her wrist ice skating in Central Park, or the painting she gave me on my birthday—one of a tree using a tube of my favorite color blue paint. She loved to paint trees, with branches reaching toward the sky and thick trunks firmly rooted on the ground. Her art adorns our walls and makes us smile.

When Virginia died, family and friends asked what they could do as a memorial. Virginia was a sophomore at Davidson College when she died. Already an accomplished artist, she was continuing studies in art at Davidson and had been the subject of a special article in the campus newspaper. So with the contributions in her memory, we funded an individual art studio at Davidson. Davidson is unique among colleges, especially liberal arts colleges, in that it has individual studios available for senior art majors. By having such facilities, young artists can experience what it might be like to be a practicing artist, with one's own private creative space. On Friday, May 10, 2002, Mark, her father, Bret and Catherine, her brother and sister, and I traveled to Davidson to be present for the dedication of this studio. Present were the college president, her art professors and other teachers and staff, and a host of students who were close to Virginia. Herb Jackson, former chair of the art department at Davidson, himself a noted abstract artist and teacher of both Bret and Virginia, remarked that Virginia most certainly would have occupied one of these studios, for her creative talents and perceptive insights showed extraordinary promise. Etched on the glass plaque outside the room is:

Individual Art Studio, Given in
Memory of Virginia Baker Logan,
2003, By Her Friends and Family.

A letter written to all donors reads, in part, "Though we grieve Virginia's loss, we even more miss what she would have become. In providing this space, you help to keep her creative spirit alive, through the work of the students who will work in this studio and who may one day ask, 'Who was Virginia Logan?'"

JOHN PHUA
[From an interview]

Through the auspices of the Lance Armstrong Foundation, we began a bike ride for children called Ryan's Ride, which benefits cancer survivorship programs in the San Francisco Bay Area. We have had a great turnout and a celebration of Ryan. As a parent who has lost his child, I would do anything to feel the presence of my child again. On this day as the air was filled with the excitement of children laughing on their bikes, I felt Ryan's presence. A gift to Matthew, Michele, and me that will help us survive in strength and grace. Ryan's spirit will continue to help others as we raise awareness and provide hope to those who face life challenges through programs funded by Ryan's Fund.

PATTY SHAW

Well, am I ever glad you asked that question! I married Don about one to two years before Cathy's murder. As I said before, she got to meet him twice. Don has two daughters who are, literally, the same ages as my first two children. To celebrate our wedding, the following year we took all of our children and their families to Hawaii for one week. Our children and grandchildren got to meet one another and, wonder of wonders, they all clicked!

About nine months after Cathy's death, Don's two daughters came to me and for my birthday present they gave me an envelope that enclosed information about Cathy's beloved alma mater, Colorado College for Women/Temple Buell. What those wonderful women had done was to marshal $250 from each of them and my two daughters-in-law, her best friend from college, and her roommate for a donation to a new school at the college, for women who are returning to the workforce! And, it was given in her name. I do believe that Cathy's happiest years were her college ones and to have an engraved paving stone there forever is something that I feel would honor and delight her. I got permission to scatter some of her ashes at her favorite place on campus and, much to my dismay, it is no longer there. A new dorm is on the spot. But the stone is a tribute to her that will live on and on. Isn't that simply grand?

Reflecting the Personality

Amanda and Mimi were passionate young women who liberally shared their enthusiasms and opinions. The extent of their influence on our attitudes and actions continues to surprise and move us, and it always expands our experience. *Have you noticed your child's energy or personality influencing your own? In what ways? Do you think this influence is greater than it would be if your child were physically here?*

VAN JEPSON

Absolutely I am influenced, and for two reasons: one earthly and one spiritual. As a way to keep Ian's memory alive inside of me, I sometimes find myself incorporating his behaviors. I also experience his spirit's energy and presence in me many times throughout my week. Sometimes I have vivid recollections of him entering and exiting my earthly body.

JOHN LECOMPTE

Our daughter Mimi lived life with a tremendous energy and enthusiasm. Her favorite descriptive word: *amazing!* When she said it she meant it to the depths of her soul. She immersed herself in everything she did. It was true in her friendships. It was true in her work. It was true in her hobbies. She was truly present, committed, and involved in whatever was going on at that moment.

I feel a sense of Mimi's presence when I travel where she might have gone. Her memory is especially clear when I am gardening, cooking something special, eating fresh crab—some of her loves. More than her presence, I have my own feelings of joy that might approximate Mimi's feelings for things she loved. It is less a matter of imitating what she might do and more a matter of finding for myself the joy she experienced.

None of the lessons learned from the devastating loss of a precious child can be worth the price. But for me, it would be less than honorable to ignore or deny the experience of her life and the *amazing* lessons she demonstrated.

SUZANNE REDFERN

Mimi was famous for her determination. She wasn't stubborn in her relationships with others, but a peacemaker—gracious and conciliatory. However, when it came to getting something done, watch out. She'd set her jaw and march into whatever it was with all the stoicism of her Viking forebears.

My friend Nancy offered up a perfect example of this characteristic in her toast at Mimi's wedding, in the form of an aviso to Brett about the mettle of the woman he'd just married. Nan remembered an incident that had happened several years before, when Mimi was spending the summer with her and Larry in Atherton. Late one windy afternoon the three of them were in the garden when they noticed that a lawn umbrella and its attached round metal table had blown into the pool and sunk to the bottom of the deep end. As Larry and Nan started discussing whom to call, Mimi dived in, fully dressed, plunged to the bottom, and started rolling the heavy steel table and the waterlogged canvas umbrella toward the shallow end. Up for breath she came, and down again, until at last she dragged the whole shebang up the steps and, with a grin of triumph, set it upright where it belonged.

Mimi's former roommate Carolyn recalled a similar tale at Mimi's memorial service. Starting a new semester at UC Davis, the girls were moving from one apartment to another. Having finished hauling all of the small stuff, all that remained was an eight-foot couch. While Carolyn was mentally running through all the guys she knew with pickups, Mimi lifted one end of the couch and lugged it toward the door. Despite her doubts, Carolyn pitched in, and the two girls wrestled the substantial piece of furniture out into the parking lot, heaved it into the back seat of Mimi's red VW bug convertible, and drove through the streets of Davis reveling in the double takes on every corner.

In that same spirit, Mimi took on cancer. If the march of the virulent form of carcinoma that took root in her lungs could have been halted by sheer determination, she would have stopped it in its tracks.

It's that indomitable will of Mimi's that I try to incorporate more than any of her other personality traits. Whenever I notice myself turning away from something because it seems too hard, just too much trouble, whenever I feel the "Oh, well" forming on my lips, I call up images of dripping lawn umbrellas and couch-stuffed VW bugs, and I reconsider.

PATTY SHAW

No, not really, unless you could consider my truly appreciating my children more because they are precious to me and I am certainly not getting any younger. And I do try to be as charitable as possible in my opinions of people and that is definitely a positive trait from her. So, yes, I guess she has influenced me in that way.

MERRYL WEBER

If there is any one way that I feel I am living for both myself and Adam it is through a form of sound work that I was taught and have subsequently been practicing. Though I love music of all kinds, I don't understand the mechanics of music at all and have never played an instrument to speak of. Adam had a passion for music and was a pretty good musician and songwriter for his age. He had always wanted to be a musician and reach others through music. The sound work literally called to me and I knew I wanted to learn it from the first few minutes of being exposed to it. I think it is quite funny that I ended up doing something like this, so outside my supposed areas of expertise.

Taking Stock

The one question in part 5 that nearly no one chose to answer was the one that asked whether people feared losing intimacy with their children with the passage of time. Only three people responded: Patty Shaw said she has absolutely no worries about feeling distanced from Cathy, and both Van Jepson and Merryl Weber remembered having had thoughts about that possibility but found that their connections were as firm as ever. The silence from all other quarters on the matter would suggest that no one else even gave it a thought.

The conclusion we all may draw here is that the fabric of the silver cord that connects us with our children will never fray. We are forever tied to them with what Jenica, in her loving paean to her mother, Kathleen Weed, calls "silken strands of understanding" that stretch beyond the horizons of death. To paraphrase another of Jenica's poignant images, you can be assured that your son or daughter is, now and always, "an eternal moment happening inside you."

Now that you've come almost to the end of *The Grieving Garden,* it may be helpful for you to reflect on what you've read in terms of your own grief process. After all, the book was written with you in mind. We want it to be of use, and we've found from our own experience that putting words to terrible feelings robs them of some of their awful power and makes them ever so slightly more manageable. So, try imagining that the two of us, Suzanne and Susan, are sitting in your living room or your office and talking with you about your own grieving experience. What happened to *you* in the first weeks after your child died? Where did *you* look for support, and how did that work out? How is *your* family dealing with their enormous loss?

Better yet, put yourself in a garden, in the welcoming company of twenty-two understanding friends, who've felt what you're feeling, who care about *you,* and who want to keep you company in your grief. We wish we were actually there with you now, to hear what is in your heart and on your mind.

PART SIX

REACHING OUT

Setting Out

If you're a parent grieving the loss of a child, the following pages were written just for you. All twenty-two of us were asked to reflect on our own grief experiences and to offer up something we learned that was meaningful in our lives. A bit of wisdom, a piece of advice, a word of encouragement.

By now, you've gotten to know each one of us. You've read what we said, you've seen our pictures, you've learned something of our lives and our children's, and you've heard how they died. You'd probably recognize many of us in the pieces that follow even if our names weren't on them. Our personalities and viewpoints and ways of expressing ourselves show up loud and clear.

As individual as we are, and as different the messages we've written for you, we speak with one voice, one strong and insistent voice, in sending you hope. We promise you that your pain will diminish. We assure you that your life can be meaningful again, and productive, and even full of joy. And we remind you: no matter how isolated you may feel at times, you are not alone.

Sharing One True Thing

Grief is as individual as a fingerprint. One must find one's own way through it, being true to what feels right for oneself. Yet there may be something you'd wish to offer to someone just setting out on this path—a discovery, a conclusion, something you carry with you each day. *If you were to have the chance to share one true thing— about life, or death, or grief—with a newly bereaved parent, what would that be?*

STATHI AFENDOULIS

In our initial moments of grief, following the death of our children, there are so many unanswered questions. In reflection, when I looked back on all that happened, it seemed going forward with life was impossible. The weight of grief made the accomplishment of even the simplest task a Herculean effort. The thought of the ensuing years of living were overwhelming. How can I go on? How can I ever be happy again?

In these moments, I took the advice of a good friend and counselor. She told me, "Go to the source. Ask your child, 'How should I live?'" Personally, the answer came quickly and clearly. My daughter lived life to the fullest, never allowing disease to impact or define how she lived. Her advice to me, through her struggle, was to live and be happy.

Accomplishing this will not be easy, because we will always grieve the loss of our children, and this, too, must be a part of the way we live the rest of *our* lives. We cannot live for them, for they are in a different place, gone from us in this life. But we can live our lives in honor of them. In memory of them. The love and remembrance I hold for Lainie, every day, sustain me and give me the strength to go on. I can hear her voice, telling me to live. To do the things I love to do. To fulfill my dreams and to help all my family to fulfill theirs. This is her legacy to me. She left us physically, but her love and spirit remain behind, vital and alive in our hearts and minds. And when you start to forget, in moments of deep despair and sadness, remember, "Go to the source." They are there for you, all of you.

INÉS ASCENCIO
[From an interview]

I think we need to learn to appreciate our children. Sometimes parents have high expectations for their kids, but I think to just appreciate them for the individuals they are, or for whatever they bring to us, is what matters. I am sure that everyone's children have touched a lot of people. Even though my daughter did not spend much time outside of me, people tell me that her life touched their lives. I think it is important to support our kids in being who they are meant to be in life, however long or short that life may be. Sometimes it is not exactly what we had hoped for or planned.

[In her San Francisco Mission District office, Inés sings for us from Khalil Gibran's *The Prophet*. This is an excerpt.]

ON CHILDREN

And a woman who held a babe against her bosom said,
"Speak to us of Children."
And he said:
Your children are not your children.
They are the sons and daughters of Life's longing for itself.
They come through you but not from you,
And though they are with you, yet they belong not to you.
You may give them your love but not your thoughts.
For they have their own thoughts.
You may house their bodies but not their souls,
For their souls dwell in the house of tomorrow,
which you cannot visit, not even in your dreams.

That's what I believe, that they are a gift.

SUSAN BENVENISTE

If I were to share one true thing about surviving the death of one's child, it would be to know that enduring the "firsts" can be one of the hardest obstacles to face. Examples of the "firsts" I refer to are: the holidays, birthdays, Mother's or Father's Day, the death day anniversary, and any other events of significance to your family. These days can hit with a vengeance, like a blow to the gut. Planning in advance how to celebrate or spend these days gives us some control and can help soften the hurt.

In our case, the first major event we faced without Shelly was my husband's fiftieth birthday. Not being up for a party, I packed him for a "surprise destination." We flew to Palm Springs (not a normal vacation spot for us) and were met by our son Josh, who flew in from college also as a surprise. As we celebrated over dinner in a restaurant, it quickly became clear we would have to learn to be a family of three . . . even the conversation dynamics had changed. Needless to say, the celebration was bittersweet. On the positive side, we had changed our routine and discovered we had the strength to face other such events.

Our first holiday without Shelly was Thanksgiving. Instead of a traditional sit-down dinner with our small family, my mother planned a buffet so that Shelly's absence wasn't so "in our face." The following year we were able to resume our normal routine. Don't get me wrong, it was still a very difficult day, but that difficulty was lessened by knowing we had gotten through it the year before, and would again.

For us, Mother's and Father's Days are difficult especially now that our parents are deceased and our son isn't always in town to celebrate with us. We prefer to avoid restaurants or other public places where those celebrations are taking place. A good movie in a dark theater can be a wonderful escape. Some years we find comfort in going to the cemetery, other years it's just too painful.

I have shared some of our experiences to illustrate that there is no right or wrong way to endure these "firsts." Each of you will find your own way. I hope with passing time you will be able to celebrate the joy your child brought to your family, as we do Shelly.

MARY LOU COFFELT

Given the opportunity to share a bit with a newly bereaved parent, I know that there are no magic words. The instant after our child's death, we realized this: *Life is forever changed.*

So how does one reach through this hell and begin an ascent back to life? Very slowly. Very carefully. And, for me, very tenuously.

What can I say to you, the newly bereaved parent, to guide you now that I have survived nine years of this experience? Follow your trail. Walk the walk *you* need to find, to allow yourself to experience your grief. Surround yourself with people who can support you. People who can nourish you, not those that drain you.

In the past years I've found that during the difficult times, when I lacked the energy or motivation, I let myself be bounced around by whoever made themselves available, not necessarily who was good for me. In retrospect, after the third year or so, most of our dear, caring friends (who probably needed a break from us and thought we were doing well) went back to their own lives and expected that we were capable of picking up the telephone. Now I see that I should have made more of an effort to keep myself in touch and surrounded by my safety net of friends. We were still so very raw from our loss and lacked the strength to make our own way. For a while, too long, we seemed to let life knock us around. Maybe this was a part of our practical natures. But if I could, I would recommend that grieving persons be fiercely protective of which people and experiences they allow into their world, for many years following their loss. I am aware that, even nine years later, I am not the resilient woman that I once was, but with that awareness I am learning to take better care of myself.

Most important, I believe that what saved me from giving up, giving in, to our pain was *conscious choice.* It sounds like a bit of a simplification to say that I woke up one day and said, "I do not want to feel this way forever," but at some point I had to decide that I would not remain enveloped by my pain. I believe that we all have an amazing power within ourselves to shape our existence.

I will never be able to erase the day that life slapped me in the face and took away my Mattie, forever changing my life from a light-hearted and charmed one to a scarred and tender one. I no longer feel the innocence of life, I forever carry the pain of our tragedy. *But* I have the power to decide how and what I will do with this experience. I did not want to let it destroy the rest of my world: my husband, my children, my parents, my siblings, my friends, and—most important—my self.

I asked myself this very important question: What would Mattie expect of me? What would he wish for me? What would be a tribute to his life? If I chose to wallow in my pain—a very easy choice to make—how would that reflect on his ever-important life here on Earth? If I could not pull myself out of the dark and consuming hole of grief, what kind of a legacy would he have left? A torn and despairing family? A mother wracked by pain and fear? I said no to those choices. The picture was not one I could accept. People often commented, "I don't know how you do it!" I could respond, "The alternative is unacceptable."

So making that choice is the first step. For me it was followed by many other choices, often daily choices, some small and some enormous, each one critical to my recovery. I still make choices each day. I suspect, although they become easier, that I will forever be faced with them. Early on, they were as basic as whether to get out of bed or not, then maybe whether to rise from a chair. This sounds crazy to someone who has never been struck by such force, but to those of us who have lived this tragedy, we know how difficult, at first, some of our most basic acts become. Applaud yourself when you are successful at taking even the smallest step. And carry on. Keep taking baby steps. Keep making positive choices.

At first Bob and I (and our newborn baby) would hide in our home. The only part of the world we allowed in came to us from caring friends or family. There were daily or weekly visits from loved ones checking on us and, in their own way, trying to help us back into the world.

When we finally decided to take some steps back out, it was through a *conscious* decision to do so. It felt forced—it was hard. Some experiences were okay, some were treacherous, and we learned that it was all right to back up and slow down.

In our past life, "before Mattie" (as we came to call the time before his death), helping out at neighboring ranchers' cattle brandings was one of our favorite things to do. Brandings are both a social and a work-related day. Bob, Mattie, and I all loved them. "After Mattie" we stopped going to them. We were haunted by what we knew would be a giant step to take. We'd reconnect with a lot of people and would be forced to socialize. We'd be placing ourselves in a situation that, at one time, had brought us all so much joy, knowing that we had no idea if we would ever feel joy again. We finally made a conscious choice to choose life, one small branding at a time! We went to a small and safe branding where we knew we would be around people who cared about us and would respect our need to escape if we had to. It was not easy. But we were glad that we'd accomplished it.

Like the brandings, each conscious step we took, even the unsuccessful ones, brought us closer to life again. Some days we were strong enough to choose to step back into living, and other days we hid like fugitives. I think it is all part of the process. But to get through that process, much of it needs to be *intentional*.

[Added on August 16, 2007]

I feel compelled to write this, even though my "story" has long since been sent to Sue [Redfern], my writer friend, for publishing. It is my hope that sharing this later stage in my grief journey will possibly help inspire a reader in the midst of drowning to hang on and keep treading water . . . to feel hope.

This June 4 marked the ten-year "anniversary" of our son Mattie's death day. It seems so hard to imagine that ten years have passed. Ten years seems a long time and although the clarity of the day seems like yesterday, much of the years between are a blur to me.

Not long after Mattie died, I remember reading a statistic stating ten years as the average length of time it took for a bereaved parent to be able to get through a day without continual thoughts of the deceased child.

At the time I felt that ten years sounded impossible to even get through a day, let alone not be consumed with thoughts of our tragedy. I couldn't imagine a time when I was not wounded and in pain. Today, I need to proclaim, it was about ten years for me when something magical did happen to me. I didn't make the connection at the time, until one day, I found myself feeling "lighter." This is the only way I can describe this feeling. For years, "post-Mattie," I have felt heavy. Life has been work. I have faithfully trudged along and time passed. At times I have felt joy and happiness, even with the pain of my loss still with me. But I felt different even when I got to the point where I felt "happy" again. I carried a weight with me. Life was not light and easy as it once seemed. Time and effort got me back to good, but it took work. It took intention.

Then one day something seemed different about me, about my life, about the way I seemed to view my life. It was no longer so mechanical. I was able to look forward in a very different way. I felt as though there was a load lifted from me. I felt a joy; a peace. A lighthearted feeling about life that I didn't even realize was possible to feel again. It was more looking forward and less looking back.

I believe my open wound had finally healed.

I certainly have not forgotten one little bit of my precious Mattie or our experience, and it is still very present in my person, but, it does not taint each day of my life or my view of the future as it used to. It is as though I was able to surface to the top of the water after swimming forever.

I do not want to use a lot of metaphors or sound too cheery, because I have not at all forgotten how black the world can be. But I really truly hope to share that I believe and now know that there is a time when our grief wound heals and we can live, really live, like we used to, or better (amazing thought!). I will always be scarred, I am forever changed, but the horror of the experience does not weigh down my daily life or my future. I am able to throw myself joyfully into living. I am able to trust the Universe and see its beauty with a light heart and a more spontaneous attitude.

That is a change worth noting, and one I pray all grieving parents can eventually experience.

I sincerely hope sharing this gives you something to hold onto. For me, it has been worth the work and I believe it can only get better. I hope you can hang on and feel the freedom from the pain. May God guide you and bless you.

NANCY EMRO

Of all the things various people told me after my son died, some were occasionally helpful, most were not helpful in the least, and some made me angry. Most things were said to try to make me feel better and didn't make me feel better at all. But the one thing I did find helpful and would tell a recently bereaved parent is this: Eventually, you will not feel as badly you do now. I cannot tell you when, and I cannot tell you that you will feel the same about life as you did "before," but at some point you will feel significantly better about life. Do not give up hope, there is light at the end of what often seems to be a very long, dark tunnel. There is light, there is joy, there is laughter, yes, there is even happiness. One day, you will wake up and your child will no longer be the first thing on your mind. You may not believe me now, but trust me, one day, six months from now, a year from now, two years from now, eventually at some point, you will feel better than you do right now.

They say the first year is the hardest; I would say the first two are the hardest. In many ways, for me the second year was almost as difficult as the first. But there was the tiniest pinpoint of light at the end of the tunnel.

At my darkest hours, when I was truly sad and in despair, when I couldn't even think about how to lift myself out of the bottom of the pit, I could (sometimes) remember to look at the list on my bedroom door. That was a list of ten things I could do to help myself feel just a little bit better. They were simple things like: buy some flowers, go for a walk, e-mail someone, call someone, listen to music, spend a few minutes in the sun, read some inspirational words. Those simple things helped me just the tiniest bit, but sometimes that was all I needed so that I could function, get over that hump, until the next day or until the next week. Eventually, I didn't need the list anymore. Eventually, my son was not the first thing on my mind when I awoke in the morning (although he is still always the last thing on my mind). Eventually, my emotions healed. My life is not the same, and will never be the same, without my son. But along with the sorrow that he is gone, there is joy and laughter and happiness in my life. There is light.

SHEILA GEORGE
[From an interview]

I think the one thing that I would tell somebody who is grieving now is to grieve, to cry, because if you don't cry people turn inwardly, and it gets harder and harder to release if you don't do it in the beginning stages. And you do have to work through the stages—if you miss one, you're definitely going back. But to know that eventually life will get okay, though you never forget and they're ever-present in your life. No matter what's around, something will trigger a thought, and it's okay to feel that, it's okay. I mean, I used to go out to the graveyard quite often. Now I do it when I want to; I don't *have* to like I used to for a while, constantly, lying down on the grave, but if that's what it takes to get you through, then do that. Don't let anyone tell you, "You shouldn't go to the grave, you shouldn't!" Yes, I *needed* to go to the grave, I *needed* to be there, until I could accept that he was in there. I never could accept that he was in the ground, so in my mind I put him in Oakland, in my sister's house. At the graveyard my body and my mind came around to accept that he was gone because I was at the grave, but when I left that grave he was in my sister's house in Oakland. And I did that for two or three years and I finally accepted the fact that he was gone, and when I accepted that, I accepted where he is.

But what I would say is just do what you can do. I wouldn't let anybody tell you anything different. In hindsight, I didn't cry and I didn't grieve as much as I should because I was protecting my mom, I was protecting the kids—they want you to be strong. But *we're* the parents that had these children, *we're* the ones that should have the right to fall apart. Any grieving mother should have the right to do whatever she feels like doing, when she feels like doing it. Don't go to work until you feel you're up to it.

KEITH GILBERT

Losing a child feels like a very "unnatural" life event. There's a tendency to feel stigmatized: like you've done something wrong;

like others may not want to be with you anymore. And, in fact, some will shun you because they don't know what to say, or because what happened to you is so horrible that they don't even want to be close to it. And you may be surprised by who these people are. Sometimes the ones you thought you could count on are those who just can't stand to be with you except in a very superficial way.

It is terribly unfair, but you have become different in a way that is unattractive to others. Fortunately, you can help others get past that by becoming more open, and by not hiding the vulnerability of your feelings.

As painful as it is, you often need to take the first step in opening up to those who fear what happened to you. If your friend is avoiding the subject, bring it up and talk about your feelings. Don't let them get away with avoiding or changing the subject. Let them know you want to talk about your child, about your pain, and about how it has changed your feelings.

It's a real test of your courage. Try to think of it as your child's leaving you with an opportunity to grow. And that's what life is about.

SUSAN GILBERT

I made up my mind as soon as I heard the awful news that I must try very hard to hold on to life. It was the hardest thing I have ever done, but I know that it can be done. I therefore did whatever it took to hold on, and I hope you will also. I saw counselors and when they were not helpful, I found someone else. I could not continue to work, but I found a replacement for work in going to school. I also held on to relationships, especially that with my husband; there were times that it helped for the two of us to have a third party with whom to share our pain. And things got better. Not for a while, but life became worth living and held joy and contentment again.

I believe that nothing in life is as difficult as what we bereaved parents are experiencing, and we need to find appropriate support wherever we can find it. We were helped so much by being in the company of other bereaved parents who helped us see that life would be better one day. Conversely, we must let go as much as possible of what does not help. Acquaintances who are draining our scarce emotional energy must be let go, at least for now. Activities may also rob us of precious energy, and the unhelpful ones can be weeded out.

Holding on to life may mean finding forgiveness. I did not want to waste one second of life hanging onto resentments. While Amanda's accident was ultimately no one's fault, it would have been easy to blame the driver, the person who owned the vehicle, and so forth. Nothing will ever change what happened. Nothing. There is no upside to finding people to blame.

In smaller ways, forgiveness also meant understanding and forgiving the people I felt let me down. I came to see that they are flawed human beings, just as I am flawed. When the disappointment was severe, I found new people with whom to associate.

And I learned that I must forgive myself. No one is a perfect parent and no one is without faults. Our children are the proof that we were enough.

Van Jepson

Your child's spirit is safe and alive and it is going through a process of acclimatization similar to that when a child is born into the earthly plane. That you can develop a skill that allows you to open your heart and hear them anytime you want, so you can know for yourself what they are learning, playing, and creating in the place that they are.

Monica Jones

I am writing this twenty-eight years after Bronwyn died and therefore with some perspective. In the beginning I thought of her every day and was often sad. However, as I have said before, even when she was alive, I realized that although I could not control all the circumstances in my life, I could determine my attitude. After Bronwyn's death, I consciously decided to remember the good times our family had had and how she had enriched our lives, rather than bemoaning her death or wondering what life might have been like if she had been born "normal." I decided I would best honor her life by trying to exemplify the qualities she held dear: intellectual curiosity, compassion, and a fine sense of humor. This is not to say the process is easy, but with time one can remember one's child with calmness and gratitude. The following poem expresses what I mean.

HE IS GONE

You can shed tears that he is gone
Or you can smile because he has lived

You can close your eyes and pray that he will come back
Or you can open your eyes and see all that he has left

Your heart can be empty because you can't see him
Or you can be full of the love that you shared

You can turn your back on tomorrow and live yesterday
Or you can be happy for tomorrow because of yesterday

You can remember him and only that he is gone
Or you can cherish his memory and let it live on

You can cry and close your mind, be empty
and turn your back Or you can do what he would
want: smile, open your eyes, love and go on.
—David Harkins, Silloth, Cumbria, United Kingdom, 1981

MARTIN KATZ

I had partially shut down after the death of my sister and then, later, Lee's sister. They had both been flower girls at our wedding. I internally found myself somewhat withholding of complete love and affection. I guess I subconsciously thought that withholding would help me avoid feeling so much pain if I lost someone again. It hampered me from enjoying my family and friends to the fullest. It was probably one of the dumbest things I ever did in my entire life. *Never, Never,* do that! It is a *Lose-Lose* situation! The smart thing to do is to learn that life is ephemeral and that you should learn to love and enjoy it to the maximum.

Think about some hobby or activity that you have always wanted to do. Indulge yourself. Take a class and find others with the same interest. No matter how self-driven you think you are, you will not do it unless you put the date down on your calendar. You will meet new friends, learn new things, and find it wonderful mental and occupational therapy. *Remember*: join a class!

Finally, I became a lot more aware of nature. I remind myself often to really look and see the beauty around us. I also try to remember that we have only one life to live and that we owe ourselves some peace, quiet, enjoyment and that it is okay to indulge yourself occasionally.

JOHN LeCOMPTE

To any newly bereaved parents I would say: let no one rob you of your right to grieve. Let no one interfere. If you have a companion to witness your grief without placing conditions on you, it is a true blessing. I recently found a "Permission to Mourn" certificate that sums this up well.

PERMISSION TO MOURN

Is granted to the holder of this certificate

_____

Is hereby entitled to publicly acknowledge his/her loss, mourn openly, to share narratives of the loss, and to recruit social support in his/her own way and time, without apology or embarrassment.

Tears, memories, silence, uncertainty, and strong emotions are hereby enfranchised.

Please treat this griever with kindness, compassion, and love.

This certificate has no expiration date.

KATHRYN LODATO

The one true thing I would share is not an easy thing. It's not warm comfort. But for me, coming to realize this truth is, nonetheless, a comfort. A comfort that's hard and heavy, but bright and solid. It is this: The breathtaking, staggering intensity of the pain, the shattering, unbelievable quality of knowing that my child is gone, it doesn't go away. In some ways it doesn't even diminish. For me, as I write this, it's been nine-and-a-half years. Nine-and-a-half years since I saw Nick, heard his voice, had his living presence in my life. That searing sense of the full realization of his death I call the abyss. I can feel it, I know that it's always in me.

The difference, and it's a huge difference, that time and grieving have given me is that I live the great bulk of my life at a safe distance from the edge of that abyss. Those early months, and even years, I often felt that I was right on the edge of it. Living so near to that abyss left very little room in my life or my heart for anything else. And I truly didn't think that I would survive if I fell in. Now, while it's always in my peripheral vision, my field of awareness, I'm usually not at the edge. But I can go there. Sometimes I'm swept there unexpectedly. Other times, on anniversaries or simply on a quiet Friday afternoon, I can choose to go there and feel that primal grief, that bottomless sorrow. But here's why it's a comfort, why I wouldn't change this, why I wouldn't remove that abyss from my soul, even if I could: I know, as deeply as I'll ever know anything, that I will never forget Nick. I know that his importance in my life will never diminish, that his life and his death will never be just something that happened in the past. It is a bargain I gladly make. For me, to hold his life forever alive in me means that I must also hold his death forever alive in me. I hold it all: the gift of him, the miracle of his life and his being, and the abyss. And together, they have formed something more, some ineffable greater awareness of the beauty of life. I have had to grow my heart to be able to hold it all, to be able not only to go on living, but to go on living well. It is hard, but I owe it to Nick, and so I do it.

ANNE LOGAN

To the newly bereaved parent, I would say, "You are not alone." The sadness is overwhelming, your life is changed forever, the pain will never completely resolve. But you need not face this darkness alone. Family, friends, even total strangers, who may or may not have experienced a similar loss, are ready to lend their support, to share your grief, to stand by you in the dark hours. With their presence, they testify to the interconnectedness of humankind, to the common thread of life and death that binds us all. They witness to the fact that not only can life go on, but that life is good. There is a part of me that died with Virginia, an empty spot in my heart that aches still. And I am still saddened when I think of what she might have been. Oh, how I'd love to talk to her right now, to hear what she thinks about life, art, our president (I think I know what she'd say about that!). To see how her painting evolves, to watch her open her Christmas stocking with that special glee of hers, laughing at the silly presents. But I am not alone. She is with me still. In my memories of her, and in those of family and friends who stood with me in the darkness, silently professing their love, sharing my grief, and reminding me that life *is* good, even a life lost.

MICHELE AND JOHN PHUA
[From an interview]

John: Please say that it's a very hard journey. I think some people try to paint a nicer picture, to reinforce this strong attitude that everybody wants the bereaved family to have. But being the one who's going through this, maybe I shouldn't say . . . there are enough people giving that other advice.

But you're going to make this journey. There is hope, and you'll find hope through this process of grieving. Hope to at least get by from that point. Everyone will have their own ways of integrating that person—their child—in themselves. Whether he's here or not, he'll always be a part of your life. It's okay to keep them in your life and integrate your child's life into yours in some way. But you don't know what that way is at first . . . it takes time.

What the hardest thing is, is not to feel lonely. I think that's the fear, that you'll just sit there alone. If there's a book that has to do with other families, just by reading it, it could get you by another day. I can see where they're at, can see how they survived.

Michele: I'm sure I don't have advice for other parents, but I just feel that, in this society, they don't have the tools. And for me, as long as I'm living, my duty is to educate, to put myself in public so that maybe the next set of parents . . . A mom will write to me, people I don't know really well, and they say, "Michele, I know this other mom who just lost a child, or one who has this bad illness. What should I do?" I say, first, sometimes it's really hard to take time out of your busy life to be involved in someone else's life. But if you were to do it just remember that birthday or the anniversary. You know, a card when they least expect it. People are so appreciative of it. And I think for me, I hope that other bereaved parents would just be open about their feelings to others. So that in this society everybody would end up getting more tools. And then maybe in a decade or twenty years from now it won't be as hard for new bereaved parents.

Did you see the Oprah interview of the family whose teenager was killed in an airplane crash? When Oprah was interviewing that family, part of me was fearing, "How will they present them as a bereaved family?" Then I said, "Wow, they're so strong!" But then they seemed like the family was saying it's okay, when it's *not* okay that their son died. That they were reinforcing that notion. And that's the challenge, that's the tug of war. If I'm acting like I used to act or doing what I used to do, then people think that it's okay, that it's not a hard thing. You want them to know that it's really hard, but you don't want them to be shocked. And you don't want pity.

So with that family, on the Oprah show, the first thing the mother told her family was that it's okay to be sad but you cannot be bitter and you cannot be mad. That little fourteen-year-old boy *died*. I'm not sure about that comment . . . sometimes you cannot control your feelings. So I think what's important to tell the readers is this: I'm just all over the place, really. You caught me in this moment, but if it's tomorrow at 2:00 I might come across as very strong, and today—at this moment—you caught me in my grief burst. So although at one moment we might be strong, the next moment we just collapse.

But if you want practical advice, I say get tools, get in a group. I think that really helps. Like Kara, a grief support organization in Palo Alto, California. John and I were ready to roll off—we were going to announce that we were going to leave, right? And we're sitting there, that day, and there was another family that lost a twin at two months—she just went into the hospital and died—and the mother shared her story and I just went hysterical, crying. And I thought John was going to announce his departure and I would go, "Okay, John, you can leave, but I'm not ready," but he never mentioned it. My advice to men? Try to go to a support group for the sake of your wife. Keep communication open.

SUZANNE REDFERN

Mimi was diagnosed with lung cancer in February 1999 and underwent surgery to remove most of one lung. In May, just after Mother's Day, a scan showed a recurrence in the other lung. Almost overnight we watched her grow into the person she was meant to be. It was as if her life was compressed by its new foreshortened dimensions and she gained in one leap all the wisdom she might have attained in a full, long life. Her brother Peter said to me one day, "Mom, stop worrying for a minute about what's *going* to happen and look at what's happening right *now*. Mimi's become bigger than any of us . . . bigger than all of us *together.*"

I could give you many examples of how her expanded consciousness manifested itself, but there's one that changed my life. During a long hospitalization that summer, on my shift at her bedside one morning, out of nowhere she fixed me with her deep brown eyes and said, "So, Mom, what do you do that makes you the happiest? What makes you feel most alive?" Such a searching question out of the blue made me squirm, and I mumbled something inane and changed the subject.

But the question was lodged like a thistle in my mind, and I worked away at it much of the night. At her bedside the next day I apologized for the brush-off and said that I guessed I felt the very fullest when I made a difference in someone else's life. Not as much in a material way as in some sort of empowerment.

Mimi nodded and smiled, my beautiful Buddha-daughter, and said, "Then you have to put it out there, Mom. You *know* things. You have gifts you're not using. You have too much to give to waste it. Don't hide it, and don't be afraid."

That was a call I couldn't ignore. All my old excuses were suddenly shown to be as flimsy as they'd always been. So for the last seven years I've held the image of those penetrating brown eyes in my heart and marched into life. And oh, what rewards have come of it. Starting to write this book was the first leap I made into completely unknown territory, and the people I've come to know as the project developed have immeasurably enriched me. Having been shut down for years, I now consciously open myself up to new experiences and new people, and the return has been the formation of wonderful associations leading to amazing adventures, such as spending a week in Kenya helping disenfranchised young women start small business ventures through the remarkable foundation formed by one new friend.

Three years ago I took the biggest risk any of us ever takes in life. I'd gone to the Glimmerglass Opera Festival in upstate New

York in August 2002, where I was introduced to a handsome and interesting man. For a year-and-a-half I pursued him with vigor, and on April 17, 2004, at the age of sixty-one, I married him! The pay-off for taking that chance continues to compound with interest every single day.

You may not have had the luxury of great amounts of time together before your child died. But if you had a few moments right now to look deeply into those eyes you know and love, I'm pretty sure your son or daughter would say to you what Mimi said to me. He'd urge you, she'd challenge you, to find what makes you feel most alive, and do it. Put your whole heart into it, and set aside your fears. That one true thing can bring you rewards beyond your imagining.

Patty Shaw

I certainly would not tell the newly bereaved parent that things will get better and that the memories will fade. If anything, at least in my case, they will become more vivid and for that I am thankful. Because my daughter was so devoted to small children, I envisage her in Heaven consoling and caring for the young children who are there. Perhaps God needed her for that reason. I find consolation in that thought.

Lottie Solomon

Authors' Note: We interviewed Lottie several times in her sunny living room, both before and after her husband Herb died, once while he was in the next room, paralyzed with Parkinson's. Even under the combined circumstances of Herb's condition and then his death, her own crippling rheumatism, and the recent horror of her daughter's death in a terrorist attack, at each visit Lottie greeted us with a smile, beautifully coiffed and dressed, and served us coffee in china cups and sweets on silver trays. We took notes during our last visit, from which the following is excerpted:

I really had no time to recover from the shock of Naomi's death, since I had to keep taking care of my husband Herb, who had severe Parkinson's and was bedridden and completely dependent on my care. That is how I handled it, but what you do depends on your own personality.

At first I couldn't listen to music, but now I can listen to it again. I'm crazy about Brahms. I would say to a newly bereaved parent that it is good to take up things that give you pleasure, and it is especially good to do something useful.

MERRYL WEBER

My heart breaks for each and every parent who has had a child die. While I know that each of us experiences our child's death in our own way, the one universal truth of this experience is how painful it is for each of us. Pain makes us recoil and tighten up in every way, physically, emotionally, mentally, spiritually. The one thing I would say to each parent is to just take life one breath at a time, to keep in mind that if you just keep breathing consciously through your pain you will be able to get through it to the next moment, then the next, until something shifts. Don't think about the next day, or the following month, or anything else but what you are feeling right at that moment. Don't isolate yourself, no matter how much you want to, no matter how abandoned and unheard you feel. Let people help you as best they can and weed out the ones who can't be there with you.

By consciously taking one breath after another through each moment, you can keep your heart and mind open to your own suffering in whatever form it is taking in that moment. By keeping your heart open to your suffering, you keep it open to a full range of experience, your own and others'. It is hard to remember to do this practice. I put signs up at my desk and in my kitchen to help me remember. I think of it as a way of keeping yourself connected to life, just as eating food that tastes good or listening to music you love can make you feel more alive in the "good" times. Looking ahead is too frightening. Looking behind is too painful. Just give yourself a lot of room to be where you are, wherever that may be, and surround yourself with other people who can let you be there too.

KATHLEEN WEED

Although I haven't discovered a truth about life or death or grief that can somehow shift the Universe back into place, I do know that if I could have selected from every child in all the world just one to be my daughter, I would have picked Jenica. Even though she died before me, even though I suffer every day for the loss of her—no matter, I would choose her.

I am thinking that you might have experienced a similar thought about your dead child. It may seem small comfort against the immensity of your loss. Even so, it is a profound truth; we, the unluckiest of all parents, would not replace our children for other children who might have outlived us, nor would we choose that they had never lived.

Despite my broken heart, I believe, *I know,* it was good fortune that allowed me to love and be loved by this child. She died before me. So living without her is the price. So be it. I grieve for her every day. Some days are harder than others. Still, I would pay any price to have had Jenica as my daughter. Remembering this helps me to feel less of a victim. It helps me to balance light and dark.

And when I acknowledge that I haven't been singled out for pain, I am more willing to embrace the world, just as it is. My grief mingles with the countless afflictions humans endure, and have endured before me. My loss is personal and irrevocable, but choosing to view it in a wider reality heartens me. And though I sometimes tremble before this staggering vision of the world, I am grateful for its more generous, less bounded perspective. This inclusive view presses me toward a willingness to become less a sympathetic observer and more a compassionate comrade. Authorities on grief often rank death of a child as the greatest loss. But it seems true that pain is a condition of human existence, and loss shapes us all. We are all initiated, one way or another, if we live long enough.

Nothing will ever fill the gap that Jenica's death brought to my life. I am not looking for anything to fill it. When Jenica was a little girl of around seven or eight she made me a "love box." I don't know where she came up with the idea for it. One rainy afternoon she busied herself with paper, crayons, and scissors. Just before bedtime, she told me that she needed a box. She wouldn't tell me why, but insisted that it was very important. The next day I went to the Hallmark store, where I found a deep square paper box. Each side of the box was decorated with the head of an angel. The next day Jenica said she had a present for me. She handed me the same box I had given her. But when I looked inside, I found that it was filled with dozens and dozens of paper hearts. Each heart was decorated with different patterns of crayon and on each heart Jenica had written the word *love* in all the colors of the rainbow. After I had lifted out every heart, I noticed that on the inside bottom of the box Jenica had written *"you mom!"*

Some say we are here to learn how to love. Jenica taught me more about love in her short time on Earth than I could have learned in a hundred lifetimes. Those of us who have lost children experience the ferocity of what it means to love—the ever-present depth of love—the whole of it. We are the parents who can say with certainty, "I would choose this child again. Again and again. Whatever the outcome."

JANE WINSLOW
[From an interview]

Several months after my son Peter died, I heard about a "grieving group" that was starting in Berkeley, at a small Zen center. Two friends who had lost a husband and a son, respectively, attended the weekly sessions with me for approximately three months. They were discontinued when the teacher went to India for a year of study.

When my husband died twenty-one years before, I did not attend any type of "grieving" program, either because they were not as readily available or because I didn't know about any. Attending this Buddhist group twenty-one years later helped me find a place where I could hold my son in my life, although he was no longer with me in body.

The "exercise" that was most helpful to me then, and even occasionally now, is quite simple. The teacher had us each bring a picture of the loved one who died. We were told to look at the photo and think of the things that the person loved about us. When I do this, I feel very special and loved by Peter. I feel his spirit with me, embracing me with love. I feel my son's spirit is with me.

MORE ABOUT US

Stathi Afendoulis was born and raised in Grand Rapids, Michigan. He learned early the values of spirituality and volunteerism from his parents, Sam and Athena. He earned degrees in English, education, and drama at Michigan State, Aquinas College, and NYU, leading to a career as a theater professional, teacher, and businessman. He and his family live in Edison, New Jersey. From 1988 to 1995 the couple was blessed with three daughters, Lainie, Samantha, and Alexandra. On December 19, 1997, Lainie was diagnosed with Ewing's Sarcoma and received a protocol of chemotherapy and limb salvage surgery. Throughout her struggle, Lainie exemplified the characteristics that would become her trademark: a compassion for others, a strength that seemed to help her overcome any hardship, and the ability to communicate her desire to be treated like the normal kid that she was, in spite of the incredible circumstances of her young life. On Wednesday, June 14, 2000, Lainie died peacefully in her home, where she always wanted to be. She was twelve.

Stathi's story may be found on pages 4, 32, 40, 55, 70, 86, 133, 144, 188, and 236.

 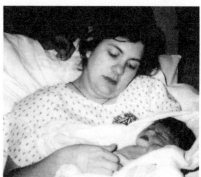

Inés Ascencio is a Cuban American, clinical social worker, and co-founder of Grupo Amparo, a Spanish-speaking support group. She lives in the San Francisco Bay Area with her two daughters, Camila, thirteen, and Liliana, ten. Though her first home was in Venezuela, she grew up in Pennsylvania, outside of Philadelphia. After graduating from UC Berkeley, she moved to El Salvador to volunteer with the Jesuit Refugee Service. Inés has enjoyed her career as a social worker for more than twenty years, feeling that it is a blessing to be able to work with others to improve their lives. She works for the City and County of San Francisco in an outpatient mental health clinic and also has a private practice. In her free time, she most enjoys dancing, hiking, traveling, and being with friends and family.

In 1992, she and her then-husband were expecting their first child. Angelita Ascencio died just before birth, in her mother's womb, on Ash Wednesday in March 1992.

Inés's story may be found on pages 6, 41, 71, 94, 126, 161, 174, 198, 208, and 236.

Susan Benveniste is a rare third-generation San Francisco native. As a teen, she rode and showed gaited horses and in 1963 was crowned queen of the Grand National Horse Show. After their marriage, Susan and her husband Ron settled into a home on the Peninsula in the Bay Area, and Susan worked for Pacific Bell until the birth of their children: Josh, in 1972, and Shelly, in 1974. They spent the next thirty years raising their children and serving the community of Hillsborough. Susan devoted her time to the public schools, the Humane Society, and developing and presenting a public education program for Wildlife Rehabilitation. The Benvenistes currently live in Scottsdale, Arizona, and Lake Tahoe.

Shelly Benveniste was a young leader who instituted the first Father/Daughter Day and a student-run Halloween carnival when in high school. She was full of life, beautiful and vivacious, attacking each day with enthusiasm. While Shelly was working as a junior counselor at a summer camp, she was a passenger in a car in which the designated driver had been drinking. She died at Bass Lake, California, at the age of seventeen, on July 17, 1991.

Susan's story may be found on pages 95, 134, 208, 216, and 237.

Mary Lou Coffelt is a California native. The youngest of four children, she was born into a warm, loving, stable Catholic family. As a child, Mary Lou developed a passion for animals, especially horses and cattle. College led her to Fresno State University in pursuit of an animal science degree. She met her husband Bob while they both worked as saddle makers. Eventually, she took a job with Bob at a local ranch; they worked as a team at various ranches throughout the San Joaquin Valley of California, settling in Hollister, where they began their own cattle operation. Their twenty-three-year marriage has produced three sons: Matthew, Joseph, and Michael William.

In June 1997, Bob had removed some posts from a rundown pasture fence and was taking them to another part of their ranch. He took his son Matthew (Mattie) with him while Mary Lou, eight months pregnant with their second son, did paperwork at home. Mattie and his favorite dog Cinch were standing on the catwalk as Bob backed the pickup to the spot where he would unload the posts. The last words Bob spoke to Mattie were, "Where are you, Matt?" "I'm right here," Mattie answered from his designated place. Bob stopped for a second and then decided to back a little closer—that was the moment, for some reason, that Mattie jumped off the catwalk and went toward the front-off side of the pickup. He was hit and died immediately. Mattie was three years, seven months old.

Mary Lou's story may be found on pages 8, 33, 42, 72, 87, 96, 110, 115, 126, 135, 140, 218, and 238.

Nancy Emro was born in Norwalk, Connecticut, in 1953. After graduating from college with a degree in business administration, she moved to California, where she met her future husband Jim Emdy while folk dancing. Their only child, Sean Aleksandr Emdy, was born on February 2, 1983, Groundhog Day. Nancy and Jim divorced when Sean was five, but have remained good friends. When Sean was in elementary school, Nancy took the college courses necessary to obtain her license as a CPA while also working full-time. Currently in her spare time, she sings in a local community chorus, periodically gives railroad safety presentations to local high school students, and remains involved with the drama department at Sean's high school.

Sean was a young man whose passion was designing and building sets for his high school drama productions. He practically lived in the high school auditorium; when he did come home for food or money, his clothes had the lingering sweet smell of sawdust. He was very bright, had a wit laced with sarcasm, but was never one to follow the crowd. He was a fan of offbeat humor, Godzilla movies, ice hockey, Formula One racing, and reggae music. Taking a shortcut home from school at 7:30 in the evening, Sean was struck and killed by a commuter train on October 11, 2000. He was seventeen years old.

Nancy's story may be found on pages 34, 57, 152, 175, 219, and 242.

Sheila George was born in Tulsa, Oklahoma, in 1944. Soon thereafter her family moved to Oakland, California, where her father was a Seventh Day Adventist minister. She met her first husband at church when she was seventeen and had a girl and two boys in three years. When the relationship became abusive, Sheila divorced and went on welfare. In her late twenties, realizing that she wanted more out of life, she entered a local trade school in electronic assembly, and later in computer-aided design. She had another failed marriage, but was always an involved mother. Sheila went ballroom dancing every chance she got. Eventually, she would found the East Palo Alto Teen Home for youth at risk, where she currently serves as executive director.

Sheila's only son Ronnie was a loner and yet a fervent defender of the underdog. In his last year of high school he fathered a baby, Ronnie Jr., and instantly became "Mister Mom." After he and the baby's mother split up, he experimented with drugs, but then voluntarily entered and completed a treatment program. He was working as a roofer while he considered his future. On November 23, 1998, in East Palo Alto, a block from home, he gave chase when a man swiped his companion's purse. Ronnie died on the street of stab wounds. He was twenty-three.

Sheila's story may be found on pages 11, 43, 73, 87, 97, 166, 190, 220, and 244.

Keith D. Gilbert was born and raised in Boyertown, Pennsylvania, a rural town about fifty miles from Philadelphia. Keith earned both undergraduate and graduate degrees at the Massachusetts Institute of Technology, and subsequently moved to Palo Alto, California, where he met his wife Sue and began his career. He held a series of management positions, including president, Electronics Group at Watkins-Johnson Co., and president and CEO of Stellex Microwave Systems. He is an ardent San Francisco Giants fan, a tennis player, and a volunteer on his club's scholarship committee.

Keith's only child, Amanda Gilbert, was born on the first day of spring in 1974 and was a bright, witty, and cheerful child almost from birth. She loved school and joined in almost every school play until she graduated from high school; she excelled at speech and debating, winning many awards. She was first in her high school class and a National Merit Scholarship finalist. Amanda was killed as a passenger in a van rollover on March 1, 1993, during her freshman year at UCLA while returning from a debate tournament. She was eighteen.

Keith's story may be found on pages 35, 97, 168, and 244.

Susan K. Gilbert was born and raised in a suburb about ten miles from New York City. She attended the University of Chicago and received a BS from New York University and later an MS in counseling psychology. After completing her education, she headed west, settling in the San Francisco Bay Area, where she soon met her husband Keith Gilbert and gave birth to Amanda. Susan worked in several health care manufacturing firms, culminating at the vice presidential level; she also consulted with several start-ups and was determined, with the help of Keith and wonderful bosses, to continue her profession at a time when not many women were both being dedicated mothers and having serious careers. She is co-author of *Women Leading* (Stephen Greene Press, 1988) and has also always been active in civic affairs.

Amanda and Susan spent a lot of time together and enjoyed similar tastes in shopping, movies, and books. On the last shopping excursion Amanda made, the night before she died, she bought Susan's birthday present, a book. Even in the midst of what is often teenage alienation, Amanda was good friends with her parents.

Susan's story may be found on pages 12, 44, 60, 74, 88, 98, 110, 115, 155, 162, 177, 209, and 245.

Van Jepson was born in Minneapolis, Minnesota, the third of four children. He played baseball both in college as well as semiprofessionally for an A-league team in California. After graduating from the University of California at Davis with a BSEE, he worked in high-technology companies in several functions and became chief operating officer of his company. He is currently CEO of an Internet entertainment company. Van married in 1986 and became the father of two children, Calvin and Ian. Both boys were smart, verbal, athletic, and outgoing. The family lived in Woodside, California, and enjoyed what they considered a perfect life until 2001.

Ian Jepson grew to be a loving, athletic eight-year-old with charm and lots of energy. He died in Van's arms on March 18, 2001, after an all-terrain-vehicle accident. Van gave his son CPR and his brother Calvin did all he could to help as well. Ian's death transformed the family instantly and forever. Van's marriage of seventeen years collapsed and he shifted from full-time work to part-time consulting in order to support Calvin.

Van's story may be found on pages 15, 36, 45, 61, 75, 88, 113, 116, 128, 136, 145, 156, 168, 178, 200, 210, 215, 221, 228, and 246.

Monica Loose Jones was born in Boulder, Colorado, in 1941 to German refugee parents. Respecting her roots, she completed part of her studies in Germany. After graduating in German from Vassar College, she married Desmond Jones, a Welsh educator. They moved to Santa Barbara, California, where Monica earned an MA. She later attended the University of London, where she earned a PhD in ESL, which she has taught at Santa Barbara City College since 1988.

In 1967, Monica gave birth to a daughter, Bronwyn, who in her second year was diagnosed with Werdnig-Hoffmann Syndrome, a rare genetic condition that leads eventually to almost total paralysis and death. For nearly ten years the Joneses' entire existence was focused on Bronwyn's many needs.

Bronwyn was bright and cheerful, had a good sense of humor, and was genuinely interested in others. She was patient with people trying to care for her. Having adopted her parents' Buddhist faith, she believed that one can welcome anything that happens as an opportunity to learn. Near the end of her life she told her parents that they should not be sad if she died, but should have a party. She thought that she had had a good life. Bronwyn died in 1977 at home. She was nine.

Monica's story may be found on pages 16, 46, 76, 163, 178, and 246.

Martin Katz and his wife Lee are first-generation Americans, born and raised in New York City. Martin served in the army in World War II and married Lee in December 1947 following his discharge. After college and graduate school, Martin launched a career as a pharmaceutical scientist and corporate executive. They soon had three children: two daughters and a son, Barry. In 1964, the Katz family moved to Northern California, where they led a comfortable semi-rural life enjoying a wide range of family activities. Lee taught college economics, and the children were fully occupied with school, work, and social activities.

While Martin's daughters progressed in their studies, Barry had a more difficult time. He was a gentle, lovable, humorous, and intelligent boy, but in his late teens he started to drift aimlessly. He tried working on an Israeli kibbutz and then got a job at the Stanford University Book Store, but the family sensed that he seemed troubled. On November 7, 1981, while his parents were vacationing in New York, Barry committed suicide. He was twenty-one years old.

Martin's story may be found on pages 17, 46, 80, 89, 98, 157, 179, 191, 221, and 247.

John LeCompte was raised in Seattle, Washington, then earned a BA in psychology at Stanford University, where he was a pitcher on the baseball team. After college John married Sue Redfern and they moved to California's San Joaquin Valley and Sue's family's farm. They had three children: a daughter, Aimée (nicknamed Mimi), and two sons, Peter and David. John actively involved himself in local causes such as youth soccer, community theater, and the public schools. After he and Sue were divorced, he operated several triple-A franchises of the Oakland Athletics. John and his wife Thalia live in the Sierra foothill town of Oakhurst, California.

In January 1999, at her grandfather's funeral in Seattle, it became noticeable to Mimi's family that she lacked energy, even for shopping. While she maintained her characteristic good humor, something was wrong. That something proved to be lung cancer of unknown origin in this athletic and beautiful, nonsmoking young woman. Mimi died on December 6, 1999, at home, surrounded by her family. She was thirty-two.

John's story may be found on pages 113, 159, 228, and 248.

Kathryn L. Lodato has lived in Northern California since she was three years old and now resides in Palo Alto. She and her husband Jim married when they were very young and had two little boys, Avery and Nick, by the time Kathryn was twenty years old. She attended college while raising her sons and graduated from law school the same year that her older son Avery graduated from high school. Always passionate about the environment, she worked for some time as a legislative advocate for an environmental group. She is currently completing a marriage and family therapist internship after receiving an MA in counseling psychology. She is also a grief counselor on a volunteer basis.

Kathryn has always said that Nick was an extrovert in a family of introverts; he had more friends than the rest of the family combined. And he had a remarkable ability to make friends with a wide variety of people. After high school, Nick went south to attend the University of California at Santa Barbara. On January 14, 1996, Nick died instantly when hit by a car. He was twenty-one years old.

Kathryn's story may be found on pages 80, 169, 200, 222, and 249.

Anne J. Logan grew up in Charlotte, North Carolina, and Richmond, Virginia, the daughter of a Presbyterian minister. After college, she studied at Columbia University and later decided to go to medical school, when she met her businessman husband Mark. Anne worked for a period as an emergency room physician. In time daughters Catherine and Virginia were born, joining Mark's son Bret. In 1984, the family moved to a farm in Orange, Virginia, where they raised horses, dogs, and hay. Anne became a country doctor.

Virginia rode as if she were part of the horse. She was an infectiously happy child, always with a smile on her face and curious about the flowers and creatures she found on the farm. However, after entering boarding school, Virginia began to exhibit signs of unhappiness and struggled with anorexia and depression. She went under the care of psychiatrists, but began to experiment with street drugs as a form of self-medication. She entered Davidson College, where her struggles continued. On October 7, 2001, Virginia Logan died of a methadone overdose. She was twenty years old.

Anne's story may be found on pages 18, 99, 129, 137, 140, 181, 225, and 250.

Michele Phua was born in Hong Kong and came to the United States when she was ten years old. She received her BA and is a certified public accountant. Michele met her husband John at a party in 1989 and the pair was married in 1992; they settled in San Mateo, California. Michele and John had several severe trials early in their marriage. An avid cyclist and fan of Lance Armstrong, John performed a self-examination for cancer and found something suspicious; the next day he was diagnosed with testicular cancer and underwent treatment. Compounding that ordeal, Michele's father was diagnosed with and died of lung cancer in 1998. Michele was his full-time caregiver and supporter during his illness. Before the birth of her children, Michele routinely worked a seventy-plus-hour week. With difficulty, Michele and John conceived twins, and on December 15, 2000, she joyfully gave birth to Ryan and Matthew. She stayed at home with them for seven months and later found a consulting job that allowed her to work only 25 percent of the day.

Ryan brought a smile to everyone he met. He was the leader of the twins, and Matthew was a loyal fan. Ryan knew how to charm and light up the room, even at such a young age. He was quite particular about his desires, from the color of his shoes to the music he liked. Ryan died in his crib on July 8, 2003, of Sudden Unexplained Death in Childhood. He was two-and-a-half years old.

Michele's story may be found on pages 22, 36, 48, 62, 83, 90, 101, 116, 131, 164, 172, 184, 192, and 251.

John Phua was born in Washington, D.C. His family is from Singapore, of Chinese origin. His education culminated in a degree in computer science and electrical engineering, which he applies in his career in the computer entertainment industry. He lives in San Mateo, California, with his wife Michele and their surviving son Matthew. John feels very fortunate to have had his cancer diagnosed relatively early and to have been able to father his twin miracle children Ryan and Matthew.

Ryan died in his crib on July 8, 2003, of Sudden Unexplained Death in Childhood. He was two-and-a-half years old.

John's story may be found on pages 21, 47, 101, 131, 164, 172, 226, and 251.

Suzanne Redfern grew up in Dos Palos, a farm town in California's Central Valley, the only child of a farmer and the former school nurse. In 1964, she received a BA in political science from Stanford University. She later did graduate work in expository writing. After marriage to classmate John LeCompte, the pair returned to Dos Palos, where Mimi, Peter, and David were born and raised. When they amicably divorced twenty-three years later, Suzanne took the helm at Redfern Ranches. Today she serves on several agricultural water boards and advocates for California's family farmers. In 2004, she married the publisher Robert West. They live in Palo Alto and on the ranch.

As a child and an adult, Mimi was interested in virtually everything, but found her greatest joy in creating beauty. She earned a BS at UC Davis, but preferred decorating her apartment to studying. She was a fearless world traveler. In 1994, she married Brett Taylor and the couple settled into a Sacramento suburb, where Mimi created an online gift business and was a gifted gardener and cook. In January 1999, she spoke of starting a family. In February a doctor spotted something on a chest x-ray; that something turned out to be bronchial alveolar carcinoma. Mimi died of lung cancer on December 6, 1999. She was thirty-two.

Suzanne's story may be found on pages 23, 50, 102, 142, 146, 165, 203, 229, and 252.

Patricia W. Shaw was born in Chicago in 1930 and was raised in suburban Illinois. She graduated from Skidmore College in English literature and married her first husband Bill, a graduate of West Point and a career military officer, shortly thereafter. Daughter Cathy was born, followed by two boys. Since Bill was a fighter pilot, the family lived all over the world. After the couple divorced, Patty remained single for the next twenty-five years, working for a world-renowned physicist at Stanford University's Hoover Institute. She was overjoyed to meet and marry her present husband Don. They live in South Carolina.

Catherine McClelland Vanden Dries was born in 1953 and was the light of Patty's life. Cathy was a vibrant woman and a popular teacher. She was recognized for her skills and contributions in each town where she lived and taught. Like her mother, Cathy became a military wife when she married a fighter pilot. Due to his various assignments, she was alone much of the time. They had two sons. In January 2002, Cathy, who was seeking a divorce, was shot and killed by her husband, who then turned the gun on himself. Cathy was forty-eight.

Patricia's story may be found on pages 25, 37, 52, 83, 91, 105, 166, 184, 206, 215, 227, 230, and 254.

Lottie Solomon was born in New York City during the Great Depression. She began playing violin at seven and got the best musical education then available in New York. She earned a BA from Brooklyn College at the age of nineteen and an MA in music from Columbia. At twenty-one, Lottie married Herb Solomon, a mathematician and statistician, now deceased. They moved west when Herb founded the statistics department at Stanford. Their daughter Naomi was born in 1949, followed by two sons. Lottie was famous on campus and off for her cooking and entertaining. Active in her community, she co-founded Kol Emeth, a local conservative temple, and also founded the Palo Alto Yiddish Chorus. She has taught music and music history at the college level. Later she earned a second master's in health care administration.

Naomi Solomon received her BA in French from Stanford University at age twenty and her MA soon thereafter. She spoke five languages and was an accomplished pianist. Naomi worked at the vice presidential level at two major banks in the field of computers. She was attending a meeting on the 106th floor of the World Trade Center on September 11, 2001, when terrorists struck. Naomi Solomon was fifty-two years old.

Lottie's story may be found on pages 28, 63, 92, 105, 131, 159, 185, 192, 206, and 254.

Merryl Weber was born and raised in Chicago and left the Midwest after college to move to Los Angeles with her husband Steve, a California native. Her lifelong commitment has been to family, service to the community, and the daily practice of yoga and meditation; she has taught hatha yoga. She is immersed in the study of Jewish text and spiritual practice and is the chair of the board of Metivta, a Jewish contemplative organization in the Los Angeles area. Merryl has studied numerous healing modalities, which she has adapted and developed, helping others to cultivate inner alignment and harmony. She currently lives in Southern California near daughter Sonya and her family.

Adam Weber had a sweet, wild, and generous spirit combined with an impish sense of humor, a wide smile, and an infectious love of life. He had an open, inquisitive mind and was highly gifted in mathematics; he wrote poetry and loved music from an early age. He dreamed of becoming a rock musician as a teenager, and played in a band. Adam died in 1995, during the spring break, in a boating accident off the North Carolina coast. He was twenty years old.

Merryl's story may be found on pages 29, 38, 52, 63, 84, 92, 106, 117, 132, 138, 143, 160, 173, 186, 210, 215, 230, and 255.

Kathleen Weed grew up in Palo Alto, California. She graduated from UC Berkeley in 1973 with a degree in English literature. She is an avid and voracious reader. She has always loved writing, especially writing poetry. She is a volunteer counselor at Kara, a nonprofit grief support facility in Palo Alto, California. Her clients are other mothers who have lost children. Her husband Steven Weed, although not Jenica's father, has been supportive and understanding of Kathleen's grief.

The first thing most people noted upon meeting Jenica was her striking physical beauty. At five foot nine, she was statuesque with a slim yet voluptuous figure and pale green eyes rimmed in blue, which seemed to change color on whim. She was the kind of young woman who spontaneously reached for the hands of her companions when they walked with her, as she leaned in close to them, listening intently. She jumped into life with grace, enthusiasm, and tender-heartedness. Jenica died from sepsis caused by meningococcal meningitis on June 10, 1999, three months shy of her twenty-second birthday, while at school at Dartmouth College.

Kathleen's story may be found on pages 53, 107, 117, 211, and 256.

Jane Winslow was born in Los Angeles, California. At the age of nine she contracted polio and currently wears a leg brace and has post-polio syndrome. Jane graduated from Pacific Lutheran University in Tacoma, Washington, with a BA in elementary education. Her first teaching job was in the San Francisco Bay Area, where she met her husband Pete, a journalist and poet, when he was doing a story on polio. They married and son Peter was born in 1967. Pete died following surgery for a stomach ulcer when Peter was just five years old. Jane worked as a teacher and had other positions, including consulting in civic affairs, while she raised her son on her own.

Peter Winslow was always a happy, cheerful kid. He was creative, open, and talkative. He liked offbeat humor and artistic endeavors and was a musician, playing guitar in a band called Less Is More. In 1993, he was working in a hardware warehouse while he considered options for continuing his education. Peter died when he was driving home from a band engagement, the victim of a driver who ran a red light. He was twenty-six years old.

Jane's story may be found on pages 39, 64, 85, 94, 109, 119, 187, 193, and 257.

Hampton Roads Publishing Company

. . . for the evolving human spirit

HAMPTON ROADS PUBLISHING COMPANY
publishes books on a variety of subjects,
including spirituality, health, and other
related topics.

For a copy of our latest trade catalog,
call 978-465-0504 or
visit our website at www.hrpub.com